MR. MILLER
OF "THE TIMES"

CHARLES R. MILLER
From the painting by Haskell Coffin

MR. MILLER OF "THE TIMES"

The Story of an Editor

By F. Fraser Bond

> ... the Editor in his den ... with the rumble of his machinery about him and fresh material arriving and flying into the printing press. It must be like being in the very furnace-hissing of events.—MEREDITH, *Diana of the Crossways.*

CHARLES SCRIBNER'S SONS
NEW YORK · LONDON
1931

COPYRIGHT, 1931, BY CHARLES SCRIBNER'S SONS

PRINTED IN THE UNITED STATES OF AMERICA

A

TO
MY FATHER

ACKNOWLEDGMENT

The Editors of the New York *Times, The Century Magazine, The Youth's Companion,* and *The Forum* have given kind and ready permission for the reprinting here of material which had its first publication in these periodicals.

FOREWORD

When the man died who for over forty years had served as editor-in-chief of the New York *Times,* an editorial in a weekly review remarked: "The general public did not know even the name of this great editor until they saw it in the obituary notices." This was perfectly true, for Charles Ransom Miller had kept consistently to the anonymity of his craft.

This volume comes into being therefore to perpetuate his memory not so much as the great editor but as a human personality "in his habit as he lived." It will not attempt to analyze Mr. Miller's half century of influence which shows in the growing independence of the press and in the public's taste for better journalism. All this rests in the minds of his own generation and remains in the heightened prestige of the paper that he served. It will not to any great extent reprint his editorial writings. To do so would be to rob them of their chief virtues—their appositeness and timeliness at the moment of publication. But it will try to give the human side of the man who to his friends and co-workers lived and moved and had his being as a most human and vivid figure. It will record the incidents, the sayings, the casual notes that made up the daily round.

Old Israel Disraeli, father of the great Beaconsfield, had small patience with the pretended geniuses of his time who affected to exclaim: "Give me no anecdotes of an author, but give me his works." For his part, he said: "I have found the anecdotes more interesting than the works." To this comment John Hay adds this agreeing footnote:

Real history is not to be found in books, but in the personal anecdotes and private letters of those who made history. These reveal the men themselves and the motives that actuate them and give us also their estimate of those who are associated with them. No one should ever destroy a private letter that contains light on public men, or *willingly let die an illuminating anecdote* disclosing their individuality.

If some of the anecdotes here recorded appear too trivial, the author begs to say that to him at least they had this "illuminating" quality and added to the lifelikeness of the portrait. In any case, here they must stand, wheat and chaff together, to await the winnowing of time.

F. F. B.

CONTENTS

CHAPTER		PAGE
I.	A New England Youth	1
II.	Dartmouth in the '70's	10
III.	The Springfield "School of Journalism"	30
IV.	Early Days in Park Row	42
V.	"The Times" Out of Joint	57
VI.	The Daily Round	71
VII.	Out of Office Hours	89
VIII.	Times Office and White House	104
IX.	The Senate Inquisition	123
X.	The War and the League	137
XI.	The Editor Talks Shop	155
XII.	The End of the Day	176
	Appendix	
	Grover Cleveland as President	189
	The Monroe Doctrine in the Venezuela Dispute	201
	Why Socialism is Impracticable	217
	Demand and Supply in Literature	225
	Has the Senate Degenerated?	235
	For the German People, Peace with Freedom	244
	Woodrow Wilson	247
	Index	257

I

A NEW ENGLAND YOUTH

A now yellowing cabinet photograph, taken at Hanover, New Hampshire, in April, 1849, shows an obviously proud young mother with a three-months-old baby in her arms. She wears a dress of black satin cut in lines of Sabbatical primness. Yet it needs no billowing of lacy ruffles to enhance the sitter's beauty or dignity. Beneath the broad brow and the smoothly parted hair shine out two large, dark, humorous eyes.

Six months after the taking of this photographic record, the young mother, Chastina Hoyt Miller, "dearly beloved wife of" Elijah Tenney Miller, died. Thirty-four years later her tiny son, Charles Ransom Miller, was appointed the editor-in-chief of the New York *Times*. He came to rank in the great city of his adoption as a sound scholar and accomplished writer; he helped mould the policies of statesmen; he became the friend and advisor of presidents.

A tenet of good newspaper writing demands that it begin with its subject. Let that rule hold in this chronicle of a newspaper writer. The sociologically minded, who needs must wade through the conventional tables of "begatting," we refer to the existing published genealogies of New England families. Certainly the baby born on January 17, 1849, lost no time in ancestor worship. He remained content with the family presumption that the yeoman stock from which he sprang originated in New England from one Captain Thomas Miller of Bishops Stortford, who sailed with his brother, John, for Massachusetts in 1635.

His immediate progenitor, Elijah T. Miller, farmed a small holding in a hamlet adjacent to Hanover, called Hanover Centre.

Time and the real-estate agent have now blurred somewhat the lines of demarcation, but up to forty years ago Hanover Centre remained a community apart, with its dozen homes, its meeting house, its school house, and its blacksmith shop.

The Miller homestead stood about a hundred rods out of the village on the Enfield road. An uncle, John Miller, a sheep farmer, lived in the next house, and through the joint holdings ran a fine trout stream. Like most of his neighbors, Elijah Miller wrung a hard living from that reluctant northern soil. But it was the recompense of his generation that much of the quality of the indomitable New Hampshire granite entered into the fibre of their lives and characters. Students of agriculture in America have divided it into three main periods. And this first period from the Revolution to 1873 they note as characterized by extreme self-sufficiency and by great adherence to local prejudices and customs. But the self-sufficiency in the temperament of the New England farmer of this time had no trace of complacency in it. Rather, it took the form of a marked individualism which endorsed the belief that a man's property was his own and that what he was able to make through his own ingenuity was his by right.

The migration of this hardy stock New Yorkward and westward provided in its day a stabilizing force for expanding metropolis and nation, and in ours, a fertile field for sociological researches and surmisings. Professor James Mickel Williams in his meaty book "Our Rural Heritage" gives some indication of the debt which present-day America owes to these same hard-toiling New England farmers with their "rural attitude of austere self-restraint and resulting rigorous standard of morality," and along with it "their vigorous attitude for the enforcement of law." From all accounts Elijah T. Miller typified his time.

Although well in advance of this day of "reactions," young Charles Miller from boyhood on let it be known that he had small taste for farming. His predilection lay rather in the direction of the trout stream, already referred to, which meandered through the parental acres.

Partly from this fact, but more largely because the local prejudice ran strongly in favor of book-learning and regarded knowledge with real respect and reverence, the father saw to it that his non-conforming son should have the chance at least of securing the best education that his means would permit. For his early training, the schools in the Hanover neighborhood sufficed. Naturally the village drew from the Dartmouth reservoir. True, that institution at the time was sicklied o'er with an anything but pale theological cast of thought. Yet along with "true religion" sound learning undoubtedly flourished. The Hanover schools took advantage of the wide choice of available teachers at their disposal. They earned an enviable reputation.

This excellent early schooling young Charles shared with an elder brother; Fayette, a younger sister who shortly died; and, as his father had married again in the interval, with a half-brother, Edward, and a half-sister, Fanny. But neither during work nor in hours of ease, did his schoolmates see young Charles relax in the beloved masculine *deshabille* known as "sitting in one's shirtsleeves." And why? Because his early personal pride could not permit it. His stepmother in her efforts to make ends meet, made his shirts herself and fashioned them so that only the collars and cuffs were of bleached linen. The bodies of the shirts were of plain homespun. Although no doubt many of the boys around him had similar raiment, Charles never publicly exposed this outward and visible sign of poverty. In fact, throughout life he disliked the newspaper practice of working in shirtsleeves.

In the fall of his sixteenth year, young Charles journeyed southward a few miles to Meriden. On the hill in that New Hampshire village rose a typical white-pillared "academy." At the time its fame stood high, ranking with Exeter and like foundations.

One of these days, some inspired student looking Ph.D.-wards, will give up deducing deductions from the t-endings in Shakespeare, and will turn to these New England schools. What a contribution they have made to the development of this country. What a strong and sterling breed of men it was that went out from under their Georgian bell towers and their mock-heroic porticos.

Of the "honestly old-fashioned" methods of instruction prevailing at Kimball Union Academy, and of the rigors of co-education in the 'sixties, Mr. Miller himself left a record. Let it go into the chronicle in his own words:

> My four terms at Kimball Academy were in the early sixties—'63 and '64—sixty years ago. In that day Prof. Roe had the department of Chemistry; Wood was professor of mathematics; and Miss Nudd—invariably "Marm Nudd"—had astronomy.
>
> But the dominant figure was Principal Cyrus S. Richards, whose strong hand had built up and firmly controlled the institution. There must have been other instructors, but my recollections of them are effaced by these stronger figures. Roe really interested us in chemistry, and was a good instructor. Dr. Richards we feared not a little, but we respected him thoroughly for his strength and efficiency; besides he was reputed to be deeply learned in Greek. On clear evenings Miss Nudd used to take the classes out to inspect the constellations which she pointed out to them. No doubt that was the first most of us knew about the Great Bear, Orion and Vega. She introduced us to Betelgeuse which we contemplated with placid indifference not knowing upon how great a star we gazed.
>
> Mr. Duncan was postmaster and was the principal citizen of the place. Mr. Blanchard was the minister and Mr. Cole the leading merchant. There was another store kept by Mr. Morgan. Of local residents I recall Mr. James Wood and Mr. Scalees who lived over the hill, besides Mr. Davis and Mrs. Smith and Mrs. Strowbridge and her daughter.
>
> Out of the student body my memory plucks here and there a name. Those who lived in Meriden and attended the classes included "Con" Smith, celebrated for his mighty prowess upon the football field; Ora Davis; Miss Blanchard, daughter of the parson. From farther afield came S. Mitchell Smith of Ohio; Charles E. Cowne of Chicago, who was my roommate; Miss Ella Bragg, Queechee, Vt.; Otis Marion of Boston; Miss Stella Redington; Samuel Powers of Cornish, now politically prominent in Boston, and Miss Alice Powers his sister.
>
> The discipline at K. U. A. was stern and unbending. Rule 6. governing the relations of the two departments, male and female, simplified the matter immensely by forbidding all relations. As I remember it now there was absolutely no exception. At another mixed school I attended later there was a similar rule but once or twice during the term levees or assemblies were held at which boys and girls had a chance to get acquainted. Nothing like that at Meriden. We passed each other on that famous plank side-walk. Though the young gentleman might know the young lady's name, and the young lady might know his name, although all the essential elements of

acquaintance existed, we could only glare at each other. I have understood that infractions of this rule were not unknown; they were certainly dangerous. Dr. Richards kept a keen eye upon his flock. It was interesting at chapel to see him look about to make sure, so far as possible, that the students were in their proper slips of pews. As he turned his head to look to the right or left the profile and look were aquiline.

I can hardly speak of the methods of instruction employed in that day. I suppose they were honestly old-fashioned, but they had existed for a century or two; they sufficed to give the boys and girls who attended the Academy a satisfactory education, and since colleges taught in the same way they fitted boys for the entrance examination. K. U. A. was exceedingly prosperous and well attended in my day. In the Fall and Spring terms there were something like three hundred students. And the Academy stood on a par with Exeter and other well known academies of the East. It must be remembered that academies like K. U. A. at that time did not have the competition of the high schools, which did not then exist.

I do not suppose Meriden has changed physically very much although the Academy is a very different structure. In my day it was like any one of five hundred or a thousand brick churches you might find in New England. The worst thing about it was its bell. To live at the bottom of the hill and twice a day be compelled at the behest of that awful instrument to climb that long ascent to attend Chapel made an impression not easily effaced. To this day the sound of a bell of the same tone fills my soul with melancholy. But the Academy stood four-square based upon the confidence of New England and of the country who knew that it conferred a useful discipline and a sound education.

From the foregoing we cull a sentence or two, append two facts from the chronology, and let the reader read between the lines.

Rule 6. governing the relations between the two departments, male and female, simplified the matter immensely by forbidding all relations. . . . I have understood that infractions of this rule were not unknown. They were certainly dangerous.

Two facts, in the light of this quotation, should go into the record just here.

At Kimball Union Academy young Miller first met and became attracted by Miss Frances Daniels, of Plainfield, New Hampshire, who was later to become his wife.

In 1865 Kimball Union Academy expelled the same Charles Ransom Miller.

Parental displeasure took the form of a year's interim in the father's efforts to secure an education for his son. Charles spent the time helping round the home farm when he had to, and off in the woods hunting or down at the beloved trout stream whenever he found opportunity. He was already a crack shot and his success as a marksman remained with him to old age.

In 1866 Elijah T. Miller decided to send him back to school. This time he chose an academy known as the Green Mountain Liberal Institute, but more usually referred to simply as the Green Mountain Institute at South Woodstock, Vermont. This school also maintained a co-educational system but with the cleavage between the two departments less rigid than at Kimball. This we can infer from the sentence in the foregoing Meriden jottings which reads: "At another mixed school I attended later there was a similar rule, but once or twice during the term levees or assemblies were held at which boys and girls had a chance to get acquainted."

Green Mountain Institute has since closed its doors. Recollections of it survive chiefly in the memory of a dwindling group of former students and in a published account left by one of their number, Doctor Almon Gunnison, for years an outstanding educational figure in Brooklyn. Doctor Gunnison preceded young Miller at the Institute by several years, but his account of it when sent to the editor-in-chief of the New York *Times* by Doctor Gunnison's brother, Herbert F. Gunnison, President of the Brooklyn *Daily Eagle,* recalled to Mr. Miller's mind quite vividly his days at South Woodstock.

In particular, Doctor Gunnison told of a fellow student, John, who with more ambition than he had attributes, desired to shine as an orator. Young Gunnison with some kindred spirits played on Master John's vanity. They wrote for him a most extravagant speech and coached him in its delivery, embellishing its reckless rhetoric with all sorts of foolish gestures.

This brought back to Mr. Miller the memory of a somewhat similar incident at Green Mountain, as this letter shows:

THE NEW YORK TIMES
TIMES SQUARE

DEAR MR. GUNNISON: May 3, 1919.

I have read with much pleasure your brother's book. His story of "Orator John's" exploits vividly recalls the unfeeling behavior of some of us in my time to a chap in the school who was so much like "Orator John" that he ought to have been his twin brother. We gave that boy some translations of Caesar's Gallic war that made the professor gasp.

Your brother wrote a most agreeable and entertaining book, and in a very pleasing style. I thank you for giving me the opportunity to read it.

Yours very truly,

Herbert F. Gunnison, Esq., C. R. MILLER.
Brooklyn *Daily Eagle,*
Brooklyn, N. Y.

The following human and humorous document indicates that despite his expulsion from Kimball Union Academy and the existing barriers at Green Mountain Institute, young Miller still sought and found the delights of feminine society. Although the sheets of the letter bearing the address and name of its sender have been lost or destroyed, the body of it remains to throw a happy light on some of Charles's extra-curricula exploits at Green Mountain and on the sunny philosophy and good temper of its writer:

Nothing for years has brought up recollections of the Green Mountain Institute, South Woodstock, Vermont, so much as seeing the picture of Charles Ransom Miller in *The World's Work* magazine. Only the forehead looks natural, for Father Time has followed you on your life journey, whitened your hair and rubbed out all the youthful looks of the face; but I can easily believe it is the Charlie Miller of my school days. What a joke if not the same! In all the years since G. M. I. was a thing of the past, I have never seen one scholar nor heard anything of any one scholar good or bad who went to the school when I did, except Norman Wood "the orator" who is a physician in Northfield, Mass., and Dr. Brewster of Windsor, Vermont, who was a brother of Mr. Burrington's wife. I recall the pleasant moonlight rides I had with you when I was teaching in South Woodstock, the gray horse you used to drive and how you would take the hilliest roads you could find, I suppose to put an extension on the hours we were out. I remember, too, the night we went to a theatre at Woodstock

Green to hear a travelling company who were playing "Uncle Tom's Cabin" and in one scene I laughed aloud. "'Member the time?" One night your thoughts and feelings seemed to be tinged with indigo color and you asked me to sing the song, "What is home without a Mother?" You didn't say why you called for the song, but I judged your thoughts were of home. I left off teaching years ago, for I was getting very nervous. Acting on the advice of a doctor, a good friend of mine, I went to live with an invalid lady as a companion, the lady a refined, intelligent, lovely woman. Had she lived a few months longer, I would have been with her twenty years. After she died I didn't care to resume teaching, and I had no ambition to take up any new work. "'Tis true and pity 'tis 'tis true," I never married, but have found homes with some congenial and some uncongenial widowers but none of them ever said: "Wilt thou be mine." If any one of them had asked me the question, maybe I would have wilted. The Chinaman's rhyme is very applicable to my case:

"No one kissee, No one huggee,
Poor old maidee, no one lovee."

Even on "the hilliest roads" no doubt young Charles Miller proved a welcome companion. Already he blossomed as a raconteur. Already he loved good stories and loved passing them on, preceding each with a premonitory chuckle. Doubtless his fair partner on these moonlit buggy rides listened to this favorite of his that comes down from his school days:

A Dutchman calling on a friend was afraid to go up to the door on account of the dog. The owner called out:

"Come along, the dog won't bite you." To this the Dutchman replied:

"You and I may know that he won't bite. The trouble is that the dog don't know it."

Charles remained at South Woodstock till the end of the spring term 1868. He was now nineteen, but with no apparent plans or ambitions. As usual during the summer vacation he helped on the farm when he couldn't avoid doing so, and fished when he could.

Although uncertain as to what he wanted to do, he knew well what he did not want to do. He disliked farming and showed no aptitude for it.

Probably this negative but well-defined fact rather than Charles's very meagre success as a student either at Kimball Academy or at the Green Mountain Institute, prompted his father to send him to college. The problem of which college to choose did not exist. Dartmouth quite naturally dominated Hanover. And to Dartmouth, quite logically, young Charles was sent.

II

DARTMOUTH IN THE '70's

Hanover and Dartmouth were an old story for Charles Ransom Miller. He had grown up within seven miles of the college green. He had known the community and the institution itself all his life. Coming over from his home in Hanover Centre, he gazed at the Dartmouth panorama with eyes that took its beauty for granted. The college on its wooded hill, the tower of the village church against the blueing mountains of Vermont, the evergreens of the old burying ground, and beyond, the rising hills of his own New Hampshire—all these had formed the familiar sights of his boyhood. He gave it all no thought, but made straight for the white frame house of President Smith, then in the most successful years of a successful administration.

In the light of the present elaborate plan of student admission at Dartmouth, President Smith's little system of personal examination by the faculty appears as highly informal. Our entering freshman followed the usual rule. This consisted first of a call upon the president himself. Doctor Smith had just passed his sixty-fourth birthday, and photographs taken at the time show him robust and healthy. They indicate the erect bearing, powerful physique, well-poised head, and firm mouth, fine brow and kindly eyes, to which his students testify. And no doubt he faced the lad who had gone over from Hanover Centre with the gracious and courteous manner characteristic of him.

Doctor Smith had come to Dartmouth from ministerial triumphs in New York, and retained a certain florid and high-sounding mode of expression, even in conversation. He had the habit of addressing an individual caller as Gladstone addressed his Queen, "like a public meeting." Students were struck at once by his marvellous command of the English language. Our freshman left no record of this meeting, but a fellow-student, Congressman Samuel L. Powers, gives a clear-cut impression. President Smith reminded him, he writes, "of a pen and ink portrait in black and white. There was nothing in his dress that was not either jet black or of the purest white. Even the shirt studs and cuff links attached to the immaculate linen, were black and his pale face and white hair were in striking contrast with his black coat."

President Smith gave young Miller three cards. Across each he wrote the name, "Charles R. Miller," and addressed them, one to Professor Parker for examination in Latin, one to Professor Packard in Greek, and the other to Professor Quimby in mathematics. In turn, young Miller sought out this professorial trio. In answer to their oral questionings he laid bare his knowledge and his ignorance of the humanities and the science of mathematics. Each inquisitor marked his card with a Greek letter and instructed the would-be freshman to return it to the president. No record states of just how near the examiners' hieroglyphs approached to the altitude of "alpha" on the one hand or the ominous depths of "omega" on the other. Probably they approximated a happy mean. Certainly upon their presentation the president with a spacious gesture and a manner which with a few words indicated that he had passed the best examination of anyone, stretched forth the right hand of fellowship and admitted him to all the rights and privileges of the Class of 1872.

For the first part of his freshman year young Miller lived in what was then known as Power's House on the opposite corner from the gymnasium. He there had as his first room-mate, George Fred Williams, of Boston, later to have a distinguished career at the Massachusetts Bar and in the Massachusetts Legislature, in Congress, and as United States Minister to Greece. At the end of his freshman year Williams left for two years of study abroad in Heidelberg and Berlin and Miller moved over to a room in Wentworth Hall.

This building along with Thornton and Reed formed the Old

Row. Wentworth Hall had been built in 1829 and named after an early benefactor of the college, Governor John Wentworth. Originally of red brick, it had at this time just undergone a sprucing up. Coats of yellow wash applied in the spring of 1868 brought it and Thornton in harmony with Reed, which had been yellow from the beginning.

Edwin J. Bartlett, also of '72, and later faculty member and ardent Hanoverian, writes of the Dartmouth of '69: "The total enrollment of the College that Fall was 370. Fifty-three were from without New England, and of the remainder, more than half were from New Hampshire. The list of all the faculty, including non-resident medical lectures, was 28. The 'Academic' faculty numbered 14, with the addition of one non-resident lecturer. There were 261 'Academies.' "

In the classroom of those days, the recitation system flourished. Three times daily the student had the opportunity to show the extent of his acquaintance with the subject under consideration. In the presence of his classmates, he faced a cross-examination by an expert cross-examiner. Congressman Powers holds to the belief that "the recitation system is the best method of instruction ever devised, and is especially well adapted to classes of limited numbers. It is a test in which ambition and pride stimulate the student to do his best work. The average boy at Dartmouth in the 'seventies did about as good class room work as he was capable of doing." Along with a uniformity of system of instruction went a uniformity of curriculum. "There were no 'snap' electives because there were no electives of any kind," writes Professor Bartlett. "Everyone in the Academic Department studied the same things if he studied at all. And if sitting beside the same men for four years and unitedly learning how much each professor manipulated his cards and applied the working scale had its disadvantages, it also had advantages which will never come again. That scale was a wonder: 1 was perfect; 5 was absolute zero; and as it was worked the average marks of the first third of the class seldom got any nearer 5 than 1.30. Greek appeared as mental pabulum in 9 of the 12 terms, and Latin in 8, and what was the matter with the other 3 or 4 terms, I cannot tell."

But a curriculum depends for its effectiveness on the personalities behind it. A subject succeeds or fails with the instructor who teaches it. What manner of men, then, composed the Dartmouth faculty in 1869?

Of them all, Professor Sanborn, head of the English Department, exerted the wisest personal influence. "He was a typical New Englander—the blood of the Websters flowed in his veins. He entertained positive views on the political and religious issues of the day, and did not lack the courage to defend them." "Professor Bully," as his classes called him, loved to advise the young fellows who came to him to enter political life in the expressed belief that they could be of more use to mankind in that field than elsewhere. Himself enthusiastic, he had the happy gift of arousing enthusiasm in others. His was the influence behind the renewed interest in literary expression, written and oral, which distinguished the Dartmouth of the later 'sixties and early 'seventies.

After him comes the head of the Latin Department, Professor Parker. He stands in the memory of his students as an interesting and charming personality. He impressed the young man from Hanover Centre to such an extent that Miller's first announced ambition was to become a professor of Latin. Doctor Parker had studied for the ministry, and had served as a chaplain through the Civil War. He brought to his Dartmouth classroom a certain pastoral gentleness. Indeed the rumor ran that Professor Parker possessed such a sympathetic nature that he was incapable of inflicting a low mark, however poor the recitation. He had the habit of giving his own interpretation of the passage, after the student called upon had reached the end. This he did in an English so glamorous and expressive as actually to win the admiration of his students.

A forerunner of the present era of youthful instructors was John C. Proctor, professor of Greek. He graduated with the

Class of '64, and became professor six years later at the age of thirty. He looms in the Dartmouth annals as an able scholar, but one whose energies went to the high-ranking men in his classes. He had small patience for the vanguard of that mighty army of collegians who boast the gentlemanly grade of C.

The Department of Mathematics and Engineering had at its head Elihu T. Quimby. His students recall him now as more engineer than college professor. He possessed all the traits of the "good mixer" and more than held his own in conversational give and take.

Modern languages got short shrift as far as the hours devoted to their study went. They had an able exponent in Professor Ruggles, and this scholarly man planted in young Miller the early seeds which later flowered in a marked lingual facility.

The other mentors included Professor Noyes, who taught Philosophy and Economics, and Professor C. A. Young, the foremost astronomer of his day. His Dartmouth students dubbed him Professor "Charley," but his later Princeton ones substituted the more inspired, Professor "Twinkle."

Dartmouth men all, they gave of their best in her service. Undoubtedly they could and did open up new worlds. But they stood as high priests of the old tread-mill system of education, and the great moral of young Miller's early years remains. A boy of true originality and scholarly possibilities did not get the real stimulus—until he left college. He chose while there to scorn the time-worn Baedekers and explore the new worlds on his own hook. His every action seemed to shock a faculty which offered the least possible resistance to a shock. He read everything he could lay his hands on, except the material required. Accordingly, he received, not the laurels of scholarship, but the "wooden spade." This trophy went to the "digger," the burner of midnight oil, somewhat in the plan of *lucus a non lucendo*. And his classmates were not surprised when the spade's recipient rose to his feet and the occasion, and accepted the presentation in a sparkling speech.

The college, however, did provide a favorable atmosphere for young Miller's definite literary trend. Professor Sanborn's revival of interest in writing and debating resulted in the re-establishment of *The Dartmouth,* by the senior class of 1867. This college monthly had not appeared since 1841. In its rebirth it kept to the earlier tradition and consisted of essays, poems and short editorials. Young Miller found in *The Dartmouth* just the impetus he needed for early flights in poetry and prose. These resulted in his election to the editorial board of the magazine in his senior year. In view of his career as a prose writer, it is interesting to note that poetry claimed his first love. His personal library consisted chiefly of volumes of verse. And he emulated the varied metres therein conned, with frequent adventures into rhyme. His class, impressed by the excellence of these productions, elected him to the post of class poet.

His desire to read anything and everything that came his way brought to him a realization of the advantages of an extensive vocabulary. He passed on an enthusiasm for words and their meanings to his friends. At the "eating clubs" at which his particular coterie met, Miller ruled that each member bring to each meal a new word. This, with its meanings, the group bandied around in its conversation, until the word became the common property of the table.

At first he found his urge for reading thwarted by the very institution organized to satisfy it—the library. The rules of the library, or rather libraries, for the college library and the literary collections of the Social Friends and the United Fraternity were kept apart as three separately administered entities, seem at this date as if devised to discourage wide reading or eclectic study. Despite the fact that Miller entered Dartmouth during a period of renewed interest in literary pursuits, and that the rules had been relaxed to permit a freer use of the volumes, he found the library still of little actual value. Students were not allowed, for one thing, to enter and inspect the books. As there existed only a very imperfect catalogue, they had no other means of making selections. Furthermore, the library opened its doors but one hour each day.

If a student knew what book he wanted, and thought that it was in the library, he might come and inquire at the proper hour at the window in the door of the library room. But it often happened that, through the deficiencies of the catalogue or the ignorance of the assistant, books could not be found that were in the library. Again, all winter long the room had no heat. Indeed it seemed as if everything conspired to prevent the college library from being of service. Accordingly the students relied chiefly upon the collections of the two societies. Even here, Miller found regulations a stumbling block, until the happy day when he rose above the law. This came in his senior year with the securing of the post of assistant-librarian of the Socials. The position of librarian in each of these fraternities ranked as one of high honor. Prospective candidates canvassed supporters and conducted energetic campaigns. In 1871 Charles Dana secured the election. The office carried a salary, the duty of administering the library, and a number of privileges. The librarian appointed his own assistants. Accordingly Miller applied to the successful Dana for the job of first aide. He secured it, and along with it, that which he chiefly desired, free access to the library at any time. In this period of unrestricted browsing, his uncannily retentive memory stocked itself with the beginning of that fund of information which later amazed his fellow-workers in journalism. A reading room, founded four years before his coming to college, introduced him to the chief current periodicals.

From these, he learned of a new voice in American letters—that of Walt Whitman. When the time came for the Class of '72 to follow an annual custom and invite a distinguished poet to deliver an address and to read from his own works, Miller persuaded his fellows to ask the new poet. True the choice had its chief inspiration in a desire to outrage the faculty. The action of '72 in passing over the approved list of New England respectabilities and sending for this stranger was regarded as a violent blow to a sacred tradition.

Young Miller fitted quickly and pleasantly into the social life of the then small New England college. He found himself with boys who had come from homes and communities similar to his own. He possessed a sense of fun, plenty of spirit, and a humorous twist in thought and expression. His Christian name Charles soon gave place to the shorter and more familiar "Chuck." His fellows regarded him as a likeable, human chap, a little free perhaps in thought and act for the theological atmosphere of his time, but never scatterbrain.

But in the later 'sixties, and particularly so at Dartmouth, the collegiate social life lacked most of its present-day complexities. For one thing, Hanover's inaccessibility threw the student body more on itself and its own resources. Then the long Winter imposed a very literal hibernation, unbroken by any "prom" or "carnival" with the attendant emotional upheavals and economic depressions. The practice of "dragging" a girl to this or that college function had yet to be born.

A present-day Dartmouth professor, writing on "What the Students Think About and Why," puts down eight general heads in the order of their importance. "His first and primary interest —and mental question—is the same as it has been through the ages, namely Himself." Then follow: Women, Activities, Studies, Religion, Movies, Liquor and Men.

Eliminate "movies," and move "women" to its vacant position in the sequence, and the list may well stand for that of 1869. Naturally time changes a detail here and there. "Activities" then put more stress on athletics as an outlet for the individual student's animal spirits, and nothing at all on athletics as a commercial proposition or as a bid for wide publicity. They put major emphasis on the "oratorical" and "literary." Studies probably suffered somewhat as an "interest" through the cut-and-dried nature of the curriculum. And religion? Surely as much vain speculation on its mysteries filled the winter evenings then, as fills the collegian's "bull sessions" now. What if Doctor Leeds, the college parson, was a preacher of the old school, who "kept well within the articles of the church creed," and "was not easily led astray by new views on theological questions"? Rumbles from the Victorian iconoclasts overseas must have reached even snowed-in Hanover to set the boys' tongues wagging. As for Women? New England boys turned naturally enough to New England girls. Young Miller for one found his romance in the neighborhood. With Men he proved a good mixer, and Liquor? Well, in those days Dartmouth undergraduates did not need to place proximity to the Canadian border among their alma mater's outstanding attractions. Each class divided temperamentally into "seeds," quiet, law-abiding souls on the one hand, and gayer dogs, known as "beats," who were whispered to "keep liquor under their beds," on the other. "Chuck" Miller threw in his lot with the more convivial crowd.

Indeed his lack of interest in studies as such became notorious. *The Times's* formal obituary of its distinguished editor stated that while at Dartmouth, he stood "near the head of the class." His classmates, with one accord, reverse that dictum and that position. His place in a class was nearer the foot. In fact he strove to attain that undistinguished ultimate. He entered into a contest with his fellow sophomore and roommate, John Bailey Mills, later of the Grand Rapids *Daily Herald,* as to which one should stand at the foot of the class.

Augustine V. Barker, a fellow scapegrace, but a judge-to-be, has this to say on the subject: "Miller could have stood near the head through the entire course with less effort perhaps than was exerted by any of those who did so, but *he did not do it.* He was entirely indifferent to marks, to rank in the class or to the rules and requirements of the institution. He had such a wholesome contempt for those reputed to get better marks by toadying to the faculty, that he leaned backwards in the other direction."

This leaning backwards reached an acute angle in his junior year. He made a point to express opposite views from those expressed by the professor in each course. He did not buy or use a text book that whole year. Instead he bought and used in the classroom, French novels. These he perused while others recited around him. When pounced upon by high Olympus and called to recite, he had the knack instantly to grasp the subject and astonish the interrupter.

Nor are his fellow students now wise after the event. At the time, both classmates and faculty sensed the brilliance of young Miller, saw the light he laboriously tried to hide under a bushel.

Very occasionally he would take his place on the side of the angels. It would so happen that a piece of work would attract him. He would then even go the length of investing a modicum of time in its preparation. One incident of this type stands out vividly in the memory of the Class of '72, and even entered into the official classday chronicle.

The Scene: a Dartmouth lecture room. A class in Euclid dragged its slow length along. One "rider" more devilishly involved than its predecessors baffled the intelligentsia. The professor, disappointed in his bright young mathematicians, drew a bow at a venture. He called on Miller, Miller the surreptitious classroom connoisseur of French fiction. Miller went up to the blackboard, took up the chalk and unhesitatingly and straightforwardly led the bewildered class safely through each successive intricacy to the final flourish of a Q. E. D. The resulting applause made the windows rattle. The class chronicle entered on its records that " 'Chuck' astonished the class by making a 'dead rush' on one memorable occasion." Something had inspired him to work up this particular problem, and he just happened to be called by the professor.

But if he gave the claims of the formal curriculum short shrift, young Miller did enter with zest into all the undergraduate literary activity. Like all remote communities, the Hanover of the time was thrown upon itself and its own resources for entertainment. For the lectures, concerts and the like, he concocted the "mock programmes," then in vogue, exercising his talents for raillery, burlesque and satire. Much of this work took the form of rhymes and jingles. But as class poet, he doffed the cap and bells and put on—becomingly at that—the singing robes of the prophet. In later years his classmates still regarded his chief formal poem, "Fancy's Art," as remarkable. Certainly the logical manner in which the young laureate held to his theme throughout foreshadowed the dominant trait of his later editorial style.

FANCY'S ART

CHARLES R. MILLER, HANOVER, N. H.

'Tis passing sweet to pause amid the ways
Wherein we pass our round of weary days,
The close-girt robes of toil aside to lay
And for a while to let the fancy play;
To let dim visions soothe the weary brain
And in light dreams forget the body's pain.
A power to cheer is magic Fancy's art,
To light again the dark desponding heart;
To lift the heavy clouds of doubt and care,
Far hence to drive the shadows of despair,
Grief to assuage, deep sorrow to console,
And with bright sunshine brighten all the soul.
All potent Fancy! Painter of the mind!
Within no limits is her skill confined.
A greater limner she than one who paints
With hand all trammelled by the dull restraints
That matter puts on man and keeps, because
He is of matter ruled by matter's laws.
A fitting thing she is that knows no stay
No let or hindrance in her fitful way.
All climes of earth, all places, howe'er far,
To her are near and known; space cannot bar
A thing that is no thing, a form of air,
An elfin that can well with elves compare.
But not in earthly ways her steps she keeps,
She spans the stars and heaven's arch o'er leaps;
She strips the splendors from the burning sun,
And with them boldly paints the course she's run.
From dim, forgotten niches of the past
She brings remembrances, that crowding fast
Upon the soul, bring back the olden days
With golden mem'ries flooding all their ways.
To every sense her light appeals she sends,
O'er all our being her fair sway extends.

With every tone she fills the listening ear,
Alike at her sweet will we seem to hear
The clang of arms, the harsh, hoarse battle's roar,
The silvery music of the wave-lapt shore,
The howling storm, the wild tornado's wrath,
The pine's soft whispering in the breeze's path.
She paints the splendors by old Phœbus cast
O'er Western skies when late the day has passed,
And shows the pale, gray tints of morning light
That rouse and rout the startled hosts of night.
On all alike she throws her joyous glance
And with impartial hand her favors grants.
Twin sister, she, of thought; where Reason reigns
With equal sceptre, she her state maintains.
All walks of life are hedged about by care,
And unremitted toil too soon will wear
Existence's sweets to nothingness away,
And leave what's left of life, blank, cold and gray.
Let all subservient be to greed of gold,
Gray hairs come on, we're prematurely old.
But give an hour to Fancy now and then,
Our spirits are refreshed, we're young again.
No more attractive form these day dreams wear
Than when they picture out a future fair,
And blandly to our willing ears relate
What haps to make or mar our coming fate.
To him whose life in business ways is spent
They come in whispers when his mind's unbent,
And in his ear a flattering they tell
Of wealth to come that will his coffers swell.
Estates he sees, and houses all his own,
He feels himself a man of riches grown.
He who of learned life a choice has made,
Whose mental wealth is all his stock in trade,
Dreams over of the progress he will make,
The high positions he is bound to take.
The statesman sees in fancy his proud name,
In splendor written on the scroll of fame.
The lawyer to the judge's bench aspires,
Once there, from legal ways he soon retires,
In politics some rival to defeat,
And in the nation's council takes his seat.
Such aspirations men do all possess
From higher ranks to low ones to progress.
Though never may the higher place be won

Sweet are the visions that entice them on.
But one there is who ever ready seems
To turn from cold realities to dreams;
To leave behind the heavy, thankless task
That pleases not, in Fancy's smiles to bask.
That one the student is; dreams are his light,
His life, his soul; he sees before him, bright
In its approach, the time he's longed to see,
The wished-for time that comes to set him free.
Grown weary with much poring over books,
He longs to leave them, and impatient looks
To that glad day when college life complete
New paths shall open to his untried feet.
Not yet arrived at man's full, proud estate,
He ill can brook delay and patient wait
For time's slow march to show his future's plan,
He would at once step forth and be a man.
Too soon will end his happiest days of life
Too soon will come the struggles, cares and strife;
He knows it not, to him 'tis all untried,
He only sees the bright, the golden side.
Fair structures are the castles that he builds,
And every part, his teeming fancy gilds.
Light forms flit over in their stately halls,
Gay banners graceful float upon the walls.
What wonder that bright visions round him play,
When fancy holds her undisputed sway.
As when the ivy up the rough-hewn side
Of some old wall climbs, ever spreading wide,
Its wealth of sinuous, interlacing vines,
Round every point its leafy trail entwines,
Through every crevice sends a living root,
On every corner plants a clinging foot,
And daily growing ever upward steals
Until at length it all the wall conceals;
And what was rude, unsightly, rough before,
Concealed from sight, by verdure covered o'er,
Becomes a thing of beauty richly drest
In robes of living green, its form expressed
In flowing lines and graceful curvings new
With all its roughness hidden from the view;
So Fancy, with a web of brilliant dyes,
Hides all the future's trials from his eyes,
Decked gaily out by her consummate art
He fails to see the rougher, ruder part:

DARTMOUTH IN THE '70's

In such a splendid, many-coloured dress
It looks all sunshine, gladness and success.
But as the leaves from off the ivy fall,
And show again the rude-built, rough old wall,
So, from his future, falls the tissue light
That kept its troubles from his trusting sight.
Time rudely strips it from the coming years,
And shows their ills, discomforts, pains and fears.
What if the end of dreams he knows full well,
How false and flattering are the tales they tell,
He still dreams on, enjoys them while they last,
Regards the future rather than the past,
And oft forgets connections with the Real
In fondly dreaming of his loved Ideal.

> But time is passing, let us leave
>   The dreamer to his fate;
> Our Prophet knows full truthfully
>   His future to relate.

> Our Chronicler is waiting too,
>   His pleasing tale to tell;
> The history of our four years,
>   And what each one befell.

> We've yet to sing our farewell song,
>   And give our parting cheer;
> We've yet to smoke our calumet;
>   The time is drawing near.

> We've followed Learning's pleasant paths,
>   Have walked in Wisdom's ways;
> The course is done, the end is come
>   Of happy college days.

> The "parchments" wait our eager hands,
>   And we are waiting too
> To see'f diplomas and degrees
>   Will bring us work to do.

> A.B.'s are very common now,
>   And not much in demand;
> We feel a strong desire to know
>   What task awaits our hand.

Our self-made Greeley will not have
    A college man about;
He swears that one he'll not e'en hire
    To sweep his office out.

'Twere sad indeed if all our hopes
    Of fortune, fame and fees
Were ruined by the fact that we
    Have taken our degrees.

If our diplomas drag us down
    Instead of helping on;
We'll sell them though they'd brought us more
    Before the wool was gone.

Then for some farmer we can work,
    With board and clothes for pay;
And go to school three months each year
    To pass the time away.

And in that humble sphere of life,
    We'll toil and patient wait,
Until we find our talents can
    Command a higher rate.

Small matter where our lot be cast,
    If when the race is won,
In viewing what our hands have wrought,
    The Master says, "Well done."

Young Miller's power of concentration, used only in his formal studies as a last-minute resource to escape the executioner's axe, came to the fore in his play. He excelled in any game he took up. His friend Barker recalls a triumph in chess:

"Once he and I were calling on some classmates who roomed in Professor Quimby's house; as we passed the Professor's study on our way out he called us in and in a rather patronizing manner asked if we played chess and offered to teach Miller to play. I do not think either of us had ever seen the game and I, not being interested, went to my room. Some time afterwards when Miller returned he said that he could have beaten Quimby easily the first game they played but did not think it was good policy to do so. He also stated that Quimby was boasting about taking part in a contest by mail and stated that if he could get into it without Quimby knowing his identity he would like to beat him there and believed he could do it. I suggested mailing under another name and he did so and defeated Professor Quimby in every game that he played with him. I think these contests were in *Bonner's New York Weekly* and I doubt if Professor Quimby ever knew who his real antagonist in the contests was."

As none of the national fraternities then having chapters at Dartmouth had asked Miller to join, he met the situation with characteristic resource. He set about starting one himself. Through his efforts the Omicron Deuteron Charge of Theta Delta Chi came into being. It was instituted with fitting pomp and circumstance; the president of the Grand Lodge of that fraternity came up from New York personally to officiate. In the room of A. N. Ward (later Reverend A. N. Ward), No. 17 Thornton Hall, this fraternal official admitted the first Dartmouth initiates.

When the choice of a delegate to send to the annual convention of the fraternity in New York came up for discussion, the "brothers" voted naturally enough for Miller. Accordingly as a Dartmouth undergraduate he made his first trip to the metropolis that was later to hold him in such high esteem. While in New York he went about sight-seeing with a fellow Theta Delt from Princeton. Somewhere in his travels the Princetonian picked up the germs of small-pox. He took them back with him to Princeton, where, after due process of incubation, an epidemic developed. For a time Princeton had to close its doors. Miller escaped the small-pox but brought the measles back to Dartmouth. His friends there decided that of the two, Miller had made the better choice.

At the end of his sophomore year, Dartmouth College decided to expel the future editor of *The Times*. In this action it followed the precedent already set by Kimball Union Academy. The exact cause of the decree remains shrouded in academic secretiveness. Faculties have before 1869 and since moved in a mysterious way their wonders to perform. His classmates attributed it to the growing sum of Miller's minor offences. He had a way of being a very annoying young man, this brilliant but dilatory student. Perhaps his chief irritating habit was the one already noted; the fact that he never let a chance pass in a recitation room to express opposite views from those of the dignitary in charge. But the fact remains that at the end of this college year he left Dartmouth with the understanding that he was not to return there in the fall.

Up to this time he had spent his summers—as did the sons of most New England farmers—in helping to till and tend the parental soil and garner the crops. But this June, shortly after Dartmouth shut its doors, he left Hanover in disgust for—nobody knew where. Presumably this sudden departure formed the one exit left open in what was otherwise a domestic impasse. Miller, senior, never anywhere near affluent, had done his best to give his son a sound education. That son, from all accounts, had done his best to dodge the opportunity so provided. We may well imagine that parental wrath waxed, as only wrath self-consciously justifiable knows how, at the news of this second expulsion.

Certainly when his classmates returned to commence their junior year they found neither "Chuck" nor trace of him. Finally when the term was some weeks underway, word reached his friends from some Dartmouth men that they had seen Miller in Tilton, New Hampshire. The report proved correct. Miller had found work in the tiny printing office at Tilton. His classmate, A. V. Barker, was delegated to seek him out and if possible induce him to return. This class representative went to Tilton and found "Chuck" at the case setting type. Let Judge Barker himself recall the interview that followed:

"I went to Tilton and found him at the case setting type; in his usual indifferent manner he said that the exhaustion of brain tissue at that job was not so great as trying to compete with the man who had led our class up to that time, and that it was more remunerative.

"He told me that he had been canvassing for one of Mark Twain's books and had about starved at the job, whereas he was getting three meals a day at this one. He declined to treat the matter of returning to Hanover seriously and in the midst of an earnest appeal of mine to do so interrupted me and said he would rather discuss with me 'The Infinite Ramification of the Ideal.' Beneath this air of indifference however, I could detect a note of utter discouragement, evidently resulting from his inability to return to college."

Barker, however, kept on endeavoring to persuade his friend that Dartmouth wanted him back, but left without any very sanguine hope that "Chuck" would return to Hanover.

A few nights later, towards morning, Barker was awakened by someone in his room, and Miller crawled into bed with him. "Chuck" slept on until Barker had returned from his first recitation and announced his intention of staying in bed until Barker had discovered the lay of the land. Barker went at once to see the president's daughter, Miss Sallie Smith, the usual intermediary. Later in the day, she sent him word that if Miller would call on the president he would be allowed quietly to take his place in the recitation rooms. To this Judge Barker now adds:

"I am quite sure Miller did not call on the president or make any promises, but he did take the place quietly in the recitation rooms. The episode was never mentioned between us afterwards."

As the son of a small farmer, the future editor's material resources had always been slight. Coupled with this went an indifference to money matters verging on ignorance. One classmate records that:

"Miller was absolutely irresponsible in money matters in those days. He did not seem to know what money was for; perhaps I should not use the word, Indifferent, because there was no thought of dishonesty or anything approaching it on the part of any one who knew him. While always hard up I never knew him to borrow a dollar from any one, although bills gave him no concern."

Another says: "I am inclined to think that if the Class had been polled upon the question of chances of financial success, Miller would have stood very near the foot of the list." Still another amplifies the point: "None of us who knew him in those days would have dared to predict that he would ever become an accomplished student of Greek and the modern languages. Neither did any one expect that he would become the wealthiest of the class."

But while his subsequent fortune cast no shadows before it at Dartmouth, his coming connection with writing and with journalistic writing at that, did. His classmates even then perceived him as preordained for the fourth estate. Despite his negligence as a student, they knew his large, well-formed head contained an active brain with plenty of gray matter. They had marvelled at his facility in the correct use of big words; they had heard him often express himself with pungency and force. The class prophet, Charles H. Clement, voiced but the general feeling when with mock gravity he looked into the future and declared:

"I learned that Miller had succeeded to the management of *The Day's Doings,* where by his pleasantly caustic remarks, and the chaste as well as artistic production of his pencil and muse, he is daily winning himself laurels."

Into the pre-graduation celebrations "Chuck" Miller entered whole-heartedly—too whole-heartedly to please the faculty. In fact he felt he stood in such ill-favor as the result of last-moment convivialities, that the college might withhold his degree. Accordingly on Commencement Day, he disappeared from the campus. Some friends started out to search for him. Finding him, they rushed him back to the college, with barely time enough to change into the cutaway coat, striped trousers, and tall silk hat, the then approved regalia of the graduate-elect.

Later, the same day, Augustine Barker, on his round of good-by visits, called at the home of Mrs. Paige, whose house had catered for his boarding club. There on the lawn, he discovered Miller playing croquet with his friend from Kimball Academy, Frances Daniels. Miss Daniels, Mrs. Paige's niece, had come up from Plainfield to assist her during the Commencement week.

Miller at the time appeared to have neither plans nor prospects, and his friend, before leaving, was anxious to talk over what the future might hold. Calling him aside, Barker, in a most serious and earnest manner, asked:

"'Chuck,' what *are* you going to do?"

Putting his hand up to Barker's ear, and in a tone equally serious and grave, Miller replied:

"By George, I am going to beat that girl playing croquet."

III

THE SPRINGFIELD "SCHOOL OF JOURNALISM"

"Chuck" Miller carried from his graduation platform two things—his diploma and an urge to write. With them both, he turned naturally enough to daily journalism. For it happened that in 1872 that calling had even more than its usual appeal. True, the college man in newspaper work then lacked his present-day growing supremacy in numbers, but he had already won a respected place. Each Commencement season added fresh recruits to the ranks—boys who eagerly accepted the light pay and the heavy work of the reporter, lured then as now by the chance offered to watch the drama of politics from behind the scenes, to take an actual part in the pageant of each day as it unfolded, to get a "press pass," as it were, to the ringside of life. In 1872, in addition to these omnipresent charms, a presidential election of more than ordinary interest loomed ahead.

Then, too, along with the reconstruction period in politics had gone, hand in hand, a companion era in newspaper offices. Everywhere they hummed with the quickening of a new life. Mechanical changes had speeded up the whole process of production. New inventions entered one door; much of the old tedium went out the other. The flat bed of type gave place to the revolving cylinder. The stereotyping method meant the multiplication of pages to any needed number. Giant rolls of mile upon mile of white print paper superseded the individual sheets and formed the fodder of the new presses. And in the immediate future lay the invention of the linotype.

Small wonder that our ambitious collegian turned from thoughts of professing a dead language to the desire actually to practise a living one. He looked over the field. Near at home, in his native New England, the Springfield *Republican* stood out, as it stood out in the larger setting of the whole country.

Founded as a weekly by Samuel Bowles, the elder, in 1824, its reputation and its fortune grew steadily. *The Republican* took cognizance of that day's prevailing diversions, politics and diseases, and its pertinent comments and numerous patent-medicine advertisements made for it a welcome place in the Springfield community and in the surrounding neighborly towns. But when in 1844 the eighteen-year-old Samuel Bowles, 2d, persuaded his father to inaugurate a daily edition, the Springfield *Republican* began to win its way to the highest rungs of journalistic fame.

By 1872 it ranked as perhaps the most carefully edited paper in the whole country. Certainly it flourished as the most independent and fearless. Its youthful inspiring genius had ripened now into "the great Sam Bowles," a born leader of opinion and a born newspaper man. He had already achieved his announced aim, to create a newspaper "that should stand firmly in the possession of powers of its own; that should be concerned with the passing and not with the past; that should perfectly reflect its age, and yet should be itself no mere reflection; that should control what it seemed only to transcribe and narrate; that should teach without assuming the manners of an instructor, and should command the coming times with a voice that had still no sound but its echo of the present."

"Chuck" Miller took his courage in both hands and wrote to this great editor and asked him for a job. He wrote of first flights at Dartmouth, of his association with the college magazine, and gave as a reference his literary mentor, Professor Sanborn. As it happened, this letter arrived at an opportune time. *The Republican* had need of new men. A number of the old staff had just given up their positions when the paper came out in support of Greeley, and gone over to a local evening sheet, the Springfield *Union*. This independence of party had long figured as one of the Bowles principles. It had its genesis away back in 1854 and 1855 in repeated declarations that the Whig Party was a dead and useless relic, and that a new party free from this clammy grasp formed the only hope of a successful opposition to slavery. But in 1872, *The Republican* announced its political independence as a foremost tenet of its professional faith.

Mr. Bowles wrote young Miller from Dartmouth College to come along, in much the same manner as he had just written young Solomon Bulkley Griffin at Williams College, and to several others. Griffin arrived first. He found lodgings in Elm Street, and began work as a "freshman" in *The Republican's* "school of journalism." A few weeks later, in July, young Miller came. He presented himself to Mr. Bowles, who advised him to look up the boy from Williams as a prospective roommate. Later, as the distinguished managing editor of *The Republican,* Mr. Griffin recalled that meeting in his published reminiscences, "People and Politics." "I heard a voice at my elbow say, 'Is your name Griffin? I'm going to room with you.'

"The impulse to say 'The dickens you are' was suppressed, as I looked up and saw a clean cut youth clad in a green cutaway coat and vest, with striped trousers, and wearing a silk hat not of the latest vintage. 'How's that?' I answered.

"'My name is Miller; I've seen Mr. Bowles and he advises it, and I have been to the Elm Street mansion. You were asleep when I was shown the room.'

"I looked up and liked him."

In that look and that liking it was all settled. The two embarked on a lifelong friendship. At Mrs. Van Dusen's boarding house their humor and high spirits attracted to their circle similar convivial souls. But one fellow boarder, a serious-minded youth and a pillar of the local Y. M. C. A., objected to their somewhat rowdy mirth. He complained to Mrs. Van Dusen, and threatened to leave. For a time it looked as if her decision might go against the two joyous journalists. But they skilfully shifted the discussion from the plane of ethics to that of economics.

"If he leaves, you only lose one boarder."

"If we have to leave, you lose two."

THE SPRINGFIELD "SCHOOL OF JOURNALISM"

Economics ruled the day. Miller and Griffin remained. The complainant could do as he pleased.

Their modest lodgings were in line with their modest incomes. *The Republican* paid them each $30 a month. As everything—board, lodging, apparel—came out of that thirty per, both practised strict economy. For one thing, they made their clothes last. "Chuck" Miller cordially hated most of the wardrobe he had brought from Dartmouth. The splendors of Hanoverian tailoring paled in the light of Springfield's metropolitan modes. His ancient silk hat bore only too obviously the earmarks of the heirloom. Still that "beaver" had graced his graduation. It shared his greatest dislike with an overcoat, a long yellow affair. This he detested and vowed he would never wear again. But pride had to give way before the chill winds of New England. In later years, amusement never quite got the better of those early mortifications. "No one liked good things more than I," he used to say.

Finally their academic wardrobe did wear out. And stern necessity forced them into buying trousers. They invested in an "iron-bound" variety which alas could only be obtained in a loud checkered pattern. Next day, the office received "Chuck's checker-boards" with acclaim.

Later on, the two friends moved from Elm Street to the Gilmour Block. Here several others from *The Republican's* staff had established themselves, and with the new arrivals arranged a comfortable suite of rooms. The menage boasted a piano, and also numbered among its attractions a convenient proximity to Sheppert's saloon. Music, good humor and foaming jugs of beer mingled to make memorable the off hours of this journalistic coterie.

For these country boys the Springfield of the day had all the lure of a big town and many of a big town's cultural advantages. Miller enjoyed there for the first time a pleasure which Hanover could never afford him—the theatre.

One play in particular captivated the young reporters as much as it apparently scandalized the easily scandalized New England conscience of Springfield. This play was "The Black Crook."

Miller and Griffin attended the theatre almost nightly during "The Black Crook's" stay, and became so thoroughly familiar with the lines of the piece that they remarked to each other that if illness afflict any member of the cast, each was well qualified to go on as substitute in any of the parts.

The following letter written during this period to his Dartmouth friend, George Fred Williams of Boston, indicates not only the continuance of his romance with Frances Daniels, but chronicles the beginning of definitely personal associations with "the great Sam Bowles." Written but a little over four months after his arrival in Springfield, it shows him enjoying the great editor's "splendid claret, fine cigars and good talk" with the prospect of many similar treats in view.

As for his love affair with Miss Daniels. That young lady's mother did her best to discourage its continuance. She looked with disfavor on his suit chiefly because she regarded the future editor-in-chief of the New York *Times* as having "no prospects." The letter shows how love found a way over this barrier. Mrs. Paige of Hanover, aunt of Frances and proprietress of the eating-house frequented by "Chuck" and his friends at Dartmouth, was apparently on the side of the two young people. And we hardly need to read between the lines as he writes of the "little Mädchen" waiting for him at the home of her aunt in Hanover, and of the invitation to travel thither for Thanksgiving dinner along with the "great and most elaborate preparation for my reception, of the progress of which I have been daily apprised."

But here is the letter itself:

THE REPUBLICAN
Springfield, Mass.
Nov. 26, 1872.
LIEBER TED:
Utterly "onpossible" my dear boy, to accept your most gracious invitation, for which, however, permit me to bubble over in gratitude with as fervent an ebullition as I should have done had some kind goddess decreed that I should accept. Your letter makes me stand "halting between two opinions," I confess, notwithstanding the advanced state of my preparations for a hegira Hanover-ward, for nothing could afford me a keener de-

THE SPRINGFIELD "SCHOOL OF JOURNALISM"

light than to break bread and triturate luxury at your bountiful board Thanksgiving Day, especially when the banquet would have been sanctified to my spiritual instruction by the pressure of such honorable gentlemen as Herrin, Farmer and Welch, and the festive scene been rendered peculiarly pleasant and attractive by the presence of such charming ladies as your Mother and Sister, to whom by the way, please present my regards. Look on this picture and then on this, thought I, and in the latter I saw a little Mädchen in deep distress sore grieved because the long-looked for came not. Her lovely eyes red with weeping and her distractingly beautiful bosom rent with the keen grief of disappointment. Excuse that clause, but I imagine that it covers all—and my heart went out in prospective pity towards that gentle damsel and I said that I would not so wrong her. Seriously, Ted, Mrs. Paige, *et al* expect me and have made great and most elaborate preparation for my reception, of the progress of which I have been daily apprised, and as I have written of my full intention of journeying thither and have received passes (R. R.) to that intent, I hardly feel at liberty to cancel the engagement. Had your invitation possessed priority, it would have been most gladly accepted.

Sam Bowles has been "gooder than pie" all day today. Came to me this morning and asked if I desired to go home tomorrow, and when I told him: "Yea Lord thou knowest that I do," he kindly told me that I need not, as I had intended, tear my shirt in hurry to get back before Friday night, but might browse around among the tender lily pads until Saturday night. But note. About six he invited Chin and me to take tea at his house which we did. Good feed, splendid claret, fine cigars and a good hour's talk with him in his library was the sum of the pleasantest thing we have had in Springfield. He invited us to come up Saturday nights and meet the elite of the city. This seems to presage a little "society." This inviting to tea is an unusual and totally unexpected proceeding on his part.

It is as late as hell, and I have written more than 10,000 pages of manuscript today, so permit me to send love to crowd and make my bow.

CHUCK.

But work preceded play. From the first young Miller had the good luck to secure the type of thing that well suited him—assignments which he thoroughly enjoyed, and which, occasionally, took his individual light from under the bushel of reportorial anonymity. *The Republican* ran a department called "Gleanings and Gossip," much in the manner of the modern sophisticated "column." Mr. Bowles referred to it as "raking after the cart." But it gave the young writer an unusual chance to display his ever-enlarging vocabulary. He had luck too in his constituency.

For Springfield, the "home town" of Webster's Dictionary, was naturally somewhat self-conscious on the use and abuse of words. He developed a flair for the garbled quotation. Old residents still chuckle over a few of them.

This one, in particular, lingers:

> "The melancholy days have come, the saddest of the year,
> A little too hot for whiskey straight, a little too cool for beer."

In 1873, *The Republican* put him to work covering Springfield's municipal government. On any paper, this assignment stands out as an important one. On *The Republican,* due to the importance which Mr. Bowles placed on local news, it was doubly so. Springfield then was a homogeneous community with a population of about thirty thousand. The newer races had not as yet swept in. It remained well in line with the best New England tradition. True, that tradition as regards the social order had already begun to change. Already the rise of a wealthy manufacturing class threatened the supremacy of the ministerial and professional coteries. But life then still lacked most of its present-day complexities. The assignment gave the young reporter the chance to meet Springfield's best minds, to get an insight into municipal management and local politics. Occasionally as his familiarity with this field grew, he would collaborate on an editorial to the extent of giving special information to the editorial writer on some municipal problem or other. But this was as near as he got in Springfield to the sacred page.

Side by side with this new work, he kept on with his old studies. Indeed his professional work showed him the necessity for filling up this reservoir. He strove to make up in special study in Springfield for the time which the Dartmouth curriculum had denied to modern languages. He endeavored particularly to master French. Griffin and he secured a French text book and started in together.

Both young men had figured as class poets at their respective colleges, and both, accordingly, enjoyed the little library of the

THE SPRINGFIELD "SCHOOL OF JOURNALISM"

then modern verse which "Chuck" had accumulated at Dartmouth. First in his heart and mind reigned Swinburne. He read and declaimed at length from Swinburne and other favorite "fleshly" poets. But pride in this library was short-lived. Mr. Griffin has told of the tragedy that befell—of the entrance into their boarding-house society of a blonde and gushing brakeman's wife, a woman of charm and professed cultivation, of her borrowing volume by volume "Chuck" Miller's entire assemblage of the Muses, and then, of her sudden departure into the void from which she came, taking with her all "Chuck's" poetry and all Griffin's new shirts.

These were the days before the Sunday newspapers. That journalistic dime museum had yet to come into being to litter the Sabbath living-room, and destroy the reporter's week-end. The boys at Springfield enjoyed a let-up in their activities from the time *The Republican* "went to bed" on Friday night till well on into Sunday afternoon when they started in to work on Monday's paper. Out of this freedom grew a pleasant journalistic lunch club. The younger men on *The Republican* desired to look beyond the horizon of their own immediate community. They got in touch with kindred souls in near-by cities—Hartford, New Haven, Worcester, and Boston. With them, they fell into the way of meeting each Saturday for luncheon, one week in Hartford, the next in Springfield, and so on. To these gatherings would come the late Charlie Russell, afterward member of Congress for Connecticut, George Fred Williams, who helped put himself through law school by doing night work on the Boston *Globe;* Frank Root of the New Haven *Paladium,* later to write with Miller for *The Times,* and enjoy with him membership in the Century Club. Naturally their talk grew out of their newspaper work and experiences. They discussed each other's communities and local leading lights; they vivisected each other's journals; and swapped ideas on policies and practices.

While this daily round and common task furnished that indispensable training which experience alone can give, Mr. Bowles supplemented it in the case of his young men with an informal but definite course of instruction. His Springfield "school of journalism" preceded by a generation even the dream of such an academic foundation. But his comment, *"The Republican* is as much an institution as any of the colleges" would seem to father the thought. He had always imposed his ideas of what a newspaper might and should be upon his staff, but the incorporation of those ideas into a curriculum, grew out of grim necessity. The year 1872 found him with an expanding paper and an increased, but to a large extent, raw staff. College seniors then, with education the prize of the high calling of the few, possessed even more omnipotence than to-day. Their campus laurels were still green— only too green. Patiently, Mr. Bowles took "Chuck" Miller and his confreres in charge for practical post graduate studies.

He sent them out on routine assignments, and strove to make them acquainted with the sources of news, and the channels through which information reached the editor. They went out, they saw, they wrote. He read what they had written and sighed. Then he and his fellow-editors took each precious effusion in one hand and the author by the other, and strove to transmute the one into workmanlike "copy" and the other into a workmanlike reporter.

He taught them, for one thing, the technique of the "lead." *The Republican* was among the first to appreciate the wisdom of summarizing in the opening paragraph the gist of the subsequent news story. Mr. Bowles accordingly trained his young writers to this convention which has now become a standardized newspaper formula. Always he insisted upon a clarity and economy of style. Reporters and editorial writers alike on *The Republican* must say much in little. He insisted on this, first because he liked copy written that way, and secondly, because the mechanics of the paper demanded it. The compositors set everything by hand; they were few in number; the space at their disposal was limited. Exigencies of makeup frequently imposed drastic last-minute contraction. Copy, written economically to

THE SPRINGFIELD "SCHOOL OF JOURNALISM" 39

start with, usually suffered a squeezing down in the composing room. History records that on occasion it even survived as many as six squeezings down in one evening. All this tended to impress upon the "cubs" the shining virtues of conciseness and crystal clarity.

Then again, Mr. Bowles possessed a consuming passion for the niceties of newspaper making in typography as well as in text. He regarded it as an art. He insisted that his writers use capitals sparingly. He economized on display type. The use of big type he felt left *The Republican* with lessened resources. It left the paper much as an outpouring of superlatives left the writer—with nothing to meet a really great contingency. Richard Hooker in his centennial history of *The Republican* illustrates this Bowles trait. A reporter had lavished extravagant praise on the local appearance of a minor celebrity. "That was a fine article," Mr. Bowles took occasion to comment. "But if Jesus Christ should come to earth to-morrow morning, you haven't left a single thing to say for Him."

Everything which the young reporters wrote received the closest editing. Their stuff passed not to a copy-reader as now, but to an editor direct. No part of the paper escaped this same careful scrutiny. "There goes Sam Bowles killing himself trying to find a misplaced comma," they would say. Small wonder that *The Republican* came to rank with Dana's *Sun* as a newspaperman's newspaper. The hour of going to press favored this close attention to technique. At that time, *The Republican* had until 4 a. m. to catch the trains. This meant that the staff could comment editorially up to the very last hour before publication. It also gave Mr. Bowles plenty of time for his laborious progress through the proofs. From this progress he came to formulate collections of "do's" and "don'ts"—forerunners of the present-day journalistic style-books.

Young Miller entered into his Springfield duties with a wholeheartedness and zest that would have surprised his Dartmouth professors. His work grew yearly in importance. His rich fund of humor and his social qualities made him popular with the municipal officials whom he "covered." The late "Bob" Morris, Springfield's Clerk of Court, recalled an incident illustrating both young Miller's "mixing" propensities and his early belief in the power of printer's ink. Mr. Morris had fallen legal heir to a "white elephant" in the form of an insolvent club's gymnasium and athletic equipment. He didn't want it, didn't know what to do with it, and publicly bewailed his acquisition. Miller came along and told him that all he needed was publicity. Merely advertise in *The Republican,* and hey presto the "white elephant" would vanish leaving the purchase price in its stead.

"All right," said Clark. "You go ahead and advertise. If I make a sale we'll 'divvy' on the proceeds." Miller did advertise, and at considerable cost. But alas for this firm believer in printer's ink, its usually potent charm did not work.

The "great Sam Bowles" did more than chasten his reporters' rhetoric; he, to a large extent, moulded their political thinking. It happened that "Chuck" Miller, "Sol" Griffin and the rest came under Mr. Bowles' influence just at the time when he turned his long-held ideas and theories into the concrete of actual practice. He told them for one thing that an editor's equipment should consist of "brains and ugliness," using the last word in the sense of combativeness. His course during the presidential campaign, the Grant-Greeley combat of '72, brought both these attributes to the fore. But why bring back the smoke and smell of an old battle? Time now has softened and almost obliterated its animosities. To Grant's military genius it has given an added sheen, while it has tended to blur all memory of his Executive incompetence. Yet out of that campaign arose a new movement in the press, a movement with Mr. Bowles and his *Republican* well in the vanguard. Small wonder that the historian acclaims this period in which "newspapers had the courage to assert their independence of the Republican Party when it fell into unworthy hands," as "the most creditable chapter in American journalism."

With the powerful editorial hammer of repetition, Mr. Bowles

THE SPRINGFIELD "SCHOOL OF JOURNALISM"

impressed, upon the young men around him, his code of personal and professional independence. He believed that a newspaperman should not accept public office, that he should keep himself free from "any entanglement that might affect his independence." This led him in actual practice even to decline railroad passes for himself and his staff, when he felt the pass business overdone. He determined that he himself should never become "a party mouthpiece," or *The Republican* "a party organ." And he chose for the paper's motto—"All the News and the Truth About It." Fortunately this attitude has now lost its pristine novelty, but in those days, as he wrote editorially, "the idea of an independent journal, meeting every separate issue on its own merits, without regard to organization or parties, seems impossible of entrance into some minds."

But it did enter into the mind of the future editor of *The Times*. Along with the thoughts of that rigorous early training, it was uppermost in his mind when a few years later he stood by the open grave of the "great Sam Bowles" in Springfield cemetery. To his friend Griffin, as they turned to leave, he summed it up in one phrase, "It was worth it." It continued to be worth it to them both throughout their lives.

Let the scene change from Springfield to the Century Club, New York. Let the time roll for a moment, thirty and forty and fifty years on. In the smoking-room's deep, leather-cushioned comfort, in a light mellowed by the wraiths of departed cigars, two gentlemen sit chatting. One is Solomon Bulkley Griffin, managing editor of the Springfield *Republican*. The other is Charles Ransom Miller, editor-in-chief of the New York *Times*.

Mr. Griffin: "You know, Miller, the older I get and the more I learn, the more I admire the great Sam Bowles."

Mr. Miller: "So do I. Nowadays, when some public question is in my mind, the thought comes, 'How would Sam Bowles look upon that?'"

Thus did the training received at the Springfield "school of journalism" remain as both an inspiration and a guide.

IV

EARLY DAYS IN PARK ROW

Occasionally Miller and his friend Griffin took advantage of their free Saturdays and the free transportation to which newspapermen were then considered entitled—though Sam Bowles's independence was soon to spurn railway passes for himself and his staff—and came to New York for the day. They would dine at the Broadway Central Hotel; they would stroll up and down that famous thoroughfare; they would watch the crowds in front of the theatres; but they chose for the most part, under the guidance of economy, to see their own matinée from benches in Union Square—the always stirring drama of a great city's daily life. And they turned with an eager interest to find the reflection of it all in the metropolitan press.

Of the New York papers of that period, one, *The Times*, happened to be basking in the warmest place in the sun of public approval. For was it not the paper which had succeeded in exposing and uprooting the municipal corruption that was Tweed? In the very recent memory of the young journalist from Springfield rested the story of that achievement. He recalled how, just a few years back, in 1870, George Jones, the partner of *The Times's* great editor, Raymond, had started the attack on the most daring and most solidly entrenched ring of grafters the city had ever known; how for fourteen months, with scant encouragement and help from New York in general, he had kept up the battle with ever-increasing vigor until, on July 22, 1871, he placed in the hands of the reading public the sensational transcriptions from the books of the City Comptroller which drove Tweed and his fellow-swindlers from the City Hall trough.

Though the metropolitan publications, with the notable exception of *Harper's Weekly*, regarded *The Times's* efforts with unseeing eyes, the nation-wide press hailed the breaking up of the Tweed Ring as the great journalistic achievement of the generation. Up in Springfield, *The Republican* warmly applauded it. And in the shop talk of the office, young Miller had heard of the flattering price—$5,000,000—which the corrupt officials, unable to cripple *The Times* in its progress, had offered for that paper's soul.

Naturally it was of *The Times* and professional connection with it that he dreamed, when he chanced to build his air castles on the bed rock of Manhattan Island. The desire stood well in line with the prevailing fashion. Abandoned farms began to dot every New England community. Too many abandoned farmers had heard and answered the call of the big city. Young Miller wished with the rest to join in that migration. Toward the end of it, he got his chance.

A Dartmouth friend, one Thayer, graduating in advance of the Class of '72, had come at once to Gotham, had established connection with *The Times* and had risen to a post on its telegraph desk. He felt "a call," as they say, to enter the ministry. Despite his creditable journalistic success so far, he decided to answer it. He wrote Miller of his intentions, and advised him to apply for his soon-to-be-vacant job on *The Times*.

Miller decided to waste no time in correspondence. He took the next train New York-wards and presented his application in person.

On July 5, 1872, he arrived and began his association with *The Times,* then on Park Row in its third home. He convinced Mr. Jones of his qualifications to start right in where the theological Thayer had left off, and went at once as assistant editor on the telegraph desk. Here his extraordinary range of interests and that miscellaneous but wide-spread reading, which to his Dartmouth mentors appeared like Sam Weller's knowledge of London, "extensive and peculiar," stood him in good stead. His Springfield studies, too, had appreciably increased his facility in reading French. He desired a like ease in French conversation, and to secure it, chose to room for his first few years in New York with a French family.

The telegraph desk then had nothing like its present importance. Nor, indeed, did it have anything like the present inpouring of news to cope with. Commenting on the difference, forty years later, Mr. Miller remarked on the changed conditions:

> An appreciation of the difference in the volume of news handled by *The Times* then and now, is indicated by what I did then. After I had been on *The Times* three or four weeks, the head of the telegraph desk went on his vacation. While he was away, I handled all the telegraph copy and didn't think I was overworked. Now I believe there are eight men on the same telegraph desk, and everyone of them is busier than I was when I handled the complete service.

And the reason? "There was less to send over the wires, and it was sent in briefer form than it is now. Subject heads had come little into vogue, and news from Washington was carried under a head naming the capital; Albany was the same and so on." Cable copy received much the same treatment. A typical column of the time went under the blanket caption, "Affairs in Europe." Beneath it came six minor heads, and the reading matter fell into four "sticks" with three subheads, "Great Britain," "France" with a story each, and "General European News," with two. Occasionally would appear a variant, "Affairs in Foreign Lands" if a rare Oriental story should chance to filter in. A comparison of costs shows that the expense of news getting was then but a very moderate item indeed. During the high peak of American interest in the great war in 1918, *The Times* often had a bill for cable tolls alone of $15,000 a week. But in the 'seventies, as that paper's historian comments, this figure "would have paid the cable tolls of all the New York newspapers for a whole year."

In the later 'seventies, the young New Englander no doubt often congratulated himself on the good fortune which had brought him to *The Times*. The paper enjoyed a pleasant period of prosperity and power. It sold anywhere from 31,000 to 35,000 copies a day, one-tenth of its present daily circulation. But the figure, though considerably less than the totals alleged by other metropolitan papers, was net, and not like them subject to generous subtractions. It enabled *The Times* to pay regularly a dividend of eighty, ninety, or one hundred per cent on its capitalization of $100,000.

It had come to the fore as a news gatherer. On the very eve of young Miller's arrival, *The Times* had performed a feat in news detail hitherto unattempted in New York. It had reported in full the court proceedings in the suit of Theodore Tilton against the Rev. Henry Ward Beecher for alleged alienation of Mrs. Tilton's affections, and misconduct with her. *The Times* saw the extraordinary news value of this case; felt the keen public interest in it; and played it up for all it was worth. Each day's story began with a "lead," a column or so in length, which summarized the essential facts much in the manner of the synopsis of a magazine serial. This preceded a complete stenographic transcript of evidence and argument, which at times ran to a full quarter of the whole paper, taking up three pages of what was then a twelve-page daily. It was an expensive item, but it showed the public that the paper was bent on giving the news.

In Springfield, young Miller had found himself lucky in his newspaper associates. He soon discovered that he had the same good fortune in New York. True the great Raymond had died in the year Miller entered Dartmouth. But George Jones, Raymond's partner and the driving force behind the paper's offensive against Tweed, now had the say in the paper's policy and the largest single interest in its stock. Associated with him as managing editor was John C. Reid, who came to *The Times* in 1872. Reid looms up as a great news editor. He had the ability and the desire to lead in the journalistic trend which shifted the centre of interest, if not of gravity, from the editorial to the news columns. Louis J. Jennings, a talented and temperamental Englishman with a varied journalistic experience to his credit, had charge of the editorial page. He had entered with zest, during the Tweed attacks, into the task of supplying the editorial invective. As he entered with equal zest but less discretion into a plot to oust his employer, George Jones, from his place of control in the paper's management, he left one day with a certain abruptness for his English home.

This plot grew out of the paper's growing independence in politics. *The Times* was a Republican paper. It had figured in the Grant-Greeley campaign as the leading Republican organ of New York. But the journal that had uprooted municipal roguery at home found it could ill stomach the goings-on in Washington. It came out flatly against a third term for Grant; it voiced the crying need for reform. And in doing all this it stirred to wrath the Administration and the profiting faithful. Jennings, *The Times's* English editor, embraced Republicanism with the ardor of the convert. Not for him such lukewarm adherence to the Grand Old Party. Accordingly he embarked on a plan to keep the paper's controlling interest out of the hands of the independent Mr. Jones. Ten shares of the paper's stock were in the market and Jennings hoped that their acquisition by the "regulars" among the shareholders might solidify the Republican control. It was not to be. Mr. Jones announced on February 4, 1876, that he had bought the ten shares for $150,000 and by their purchase had become the majority shareholder.

To the place left vacant by Mr. Jennings's most natural withdrawal, Mr. Jones appointed John Foord. Foord had come to the front in the office through his work in digging up much of the incriminating evidence against the Tweed Ring, and for his skill in turning it all into workmanlike journalistic "copy." Under his editorial guidance, *The Times's* growing independence advanced from strength to strength.

Mr. Miller had come from a Democratic home. But his Springfield training under Samuel Bowles had all tended toward independent political thinking—to the consideration of public questions on their own merits regardless of their party origins. To him, after his three years in Springfield, the internal convulsions that *The Times* kept undergoing were an old story. He had already served on a paper that had found its soul, and had dared to call that soul its own.

Professionally, he kept on advancing. After doing well as an editor at the telegraph desk, he was on New Year's Day, 1876, given charge of the weekly magazine, or, more correctly, the weekly edition of the paper. These weekly editions formed an outstanding feature of the earlier era. All the leading papers published them, chiefly for the benefit of outlying readers. By 1876, however, their value had begun to wane, and they disappeared unlamented with the advent of the Sunday paper.

While in charge of the magazine, Mr. Miller could turn his hand to whatever form of journalistic writing he felt drawn. He wrote editorials. He wrote reviews. The first edition of the weekly under his direction contained a review, several columns in length, of an important foreign dictionary. The review was impressive; it was erudite; it fairly groaned beneath its own weight. Forty years later, he read it through again with as much amazement as amusement. "My, my," he commented, "I must have known a lot in those days or—have been a good bluffer."

But his hours in Park Row and at his home just across the bridge in Brooklyn constitute by no means the record of all work and no play. He enjoyed the social opportunities afforded him, and his bachelor days and nights saw him depart with the spoils from many a jolly poker game. In Chester Lord of *The Sun* and Sandford H. Steele as well as in the members of *The Times's* staff, he faced worthy opponents.

For outdoor sports he indulged in baseball, developed a liking for tennis which remained till old age, and took up golf, at which he played a left-handed game. His friends of these years recall him as a muscular man somewhat chunkily built. Although these years kept him rather closely tied to New York, he strove, whenever possible, to satisfy his New Hampshire boyhood passion for fishing.

But bachelorhood held no compelling attraction for him. His thoughts travelled northward as did his letters to that same

Frances Daniels he had met at his first school, to that same Frances Daniels he had kept on meeting at Hanover when she came from her Plainfield home to visit her aunt. During his Springfield days the two had corresponded continually and met whenever possible. Now, apparently established in New York, he determined to marry her.

But the course of this romance had never run as smoothly as the young folk most concerned desired. William Henry Daniels and, more particularly and more potently, Mrs. William Henry Daniels, looked with disfavor upon young Miller's suit. To her, as she put it at the time, he seemed to have "no prospects." She held to this attitude throughout Miller's Springfield apprenticeship, fortified in it no doubt by memories of his Dartmouth shiftlessness.

However, the rising young newspaperman in New York considered it a case for an ultimatum.

In the fall of 1876 he wrote to Mr. Daniels:

"Next week I am coming to get Frances."

Next week he kept his promise. He journeyed north to Plainfield and the two were married there on October 10.

He brought his young wife to Brooklyn, first to Cumberland Street and later to Columbia Heights, and began a singularly happy married life. Mrs. Miller proved an ideal helpmate. She entered likewise as a companion in his sports. Together in vacation time they would go off fishing with Indian guides in the Lake St. John country. Mrs. Miller was one of the first white women to go fishing and vacationing in this district.

His domestic happiness gave him added zest for his work on *The Times*. He kept up his study of foreign affairs. He wrote editorially of them in the weekly. Occasionally, those in charge of the daily edition, knowing of this penchant, asked for expository comment on occasional foreign matter that came in. This they published in the daily; but not on the editorial page. And this, much to his surprise, they paid for.

Inspired by both recognition and reward, he began to submit

editorial contributions to the daily edition. He kept away from the ground which the regular staff could and did cover. He went off the beaten track. He wrote on foreign politics. His first editorials to appear on *The Times's* page of opinion dealt with the struggle then raging in France for the control of the Republic—the fight between the real Republicans and the Clerical-Royalists. These early writings showed two things—the clear understanding which the young journalist had of international affairs, and the literary skill which enabled him to display it. They resulted in his promotion from editor of the weekly to foreign editor of the daily edition of *The Times* in March, 1879. Here he handled for publication all the news from abroad, drawing on his already formidable background to clarify its presentation to the readers and to straighten out for them some typically devious European statement or design. Naturally the editorial page called on him for information and often for contributions. John Foord, the editor, early recognized his ability and encouraged him in mastering the arts of editorial expression. The staff felt no inordinate surprise, therefore, when at the beginning of the next year Miller received his appointment as a regular editorial writer.

Until now he had been far removed, of course, from any say in the paper's editorial councils, or in the determining of its political attitudes. Indeed in 1875, he had found himself the sole supporter of Tilden in the whole office. He was on hand at the telegraph desk on the eventful morning when *The Times* alone refused to concede Tilden's election, because *The Times* alone had the news—that the result was still in doubt.

As the paper said in an article printed on June 11, 1887:

> On the morning after the election of 1876, *The Times* had the news—which no other paper in the United States had, and which the Republican National Committee did not have. It obtained it through its own enterprise and sagacity, and it paid for it.

But in passing on that news, he took no part. That task confronted the men who gathered round him at the telegraph desk:

Mr. Foord, the editor-in-chief, George Shepard and Edward Cary, the political editorial writers, and the enterprising John Reid, managing editor, the moving spirit behind the election news.

Mr. Miller on joining the editorial staff found himself among a congenial and talented group. Mr. Jones had the faculty of seeking out ability and enlisting it in *The Times's* service. The young writer entered into his work with a will. He had reached the sphere of journalism for which he felt himself well suited. He now engaged in that type of writing for which his eclectic self-education formed an admirable and necessary background.

During this period he found time for a favorite hobby, that of woodcarving. By his carving and carpentry he even achieved an elaborate bookcase with ornamental tiles which occupied an honored place in his home. Mrs. Miller not only tolerated but applauded this handicraft. As his *Times* associate, Carr Van Anda, was to remark to him years later, he was "one of the few men allowed to whittle below the attic."

Meanwhile Mr. Foord grew somewhat restive on *The Times*. The paper belonged and seemed likely to remain in the hands of the Jones family. Though he should grow gray in the paper's service, it seemed hardly probable that he would ever attain a penny's worth of interest beyond his salary; while there was always the possibility of chance or circumstance throwing him out, just perhaps when he could least afford to go. An opening occurred in Brooklyn which attracted him. The Brooklyn *Union-Argus* offered him the controlling interest and the editorial charge. The paper held out toward him a salary of $8,000, which was more than he drew on the Manhattan side of the river, and twenty-five of the one hundred shares of stock, and a controlling interest secured to him. Probably it was this "controlling interest" that lured Foord to the Brooklyn venture.

Early in 1883, Mr. Foord told his employer of his decision, though no word of the editor-in-chief's withdrawal reached the staff. At the time Mr. Foord himself did not expect to assume his new duties until May. This left Mr. Jones ample time for readjustment. He looked over the field of prospective editors at home and abroad.

One Sunday during this period he asked his youngest editorial writer to dine with him at his home. They enjoyed an excellent dinner. Afterwards in the library, they enjoyed excellent cigars. Naturally the conversation turned to the subject which chiefly interested them both. They talked of *The Times* and its editorial page. In the course of it all, Mr. Jones shot out a query:

"Well now, Miller, if you were editor-in-chief of *The Times* what would you do?"

The young man from New England thought quickly. He answered the question by making several pertinent suggestions. Mr. Jones received them without comment and the talk drifted on.

Within a few weeks, earlier than he had first intended, Mr. Foord announced his resignation. To everyone's surprise, Mr. Jones turned to his thirty-four-year-old leader writer, who but two years before had joined the editorial staff, and appointed Charles Ransom Miller as *The Times's* editor-in-chief, on April 13, 1883.

Although notoriously indifferent to the claims of correspondence, and of preserving letters of interest or importance that came to him, Mr. Miller cherished throughout his life the cordial notes of congratulation that followed hard on the announcement of his promotion. Probably none gave him a keener thrill of pride than this from the son of his first chief, "the great Sam Bowles" of *The Republican:*

April 14, 1883.
My dear Miller:

It made my heart bound with joy and pride last night to learn from Mr. Brooks of your promotion. Nobody can rejoice more heartily than I do in your success. After the high honor it is to you personally to have climbed so fast to so great and responsible a position, I feel that it is a big feather in *The Republican's* cap. And it seemed peculiarly appropriate that we should, upon Mr. Foord's suggestion, drink to your health and success at The Springfield *Republican* dinner at the Lotus.

I wish you had been of the party yourself. I should have called on you during my brief stay in town if I had been near the office in your hours.

Yours very truly, Saml. Bowles.

MR. MILLER OF "THE TIMES"

The Republican's New York letter of the same week contained this portrait:

Mr. Foord's place is now filled by Charles R. Miller, a graduate of *The Republican* school of journalism, who is about 34 years old. Mr. Miller left Dartmouth college in 1872 and was the class poet. His production was of superior excellence and commanded the attention of a friend of Samuel Bowles, and Mr. Miller was invited to begin journalism in Springfield. He spent four years or a university course with *The Republican* and then went to the New York *Times* as assistant telegraph editor. He was afterward compiler of *The Weekly Times* and then became an editorial writer. Mr. Miller has lived in Brooklyn where he has been an active member of the young man's Republican Club and an ardent friend of civil-service reform. He is a man of sound Yankee sense and a student of brilliant capacity in many directions. For recreation he writes history, contributes to *The Industrial Review,* of which he is one of the proprietors, and has been acting editor of *The International Review*. Mr. Miller is a hard fighter, as President Bartlett of Dartmouth college can testify, and *The Times* will continue to be the leading Republican newspaper by virtue of its sympathy with the progressive wing of that party. This is the first time since Raymond's death that the editorial department of the paper has been under the direction of an American.

Another note from Springfield which he cherished brought the felicitations of his first journalistic pal:

THE REPUBLICAN
Springfield, Mass.

MY DEAR CHUCK:

You will have no more genuine good wishes and congratulations on the happy event than come from your associate of the Elm street boarding house and the chequer-board breeches. Look back a bit, oh happy and fortunate mortal! Time has dealt gently and pleasantly with you, and good work and New Hampshire sense have paid the ideal dividends. For the future I have no doubts. Deep as has always been my faith in you I never pictured so bright a thing as this in those days when Perkis gobbled our midnight lunches and we smoked "heels" in default of a midnight lunch! With cordial regards to Mrs. Miller, believe me,
Faithfully,
S. B. GRIFFIN.

The following from *The Courant* must go in the record for the sake of its expressed but unfulfilled hope:

THE COURANT

DEAR CHUCK: Hartford, Conn., April 14, 1883.
Have just this moment seen the news. You can judge whether I am pleased. Best congratulations, as the Germans say, and may prosperity improve your handwriting! . . .
                                                C. H. ADAMS.

This one from Mr. Dana recalls the Dartmouth apprenticeship:

MY DEAR MILLER:
I hear that you are now editor of *The Times,* and I hasten to congratulate you. Decidedly you are the class leader now. I have always felt that the training you received in the Social Library would tell in time!
                    Very sincerely, C. L. DANA.

His Park Row confrères received word of the appointment with high approval, as this cordial letter from Chester Lord of *The Sun* will testify:

EDITOR'S OFFICE OF THE SUN

                                New York, April 17, 1883.
MY DEAR MR. MILLER:
Please let me tell you how glad I am to hear the good news, and how sure I am that you will make for yourself a far-reaching reputation. In my humble opinion the Editorship of The New York *Times* is as high a journalistic prize as exists on this continent, and I am not sure but it is the highest, I don't know of any higher. It must be especially satisfactory to you to know that you have fairly won the high honor by downright hard work and real merit, and that it is not given to you through favoritism, or political influence or rich relatives. Yours is the kind of success that means something, and I sincerely congratulate you upon it and upon your prospects.
Alas! even in moments of relaxation you always did take the biggest jack pots. As one of the "Children" I remember the meetings of the Presbytery with great delight; I am proud to have drunk beer with you and to have been robbed by you.
With many well wishes,
                    Most truly yours, C. S. LORD.

For the first year at least Mr. Miller enjoyed a comparative calm in his new office as director of *The Times's* page of opinion. But a presidential year—always an eventful thing editorially—

lay ahead. And in 1884, the young editor-in-chief faced a presidential year of more than usual concern to his paper. Although nominally Republican and ardently so in the case of one of its leading spirts, Reid, *The Times* could not look at the Washington of the time with unblinking eyes. The paper that had ousted Tweed and but recently exposed the Star Route frauds would but naturally sniff its party's Augean stables with sensitiveness and abhorrence. Certainly the young editor with the precepts and precedents of the "great Sam Bowles" still green in his memory threw all his influence to foster and support the idea of independence which grew stronger daily in *The Times* office.

Naturally the final decision rested with the proprietor, Mr. Jones, for in any case he would have to foot the bill. But Mr. Miller's steadying influence must be reckoned with in this interim while *The Times* weighed the pros and cons.

Certainly his important editorials of this period must be noted, as they stand as historic milestones on the press's long and as yet unfinished march toward political independence.

The first to give the "regular" Republican readers of *The Times* pause appeared on May 23, 1884, and bore the heading, "Neither Blaine Nor Arthur." Of it a part may well stand for the whole, as its main purport rested in this sentence:

> The list of men to choose from is not a long one. We do not believe that this is a year when "any good Republican will do."

And side by side with it on the same page ran an editorial which pointed out the mistakes which the Democrats, with their usual knack for mistakes, had made in the House of Representatives.

The following day saw Mr. Miller illustrating the excellent editorial practice of reiteration. His article he headed, "Neither Arthur Nor Blaine," and in it he rang the changes on the sentiment enunciated on the preceding day:

> The party is not strong enough to elect a President by the votes of what may be called its regular members.

EARLY DAYS IN PARK ROW

He then catalogued Mr. Blaine's shortcomings and in the following sentence damned President Arthur with the faintest praise. The President, he wrote

> had done better than was expected, and is reported to have been a modest, quiet, inoffensive occupant of the executive office.

Swinging back to the editorial's caption, Mr. Miller set forth again that

> Neither Blaine nor Arthur is a possible President. The choice of a candidate must start from that fact. That once clearly recognized, it ought not be difficult to find a man who can poll the full Republican vote, and with it enough of the independent vote to keep the government in the hands of the party which, we are convinced, is the safest and best.

When the party thought otherwise and nominated Blaine on the fourth ballot on June 6, *The Times* announced, what it had already indicated, that it would not support him. Mr. Miller gave to this editorial a title which as the ensuing election proved had a prophetic significance. He called it "Facing the Fires of Defeat," but the scorching of the editorial's own fire he tempered with the assurance that "defeat will be the salvation of the Republican Party."

About this time George Haven Putnam put up the name of the editor of *The Times* for membership in the Century Club. The proposal caused some objection—Mr. Miller had already trod on several prominent toes. But somehow Mr. Putnam managed to over-rule the objectors. Mr. Miller became a Centurian, and in a short time even his enemies within the club accepted him as a comrade.

Years later, on the occasion of Mr. Putnam's seventieth birthday, Mr. Miller squared accounts with his proposer and arranged a party at the Century in celebration of the septuagenarian's anniversary.

The association of Mr. Miller with the Century Club stands out as one of the happiest things in his life. He preferred club life above all forms of social activity. He would drop in at the Century continually to read, chat or play billiards. With the cue he became exceedingly proficient, but the game never absorbed him to the extent that he could pass up the opportunity for conversation or badinage.

V

"THE TIMES" OUT OF JOINT

Just as Mr. Miller's years bridged the transition from the older type of American journalism to the new, so he in his mental make-up blended past and present. The old "personal editor" of the Sam Bowles type had had his day. In many respects he had had a heyday. Much of the arrogant power which in earlier years had gone to the heads of Puritan divines throughout New England descended upon the new community oracle—the editor.

In a great many cases this editorship was "personal" in the sense that the editor himself owned outright or had a controlling interest in the paper for which he wrote. In his own paper and with his own pen, such a "personal editor" wielded tremendous influence. But such papers for the most part were small affairs and had at best but a meagre circulation. Their most distinctive quality was that their seat of power lay in the editor's office.

The old order changed. A broadening of the field of newspaper appeal by the popularizing of newspaper content found new inventions for mass production ready to hand. Newspapers became not vehicles for the expression of editorial opinion so much as purveyors of the news. The new devices and equipment proved too expensive for most "personal editors" to swing. The one-man office of necessity grew with the new day into a company; the one-man editor found himself multiplied almost overnight into an editorial staff. The most distinctive quality of the present-day newspapers is that their power lies in their news columns rather than in their editorial columns.

Many influences hastened the advent of that jauntier journalism of the '90's and earlier twentieth century. Mr. Dana in his famous old *Sun* encouraged a humanizing of the news. This did not mean the release of maudlin pathos and sticky sentiment which characterized *The Sun's* imitators. But it did mean that he encouraged his reporters to take the dry bones of events and breathe into them the breath of life.

Away back in 1835, James Gordon Bennett with his *Herald* had blazed the trail of sensationalism. But along with it he also developed the science of news-gathering as it now exists. He had scant patience with the then prevailing notion that news drifted in willy-nilly to the editor's desk. To him news consisted of something that required going after; that necessitated ferreting out; and if need arose, definite stimulation. He invented the interview. He scoffed at the pompous pretensions of the editorial.

He scoffed more vehemently at the old reticences and the old insistence on decorum. As publisher of *The Herald* he announced in that journal his own approaching marriage with this headline:

> To The Readers of The Herald
> Declaration of Love
> Caught at Last
> Going to be Married
> New Movement in Civilization

Small wonder that the journalistic flood gates opened to an almost overwhelming tide of cheapness and vulgarity.

Came in 1883 Joseph Pulitzer and his *World*. From the point of view of sensationalism the early *World* went *The Herald* one better. But Mr. Pulitzer maintained a strong belief in the editorial page. His reporters might pander; his editorial writers must look always to the prize of their high calling. And along with Mr. Pulitzer came the fashion for the organized news crusade. The idea behind the crusade was of course anything but new. To right wrong and to overthrow tyranny had been aims implicit in journalism from its inception. The novel twist to it consisted in the training of all the paper's guns—news, editorials, cartoons—and firing them all together at the same target.

What *The Times* had done in the case of the Tweed Ring,

The World kept on doing as a regular news "feature" whenever it found inspiration.

Don Seitz in his "Life of Joseph Pulitzer" has chronicled the battle of multi-colored inks which followed Mr. Hearst's advent on the New York scene. Present-day newspaper readers know full well the far-flung splashes which still daub the nation-wide press as the result of that conflict.

So much for the principal phases of the new era. Its results show chiefly in vast circulations, and, concurrently, in fabulous revenues from advertising. A less patent effect but one of lasting importance lay in the shift which these changes brought about in the reader's interest. No longer did the purchaser of papers turn with eager anticipation to the editorial page. He bought the paper in most instances for its news, and for its news alone.

Much good white paper has been inked over in deploring this passing of the editorial's prestige. And much of it has been inked over quite in vain, for commentators on editorial influence have a way with them of ignoring completely the chief reason for the old-time editorial's greatness. The "leaders" in *The Times* of London under Delane did not thunder by virtue of their sound reasoning; they thundered with the importance of the news which they contained. The most famous scoop which that great paper ever achieved—its announcement of the passage of the Corn Laws—will serve as an apt illustration. Readers of *The Times* found that tremendous information in one place only. That place was the first paragraph of *The Times's* first editorial that day. American papers of the period followed this English journalistic fashion as they followed others. Accordingly, it need hardly surprise anyone that the editorial page gave right of way to the front page in the reader's interest when the front page began to headline the world's chief happenings. The new era came to stay. Subsequent changes have modified the manner of news-writing; have enhanced the field of news-gathering; and markedly expedited its delivery. They have not affected its importance—except to increase it.

Of necessity many papers felt the strain of this transition. In the case of the New York *Times* several other factors contributed to make the first decade of Mr. Miller's editorship the most depressing in the paper's history. Editorially, Mr. Miller kept on fighting the good fight in consistent support of his friend Mr. Cleveland. But already *The Times,* old-fashioned in manner as in management, had begun to slip. It hastened along the downgrade during President Harrison's administration and by the time President Cleveland returned to the White House as the result of the 1892 election, its affairs were in a really bad way.

Commentators attribute *The Times's* decline and fall during these years to its abandoning of the Republican Party in 1884. Mr. Jones possessed business methods which while highly successful were also highly individual. With him at the helm all went well. So it appeared to the staff of *The Times;* so it was presumed by the public at large. Not until after the sale to The New York Times Publishing Company in 1893 did the truth leak out that for several years at least *The Times* had been running at a loss. In the ten years prior to 1893 it had earned one million dollars—but this was in the first five years of the ten.

In his will Mr. Jones had expressly stated that he wished that *The Times* would never be sold. But the Jones heirs wished otherwise. With the paper a losing proposition, their sentiment gave way. Faced by the doleful statements on the shareholders' reports, they decided to get out while the getting was still good. Shortly they announced that the paper was in the market.

Mr. Miller in the editorial which he wrote on the day that Mr. Jones died had remarked that

his wish was that the newspaper should pay more attention to the worthy than to the unworthy side of human nature, that it should commend itself to right-thinking persons of some seriousness of mind and judgment rather than strive to satisfy the desire to know what the sinful and frivolous are about.

Mr. Miller's hopes for *The Times* coincided with Mr. Jones's as expressed in the foregoing sentiments. Nor was Mr. Miller alone. A loyal staff and a small but loyal group of friends decided that if they could possibly prevent it *The Times* should never lose its integrity.

Encouraged by this support Mr. Miller undertook to canvass backers who he thought would be interested in preserving to the city a sensible, dignified and non-sensational paper. He sought them chiefly among the friends of President Cleveland.

In due course he came to Charles R. Flint. Mr. Flint commenting on his visitor's doleful appearance asked the reason.

"I may lose my position on *The Times,* unless I can raise sufficient subscriptions," Mr. Miller answered.

"All right," said Mr. Flint. "Put me down for $50,000."

By dint of this individual solicitation, and by throwing into the effort his entire personal resources along with those of Mrs. Miller, he raised the fund of $1,000,000 which the Jones heirs had set as the sale price of little more than the paper's name.

One subscriber of $50,000, however, failed to pay up. *The Times* sued, but in vain. Apropos of the affair, *The Evening Post* came out with an article which accused Mr. Flint of watering the stock. This time Mr. Flint sued *The Post*. That paper answered by retracting its statements on its front page the next day. *The Sun* celebrated its rival's discomfiture with an editorial, "Larry a Confessed Liar." The "Larry" of course referred to *The Post's* great editor, Lawrence Godkin, and indicates that in the day of transition the "personal" died hard even in metropolitan journalism.

Finally the transaction was consummated with the Jones family and on April 13, 1893, *The Times* passed to an organization known as The New York Times Publishing Company with Mr. Miller as its president. With the editor as associates in the company were Edward Cary and George F. Spinney. Mr. Cary invested $25,000; Mr. Spinney gave lavish promises but only $500 in cold cash.

To Mr. Miller the dual rôle of president and editor proved a steady strain. That he rose to his responsibilities, responsibilities for which he had previously no training and no aptitude, caused his acquaintances to marvel. Dartmouth friends almost gasped with surprise that the shiftless and utterly unbusinesslike "Chuck" Miller should find himself at the head of such an enterprise. Mr. Miller threw himself into the task with all the vigor of his prime. In his wife he found a ready ally, eager to help with every economy at her command.

At this time he continued to reside in Brooklyn. There his two children, Madge and Hoyt, had been born. Their training devolved entirely on Mrs. Miller. By a tacit arrangement reached early in their married life, Mr. and Mrs. Miller definitely divided their responsibilities. To her fell the entire management of home and children. Accordingly Mr. Miller never knew domestic worries of the sort usually heaped upon the young husband and father. This left him entirely free for his work as editor and the new and, for him, far harder task of business executive.

But though he put all that he had in him into the effort, it failed. Probably no one under the circumstances could have saved *The Times* just then. The one million dollars which the new company had paid for the paper bought merely *The Times's* good name, which at that particular moment was, financially at least, not too good, and the right to operate at the old stand at an annual rental of $40,000.

All the outstanding accounts of the old *Times,* when paid in to the new, went by stipulation to the Jones estate. Thus with no working capital The New York Times Publishing Company had but slight stamina to face the financial panic which came in the very year of organization. That it did not go under then for good and all speaks sufficiently well for the self-sacrifice and financial sacrifice of Mr. Miller and the friends. It was a miracle that the company managed to weather three depressing years.

In 1896 Mr. Miller moved with his wife and two children from Brooklyn to Manhattan and took a house at 120 West 55th Street. In order to help out the finances, Mrs. Miller let her first floor to lodgers. Though indicating most praiseworthy co-operation, the experiment proved unfortunate. The family who took the floor later defaulted with the rent.

Even Mr. Miller's mother-in-law came to the rescue. That same Mrs. Daniels who had discouraged his suit from the first, now gave of her private means to aid *The Times* purchase. More than that, she lent money to the Millers to tide them over this period when all they had was sunk in a sinking paper.

Mr. Spinney, who had earned a reputation as an excellent reporter, proved somewhat less outstanding as a managing editor.

Mr. Miller had had slight connection with the news end of a paper since his early Springfield days. But in any case he could give practically no attention to this phase of *The Times;* his editorial writing coupled with the trying financial affairs of the paper claimed all his time and strength. The prestige of the news columns declined and fell. Sanctioned by Mr. Spinney, fulsome little personal sketches of minor Tammany celebrities crept into the paper in the hope that they would sell a few hundred or so extra copies in this or that ward. Inevitably the paper's already small circulation dwindled and dwindled.

This slump had the expected effect on the advertising revenue. It fell off even more seriously. Through the years *The Times* had built up especially the department of financial advertising. The panic quite inevitably shot holes in this. The revenue obtained barely got out the paper; certainly it left no margin to spend for news. Only editorially could the paper as it then was keep its head above water. In these years of stress Mr. Miller grew inwardly depressed, but he threw himself whole-heartedly in support of his friend President Cleveland, now back again in the White House. But though the calibre of his writing remained, the meagre circulation almost nullified the paper's influence. Daily it became apparent that *The Times* must go to other owners or go under.

Carefully Mr. Miller and his confrères of The New York Times Publishing Company looked over the metropolitan field. They went over in their minds the outstanding New York newspaper executives, gauging their ability with reference to the problem in hand. They approached those they felt best fitted to apply first aid, financial and managerial. These gentlemen one and all declined the offers made to them, holding to the opinion that *The Times* had passed beyond the point of resuscitation. Mr. Miller himself acted as liaison officer as it were between the tottering company and these prospective saviors. His depression deepened with each succeeding refusal.

Nor can we wonder at his deepening gloom. Mr. Miller's own stock had fallen with his paper. He saw himself in the fulness of his prime a failure. Despite the comprehensive background which he never ceased to acquire, despite his ever-increasing facility and felicity with word and phrase, he felt himself a failure. Apart from his club intimates, and outside the immediate newspaper fraternity, he could claim no reputation. His anonymous pen had made no mark for itself in New York. Should *The Times* go under, he and his resources and the product of his strongest years would go under with it.

No doubt his philosophic mind dallied with the whirligig notion of fortune, with its element of chance, of luck, of touch and go. We with the clear light of wisdom after the event focused on his career see both his failure and his success chiefly as a case of wrong and right environment. Luck had small part one way or the other.

What a field this whole terrain of environment presents for sociological research. Given the wrong environment, how man's powers fade and wither; given the right, how they put forth shoots and blossom. Certainly one can find no illustration better tailored to this thesis than the life of Mr. Miller.

In the wrong atmosphere, hampered, coerced, crushed by financial and managerial worries, he, to use his own phrase, faced the fires of defeat.

He did not begin to reach the heights and utilize to the full his rare abilities until he received the encouragement and the freedom which the new day in *The Times* office was about to offer him.

Adolph S. Ochs and the new day came to *The Times* office together.

"THE TIMES" OUT OF JOINT

This young Southern newspaperman had built up a substantial reputation and a substantial newspaper in Chattanooga, Tennessee. He knew every department of the work from actual experience—the whole gamut from newsboy and printer's devil to editorial writer and proprietor. He had taken over the derelict Chattanooga *Times* with a borrowed capital of $250 and turned it into a prosperous concern.

Although his name and fame are now indissolubly linked with the New York *Times,* Mr. Ochs first came to New York with thoughts of another paper in his mind. A legal friend, the late Leopold Wallach, had told him that the New York *Mercury* was looking round for a new manager.

Mr. Ochs came to New York to find that *The Mercury* had been secured by senatorial gentlemen and others eager to sponsor the "free-silver" issue. Now Mr. Ochs did not believe in "free silver." He held to the gold standard and his Chattanooga paper was at the very moment upholding principles of financial sanity in a district where Mr. Bryan's fallacies raged like a forest fire. Naturally *The Mercury* management with a silver string tied to it failed to interest him. He returned to Chattanooga.

Now it happened that in 1890, Mr. Ochs had entertained Harry Alloway of the New York *Times's* Wall Street staff. Discussing with his guest the newspaper conditions in the Northern metropolis, Mr. Ochs had remarked that *The Times* offered the greatest opportunity in American journalism. This remark lingered in Alloway's mind as did the strong impression which his host's grasp of the whole newspaper business had made upon him. When the great predicament of Mr. Miller and The New York Times Publishing Company became all too evident to the staff, Alloway thought of his Chattanooga acquaintance and wired him on his own initiative. He indicated that *The Times* might be procured for no very large sum.

As it turned out, this message held the bright seeds for the future. At the time Mr. Ochs did not take it very seriously. However, the wire came on March 12, 1896, Mr. Ochs's thirty-eighth birthday. It seemed a good omen. Business called him the next day to Chicago.

He looked up his Chicago friend, Herman H. Kohlsaat, and lunched with him. Over the cigars, he told "H. H." of the Alloway communication. He could scarcely have broached the matter to anyone better informed. Mr. Kohlsaat in reply used the word that had been echoing in the Southerner's ears these many weeks.

"Ochs," he said, "this is your opportunity."

"But," protested the proprietor of the Chattanooga *Times*, "I don't think I'm a big enough man for the job."

"Don't tell anyone," counselled Mr. Kohlsaat, "and they'll never find it out."

Mr. Ochs came to New York. In the meantime Alloway had spoken to Mr. Miller of this outstanding Southern newspaperman as the possible solution of the paper's difficulties. Mr. Miller knew next to nothing about him, but impressed by Alloway's enthusiasm Mr. Miller said, "Bring Mr. Ochs to see me at my home."

As it turned out, the busy and harassed editor of *The Times* had squeezed the interview in between office hours and a night at the theatre with Mrs. Miller and the children.

Mr. Ochs came at the appointed time. The first five minutes' conversation proved to Mr. Miller that here was a man who had the meat of the matter in him. Small-town newspaperman though he might be, he appeared to have forgotten more about newspaper management than most metropolitan executives would ever know. Here, the editor felt, was the man for *The Times*.

The hour for the theatre arrived. The family grew restive. Had father forgotten that they must leave at once or miss the first scene? Father hadn't forgotten but he had matters on foot more important than play-going. At this point Mrs. Miller interrupted the conversation.

"You go on to the theatre with the children," Mr. Miller decided. "Mr. Ochs and I have still some things to talk over; I will follow you there later."

So the family went to the play. When the lights went up after the first scene they looked around for father but looked in vain. The evening wore on and act followed act. The final curtain went down. The family returned from the play to find father and that young Mr. Ochs from the South still deep in conversation.

The two had already embarked on a scheme for the reorganization of *The Times* which had gripped the imagination of both. It was well on to morning before they parted to meet again the next day.

At about this time Mr. Flint and his associates began looking in other directions and a plan was arranged with C. D. Borden, the Fall River manufacturer, and Mr. Knapp, of the American Lithographing Company, to consolidate the New York *Recorder* (a picture paper also in a bad way) and the New York *Times,* with Charles Emery Smith as editor. This plan had gone so far that a charter for The Times-Recorder Company was applied for at Albany. Mr. Flint controlled three of the five members of the board of directors of The New York Times Publishing Company, through dummy directors, and when it was proposed that the directors approve the consolidation Mr. Miller and Edward Cary, the minority members of the board of directors, opposed the proposition, but being outvoted immediately proceeded to have the New York *Times* placed in the hands of a receiver to prevent the consummation of the plan. Alfred Ely, an attorney, was appointed receiver and for four months he assumed the duties of publisher and business manager, and Mr. Miller continued as editor-in-chief.

The receivership was simply preliminary to the complete reorganization, and immediately various plans were discussed until finally Mr. Ochs himself originated a plan.

Naturally his plan of reorganization as eventually adopted did not materialize at once; it had to undergo and survive the necessary compromises and adjustments. But Mr. Ochs in that first long talk had kindled in the heart of the almost despairing editor the fires of a new hope.

The scheme as finally decided on and put into operation has been clearly summarized in "The History of the New York Times" as follows:

A new organization, The New York Times Company, was formed, with a capital of 10,000 shares of par value of $100. Two thousand of these shares were traded in for the 10,000 shares of the old company. The holders of the outstanding obligations of *The Times,* amounting to some $300,000, received in exchange an equal amount of 5 per cent bonds of the new company; and perhaps the most exacting part of the financing of the reorganization was accomplished when $200,000 more of these bonds were sold at par, to provide that operating capital the lack of which had been so severely felt in past years. As a persuasive, fifteen shares of stock were offered to each purchaser of a $1000 bond. Mr. Ochs himself, scraping together all the money he had or could borrow, bought $75,000 of these bonds, receiving with them 1125 shares of stock. Of the remaining capital stock of the company 3876 shares were put into escrow, to be delivered to Mr. Ochs whenever the paper had earned and paid expenses for a period of three consecutive years. Thus he would have—and within less than four years did have—5001 of the 10,000 shares and $75,000 in bonds, the whole acquired by the payment of $75,000 for the bonds and by his personal services. That $75,000 was the financial investment, and the only investment, aside from his own labors, which the controlling stockholder of *The Times* made for his majority interest.

The company thus organized bought *The Times* at public sale on August 13, 1896. The receivership was terminated by court order; on August 18, 1896, the property was formally transferred to the reorganized company with Mr. Ochs as publisher in unrestricted control.

To the Ochs plan of reorganization Mr. Miller gave his enthusiastic support, and through friends was able to subscribe for $50,000 of the bonds that carried with them $75,000 of the capital stock of the company as a bonus. The bonds were in a few years redeemed and Mr. Miller liquidated his indebtedness for them and remained in possession of the stock. For Mrs. Miller's investment of $50,000 in The New York Times Publishing Company she received $10,000 of the stock of the new company. In addition Mr. Ochs provided in the plan of reorganization that $50,000 of the stock of the new company should be given Mr. Miller for the cancellation of any claims he might have against the old company. Thus Mr. Miller acquired for himself and wife about $135,-

000 of the capital stock of one million dollars of The New York Times Company. These holdings were appraised for inheritance tax after his death at $1,270,784.

In this new association there soon began a friendship established on the firm foundation of mutual respect and admiration. Mr. Miller saw in Mr. Ochs a man guided by the highest motives, with a business experience as comprehensive as it was sound, and with a flair for management and organization developed to an impressive degree. Mr. Ochs felt that here was a newspaperman with the ideal editorial equipment—an encyclopedic memory, the trained mind of the scholar and the calm judicial poise of the philosopher. This mutual regard waxed daily, never to wane.

By this time of course Mr. Miller had already won a substantial reputation as an editorial writer. Yet his failure as a combined editor and publisher had been complete. That there were a thousand reasons why he had to fail need not minimize the fact. And there were some even within *The Times* organization itself who doubted the wisdom of his retention in the editorial chair. But in the announcement to the public of his assumption of management, Mr. Ochs voiced his own feelings on the subject in no uncertain tone:

> There will be no radical change in the personnel of the present efficient staff. Mr. Charles R. Miller, who has so ably for many years presided over the editorial page, will continue to be the editor; nor will there be a departure from the general tone and character and policies pursued with relation to public questions that have distinguished The New York *Times* as a non-partisan newspaper, unless it be, if possible, to intensify its devotion to the cause of sound money and tariff reform, opposition to wastefulness and peculation in administering public affairs and in its advocacy of the lowest tax consistent with good government, and no more government than is absolutely necessary to protect society, maintain individual and vested rights and assure the free exercise of a sound conscience.

While with this new day a change came over *The Times,* a change quite as remarkable came over Mr. Miller. The failure of the old company had left him bankrupt in health, in finances and indeed in reputation; he was a broken and disheartened man.

Then with the sudden lifting of the weight from his shoulders there rushed to his lungs a deep intake of fresh air, fresh hope. Buoyancy came back to his stride. Old associates like Edward Cary rubbed their eyes in amazement at the complete transformation. Gone from his writing was the compromise that adversity had occasionally wedged in; gone from his regimen of life the slipshod habits fostered by depression. He exhibited an industry and an application to his work the like of which he had never before shown. Each day he came early to his desk and he stayed at it late. A great enthusiasm took hold of him and kindled his genius. Vigorously he brought *The Times's* editorial page from its slough of despond to the highest peak, where it ranked as the ablest in the country.

With the new day, Mr. Miller became a new man; he faced its rising sun with a new faith in himself which lured him on from strength to strength.

VI

THE DAILY ROUND

The story of *The Times's* rebirth does not belong to Mr. Miller. He would be the last to claim any credit for it. The full credit belongs to Mr. Ochs. And the word "full" goes into the foregoing sentence with all its implication of complete comprehensiveness. Out of the very same men, out of the very same machinery with which Mr. Miller and the old New York Times Publishing Company had failed, the young newspaperman from Tennessee made a going and, in a short time, a glowing success.

A study of the files of the old régime and of the new makes several pertinent facts abundantly clear. It makes clear for instance that the new publisher did not bring to the paper mere business sagacity alone; he also brought to it *principle*. Out of its columns went the old shilly-shallying, the panicky attempts already referred to of stooping to conquer. In them came a definiteness of purpose and that quality which has come so distinctively to be the paper's own—independence.

At first Mr. Miller regarded the newcomer as one would any new employer, and, as the paper's earnings increased, as one would any successful employer. But gradually there grew up between him and Mr. Ochs a warm friendship which as the years passed developed into an affection as strong as Mr. Miller seemed capable of feeling.

This happy state of affairs while not a cause certainly ranks as an important constituent in the success of the new *Times*. For in the relationship which exists between editor and publisher rests the determining factor. Mistrust on either side, with its inevitable sequel of dissension, can end only in one way; a house divided against itself may not for long present an uncracked façade to the passerby. Fortunately for Mr. Miller the confidence and esteem in which he held his new chief were reciprocated in full by Mr. Ochs. Few editors have ever received more appreciative understanding and co-operation; few editors have ever given in return a more unwavering allegiance.

Naturally all this has its bright reflection in the full flowering of editorial expression. The cordial relationship between Delane and the Walters family made it so on the London *Times;* Godkin's unharassed alliance with the Villards proved it again on the New York *Evening Post;* in the case of Mr. Miller and Mr. Ochs, the files of *The Times* itself bear triumphant witness.

Years later on the occasion of the celebration of Mr. Ochs's twenty-fifth anniversary with *The Times,* the publisher took the opportunity to say:

> I desire publicly to acknowledge, and to express my sense of obligation . . . to Charles R. Miller, who from the beginning has been editor-in-chief, whose whole-hearted sympathy with my opinions and my aims and purposes with *The Times* has been an inspiration. His scholarly attainments, his facility and lucidity of expression, broad vision, extraordinary knowledge of public affairs, having a statesman's conception of their proper conduct, and his lofty patriotism have made the editorial page of the New York *Times* consulted and respected throughout the world, and distinguished it as the foremost exponent of enlightened American public opinion.

To find himself relieved from the annoyances and depressing events of business management was to Mr. Miller like a new lease on life. He gave himself with vim and vigor to the paper's editorial page. Like the new proprietor he classed himself politically as an Independent-Democrat. The two saw eye to eye as *The Times's* editorial voice now favored one part of that compound, now the other. As vice-president of the new company and its second largest share-holder, Mr. Miller had not left business cares completely behind. But he had cause no longer to regard his business cares as worries. The entries he made from now on figured on the right side of the ledger. Although relieved from strain and with his income increasing annually he could not for years consider himself quite out of the wood. He refused to permit himself to enjoy personal prosperity until he had paid off bit by bit from his income obligations assumed in the unhappy days of the old New York Times Publishing Company.

He himself had never any illusions as to whence this refreshing prosperity came. He knew that it came straight from the directing genius which Mr. Ochs had brought not only to the paper's business management but to its editorial policy as well. When occasions presented themselves he delighted to honor the man who had brought with him *The Times's* new day.

All these expressions of regard are a matter of public record and as such rightly go into this story, as they were written by Mr. Miller:

TO ADOLPH S. OCHS

On this twentieth anniversary of the day when you became the directing mind of *The Times,* those who, early and late, have been associated with you in the labors that have made

THE NEW YORK TIMES

a great newspaper, join in this assurance of their loyal good will, their esteem, and their affection. Your guidance and your inspiring example, the ideals of public duty and private conduct to which you have been faithful, your genius for the newspaper calling, your clear sense of right and justice, have commanded their confidence and their admiration. They rejoice in the triumphs that have crowned your work and they bespeak for you long years of health and happiness and the distinction of yet greater achievements in assuring *The Times* a position of

UNCONQUERABLE SUPREMACY.

August 18, 1916.

From the Executive Staff:

DEAR MR. OCHS: New York, August 18, 1916.

In addresses recently delivered by you upon the art and mystery of newspaper making, you have freely imparted to your fellow craftsmen the principles and the precepts tried and proved sound in your own experience. Of one element of success in the art, the gift of winning and keeping the esteem and full confidence of the staff, you could have spoken with enlightening clearness only by a venture in self-portraiture.

In how great a measure you possess that gift you may not understand so well as we who have been associated with you in the labors that have raised *The Times* to its high place among the world's newspapers. We whose pride and joy it has been to work beside you know of the high regard and affection and respect you have inspired among the members of the great *Times* family.

On the anniversary which begins this third decade of your control and management of *The Times,* we join in congratulating you upon the splendid triumph you have achieved by genius, character and toil. We rejoice in it, we pray that the coming twenty years may bring in yet larger measure success for you and greatness for *The Times.*

With sincere good wishes,
C. R. Miller
C. V. Van Anda
Louis Wiley
George McAneny
Charles H. Grasty

On the Silver Anniversary of the Ochs Régime:

August 18, 1921.

Dear Mr. Ochs:

To the pleasant tide of good wishes and the congratulations from many sources called forth by the twenty-fifth anniversary of your coming to *The Times* we wish to add this assurance of personal esteem and friendship.

We have worked side by side with you during the greater part of the whole of the first quarter century of your management of *The Times;* we have come to know and appreciate the qualities that have contributed to the building up of this great newspaper property, and the traits of mind and heart that have won for you the confidence and esteem of countless friends. With each year we find our relations to *The Times* and with you more satisfying and agreeable. We rejoice in the noble success you have won, in the realization of the high aims and ideals you have always cherished and we bespeak and predict for you and *The Times* future triumphs transcending the achievements of the past.

With cordial good wishes,
C. R. Miller
C. V. Van Anda
Louis Wiley

Naturally the paper's continued progress delighted him and he adapted himself to each dazzling enlargement as it came along. *The Times* outgrew one building and then another. In fact the paper had almost outgrown the impressive Times Building on the Times Square delta before it had moved into it. Temporarily ensconced there, Mr. Miller wrote his editorials from the tower that dominates Broadway at 42d Street. Finally when the paper reached its present address, 229 West 43d Street, Mr. Miller felt that his moving editorial tent had been pitched on an abiding site, and rejoiced in an office entirely suited to his tastes and needs.

The room was a large one, ten stories up, on the southeast corner of the Times Annex. Mr. Miller's desk crossed the east end, and sitting at it, he had behind him a large window. That window looked directly on the vortex of life that is Times Square. Here he loved to stand and watch the constant movement of traffic, the seemingly endless stream of taxis and pedestrians forming into those strange geometric patterns characteristic of city crowds when viewed from above.

The Square would on occasion grow blocked with humanity—crowds waiting for ball-game reports or later in the year for election returns. It appeared to him like a "restless sea of straw hats" on the afternoon of the Dempsey-Carpentier fight in 1921. This situation of his office synchronized in a way with his mental attitude: from a point of vantage above the conflict he looked down reflectively on life.

His desk was usually as seemingly haphazard as the crowd below on which he liked to gaze. He had neither instinct nor liking for mechanical methodicity. Manuscripts, unanswered letters and the like, piled up and submerged the desk, hiding from view all but a square foot or two of space immediately in front of him. These literary drifts never seemed to annoy him. Certainly they never impeded his work. He liked things that way. A secretary might "tidy"—arrange the heaps side by side like so many graves —but he must not remove them.

On one occasion a secretary's illness and consequent absence from the office delayed this tidying process too long. The manuscripts on the desk piled up so high that Mr. Miller himself became conscious of the mass and shifted sundry heaps to an adjacent table. That table in its turn could at length hold no more. In despair Mr. Miller turned to his family. His daughter came for the afternoon and the desk and table underwent a thorough housecleaning.

Usually, however, one drastic clean-up took place annually. On Election Day Mr. Miller would spend the doldrum hours before even the first tick-tick of the wire heralded the returns, by shovelling off in a heap the year's accumulation. Off it would go into relays of wastepaper baskets—the conglomeration of letters, invitations, printed addresses, briefs, circulars, reports, together with a pathetic heap of unused editorials in manuscript, written by the staff during the year and doomed to perish thus, stillborn.

His apparent lack of any method and his all too apparent lack of tidiness, Mr. Miller admitted good-humoredly. But the editorial floor recalls one flare-up—a flare-up that broke the record of unruffled days. It followed hard on the heels of an intruder who entered the office in Mr. Miller's absence to photograph its chaos. That photograph has long since perished but the echo of the mighty editorial wrath remains.

The complete co-operation between editor and publisher coupled with their affinity in viewpoint soon showed and continued to show in the growing editorial independence of the paper. Being nominally an Independent-Democratic journal, it chose to be as Independent in as many instances as it chose to be straight Democratic. This detachment came very much to the fore during the governorship of David B. Hill. *The Times* repeatedly objected to the various party deals, and then on occasion—such is the cheering inconsistency of independence—could see eye to eye with Governor Hill. During one of these periods the governor sent the following note to a friend on the paper:

Albany, N. Y., Jan. 9, 1903.

Perhaps the article in this morning's New York *Times* "Albany Blocks the Way" has escaped your attention. It is very excellent—most excellent. When *The Times* is right it is awfully right—when it is wrong, it is awfully wrong.

When it attacked the governor the paper went hammer and tongs to such an extent that it caused Governor Hill to wonder as to whether Mr. Miller harbored any personal bitterness against him. His *Times* friend informed him that Mr. Miller wrote as the paper and not as an individual and arranged to bring the two together at lunch. The meeting overflowed with geniality on both sides and proved to the governor that though vitriol might lurk in the editor's pen it had no place in his personal make-up. Later Mr. Miller went for a weekend visit to the governor at Wolfert's Roost near Albany, and all subsequent letters from the Honorable David B. Hill to *The Times*, no matter how frequently it had been "awfully wrong" according to his lights, contained the phrase, "Kind regard to Mr. Miller."

Along with Greeley and his own contemporary Henry Watterson, Mr. Miller possessed one of the hall-marks of the old-time journalist—he wrote an execrable script. Sometimes after penning a letter, he himself was unable to make out much beyond the always legible signature. As in the early period he wrote most of his leaders by hand, and as those times were the halcyon days of hand-set type, he became the despair of the composing room.

Printers swore at the copy because it was so bad, and then laughed at their predicament. But they ended by having a very definite affection for the editor who wrote so illegibly; his fault was covered by his greatness.

"Marse Henry" would condole with Mr. Miller over the trials arising from penmanship. He told him of the "hobo" printer who "caught on" on *The Courier-Journal* and achieved fame by translating the Watterson editorial phrase "from Alpha to Omega" into "from Alton to Omaha"—and started for the latter place the next morning. And every story the colonel told him, Mr. Miller could top with one from *The Times*.

Certainly Alexander Dana Noyes, in his obituary of Mr. Miller for the Century Club, caps the famous Greeley anecdote which immortalizes the printer on the New York *Tribune* who could read Mr. Greeley's manuscript as he could read print. The said anecdote alleges that this type-setting genius became addicted to the use of alcohol to such an extent that he was discharged. In those days in the printing trade one had to have a recommendation from his last employer to obtain a position on any other paper. The printer requested one from Mr. Greeley. The editor took up his pen and wrote as follows:

"To whom it may concern: The bearer of this is a common drunkard and unworthy the respect of his craft; unreliable; in fact, an all-round bum."

The printer then presented this to the foreman of the New York *Herald*. After an effort to read it, he asked what it was. The discharged printer replied: "A recommendation from Mr. Greeley." "Then," said the foreman, "you may go to work. If Mr. Greeley recommends you, I know you are all right."

Mr. Noyes's counterpart from *The Times* office tells of how Mr. Miller's handwriting necessitated the setting apart of a special compositor, one "who could read and 'set up' Egyptian hieroglyphics," to tackle it. The story relates how a youngster, serving on *The Times* with no great satisfaction to his employers, approached his chief with insistent requests for an advance in salary. Receiving a note from Mr. Miller and finding himself unable to decode the whole of it, he had recourse to the composing-room oracle.

"This note," he explained, "has reference to a raise in salary. But I do not feel like answering it until I know just what the raise will be."

The old compositor glanced over the manuscript, then handed it back with a contemptuous flourish:

"You've got no raise. *You've been fired.*"

Mr. Miller's friend George Haven Putnam frankly accused him of trying to imitate Greeley with his "abominable script" but tacitly admitted that in illegibility he had gone Greeley one better.

"If, like Greeley, you should be nominated for President," Mr. Putnam once told him, "it would be no use for you to send a note. You would have to *announce* your decision."

Doubtless this calligraphic shortcoming lay at the back of his distaste for letter writing. Even the dictation of routine replies and brief notes of acknowledgment held no interest for him. He had nothing of the passion of his English contemporary, Moberly Bell, for this function of the editorial office. Consequently he ignored all but the imperative few.

"Why bother answering letters?" he would ask. "Leave them for three months and they answer themselves."

As years and rheumatism increased he fell back on dictation altogether. Gout had turned his always puzzling script into a thing of even greater mystery. But his signature remained strong and legible to the last.

Efficiency experts can point to Mr. Miller merely as a horrible example. He in his turn had small use for their devices. True, his office boasted a small file; but, true again, he never used it. He kept no carbon copies of his letters; he kept no list or clippings of his writings. That is, he kept no visible memoranda. But filed away all this information securely was—filed away in the vasty deep of his marvellously retentive memory. Let lesser minds go in for new-fangled office equipment; he carried all his card-index systems in his head.

Anything which came in to him which he felt he would like to keep, he tucked away in the recesses of his desk, along with his matches and his cigars. And there they stayed, this heterogeneous collection, till his death—clippings of everything under the sun, a torn photograph of himself in fancy dress, a hurried note from Theodore Roosevelt asking Mr. Miller to meet him for lunch, the church calendar which announced one of the editor's infrequent speeches, a bundle of letters from Harold Frederick, who for so long was *The Times's* man in London—all tucked in together rubbing shoulders in chaotic heaps.

In a little brass rack near at hand Mr. Miller kept those books to which he habitually referred—Abbott's guide to legal procedure, the "Congressional Directory," tariff schedules, and during the last years the full text of the Covenant of the League of Nations with its cover soon worn out through constant use.

Each year a new "World Almanac" joined this group and on one occasion gave rise to the comment:

"Everything's here but be damned if I can find anything."

The expletive stands out by reason of its rarity. Mr. Miller reserved "damn" exclusively for the golf links. He disliked conventional profanity and held that swearing indicated a paucity of vocabulary. If he had occasion to use strong language, he used it and refused to dilute its strength by falling back on any mere trite and threadbare "damn."

Immediately behind him stood two bookcases filled with works on finance, taxation, law and modern history. These books he accumulated himself; *The Times's* own reference library was near at hand just outside his office door. From the walls above him looked down portraits of Raymond and Jones and a steel engraving of Alexander Hamilton.

Mr. Miller arrived at *The Times* each day just before noon. He came there either from his home or from the Century or Metropolitan Club and had already put in several hours' study of the morning papers. As he ran through any personal mail awaiting him members of the staff would drop in for a moment or so's chat. They might touch on some particular phase of the day's news which they fancied for editorial treatment. Or like as not, they came to make some amusing comment. Mr. Miller loved the humorous, and delighted in the comical slant that even routine news so often boasts. Chuckles had a way of punctuating his comments.

He went to lunch shortly before one-thirty. Now lunch at *The Times* has evolved into a function. Mr. Ochs when he came to New York did not leave behind him in Tennessee his Southern hospitality. He established a private dining room in *The Times* building. There he began bidding to his hospitable table each day the outstanding personalities of that day's front page. One day the guest of honor would be an ambassador or some visiting diplomat; next might come a bishop, a leading educationalist or a motion-picture actress, to be followed or joined by an

THE DAILY ROUND

Arctic explorer, the discoverer of a serum, or an Olympic athlete. Mr. Miller and the main executives of the paper joined with Mr. Ochs in making the guests welcome and shared with him the interest—in some cases very great—of their visit.

Mr. Miller finished his after-lunch cigar at the Editorial Conference. While nominally set for two-thirty each afternoon this gathering of the editorial clan proved as often as not a movable feast, its hour depending as it did upon the enthralling propensities of the luncheon guests each day. The staff assembled at the given time to fume in impotent impatience as their writing time dwindled and dwindled. Upon occasion they made tactful overtures to Mr. Miller, suggesting the advisability of an earlier conference hour. But he preferred to have the conference after lunch; it had always been held then. And so it continued to be held as long as his hand grasped the helm. During his last illness, however, when all save Mr. Miller himself tacitly admitted that he would not return, the hour was changed to noon.

As practised at *The Times,* this conference transcends mere formality and becomes a practical and valuable pooling of ideas. To it, in addition to Mr. Miller and his staff, came Mr. Ochs, his assistant executives, Arthur Hays Sultzberger and Julius Adler, and the outstanding departmental chiefs, Carr Van Anda, managing editor, the then assistant managing editor, Frederick T. Birchall, and Louis Wiley, business manager.

This group of seventeen, the corporate mouthpiece of the paper's views, sat around a long conference table with the publisher, wherever he happened to be sitting, at the head. In Mr. Ochs's absence, of course, this chairmanship devolved upon Mr. Miller.

Editorial writing like everything else has followed the modern trend toward specialization. Each of the men around the table had developed background in some given field. With one it was New York State politics; with another finance; yet another studied military affairs and quite naturally kept an eye on Mexico the while. Each knew approximately before reaching the conference upon what he might expect to write that day, for each had spent the morning with the papers and with reference books and had kept the finger of the ready writer upon the pulse of his allotted study. But each knew also that in addition he must take the whole world for his parish and be prepared to make some apposite and constructive comment on any event anywhere, half the world away maybe from his specialized zone. So it invariably turned out.

One by one the topics for editorial treatment for the day would be thrown upon the table. And one by one upon it would accumulate the views, the information, the ideas of the entire staff. Perhaps the embattled farmers of the West demanding their annual "relief" were on the point of obtaining some sop from Washington. In Mr. Miller's mind the news item had its genesis invariably in the high tariff and he would say so. The writer who "covered" China and the Far East would add his comment. Likely as not it would be the most valuable contribution of all. It might chance that he had just received a note that morning from a college friend, now a Minnesota editor, which gave a clear exposition of the entire rural rumpus. The letter went into the pool. Similarly with the eight or nine subjects which merited attention that day.

The writers gathered these comments together and regarded them as welcome collaboration. Some ideas they would discard; others they intended to cleave to; but all they knew helped the prospective editorials, if only as irritating goads. This practice lies at the back of the anonymity of the present-day editorial, one of the chief reasons for the article's appearance in the paper unsigned. How could the writer of the farm "bloc" editorial for instance append his initials alone to the finished screed when its chief arguments and information came from the letter handed to him by a co-worker on the staff?

Naturally not all the ideas thrown upon the conference table concurred. Much of the stimulation sprang, as it springs in worthwhile conversation, from diverging views. Men may be of the same general cast of mind and yet within that compass hold opinions poles apart. But they are held together by a common denominator—their type of paper. Writers gravitate to that paper with whose corporate mind and point of view they find themselves most in accord. This trend is a journalistic axiom. *The Times* as a consistently conservative daily would hardly attract to its staff the rabid radical. Mr. Miller could feel assured as he sat at the conference table that his associates around him saw the world of affairs in much the same general way as he surveyed it himself. Yet he knew that the conservative type of mind had its infinite variations. It might range in mental outlook from the mauve of a forward-looking conservatism to the deep indigo of a dyed-in-the-wool Toryism; from a liberalism that took cognizance of the past, that knew there were kings before Agamemnon, to a reactionism so gravely insistent that it considered Charles the First still the martyr monarch and would venerate as a sacred relic a hair from his Vandyke beard.

It has long been Mr. Ochs's boast—a boast which Mr. Miller was to reiterate before the United States Senate—that no editorial writer on *The Times* was ever compelled to write anything in which he did not believe. The boast is merely the statement of a happy fact. In its actual working out, the staff experiences no inconvenience. If a writer senses that the point of view on his subject favored by the conference is uncongenial to him, he merely says so.

"That will be all right," Mr. Ochs or Mr. Miller would say. "So and So will handle your topic to-day, and here is some stuff for a Boy Scout appeal editorial you can write for us."

As a matter of fact, during the years in which *The Times* stood behind President Wilson and his Administration, *The Times's* editorial staff had among its members men to whom the very name of Wilson was anathema. But the world is so full of a number of things, and Mr. Miller kept these noncomformists contentedly and usefully employed in realms far beyond even the lengthening shadow of the great War President.

The editorial conference over, Mr. Miller would settle down to the main work of his day, the composing of his editorial for the next morning's *Times*. During this constructive interval he discouraged any interruption and only the most important news or personage would be permitted to sidetrack the train of official thought.

Although Mr. Miller's editorials had the appearance of springing from his head full born, they had in reality a pre-natal period which lasted practically the whole day. He would tentatively choose his subject while looking over the papers the first thing in the morning. Then he kept that subject with its implications constantly in his mind during the early part of the day, letting memory, conversation and cogitation do their ramifying work the while. Usually at about a quarter to four each afternoon he would turn in his swivel chair away from his desk, rest his chin in his left hand and half close his eyes. And so he would sit in silence for thirty, forty or perhaps sixty minutes.

Preliminaries of some kind seem indispensable to the artist in any line; he must always take a look before the leap. Gladstone once boasted that he never took the trouble to prepare his speeches. The remark drifted to his private secretary, Sir Edward Hamilton, who chuckled and made this delicious comment:

"Well, if he means that he does not sit down at his desk and actually write out the speech word for word, he is right. But what he does do is to lie down on a sofa and womble it in his inside."

Mr. Miller's period of wombling, though silent, was complete. In this concentrated interval of deliberation his editorial would take its finished form in structure and content. When he called his secretary to his side to take the editorial dictation, he embarked on no hesitating prelude, made no false starts, but began with clear-cut finished sentences embellished with neither a hum nor a haw.

During his later years, Mr. Miller dictated all his editorials.

He spoke slowly and very deliberately. Long practice with journalistic form caused him to compose in paragraphs of a "stickful" but within that compass he varied his clause lengths most artfully. He took a certain delight in following a sonorous Johnsonian period with some crisp, short, journalistic sentence. So precise was this mental habit of form that his paragraphs invariably ran two to the typewritten page.

He had an uncanny way of remembering the exact verbal form of his dictated editorial. It might chance that a second thought would prompt an alteration. Without even a look at the typed pages, he would say to his secretary:

"Go back to the second paragraph where I said so and so, and change it to this." Here he would dictate a new version or a sentence or a phrase. Later, he might ring up from his home:

"Get a proof of my editorial, read back three or four lines from the end and make this alteration."

Occasionally some important caller did interrupt the flow of oral composition. But, that caller gone, Mr. Miller would go right back to dictating from where he had left off without so much as a "Where was I?" or "What did I say last?"

Oral dictation in fact and not the written word had come to be his medium. He had so mastered this art that anything by him so composed needed slight if any changing at all, and went direct into the columns of the editorial page for the most part unrevised.

Both before he embarked on his editorial and after he had completed it, Mr. Miller would see for a short time occasional visitors. Like the very exalted in any profession he was extremely accessible. When he had time to see people, any who cared to see him might come. Old friends would drop in, of course, and strangers who felt that their business merited his attention. While he suffered bores anything but gladly, he suffered them politely. He had none of the brusqueness of manner which often proves more effective than alarums and excursions in "shooing" visitors who exasperate from any sanctum.

He had all the veteran newspaperman's dislike and distrust of the type of visitor who comes with a grievance. Likewise he could scent mere publicity hunters afar off. With all such, after he felt assured of their motive, he would part amicably, with old-school courtesy, but also with dispatch.

"I am sure," he would say to his secretary, "that—" here he named the caller, "would like to be shown the editorial floor and the library." This implied also, though nothing in the tone suggested it, that the said caller must also be shown—the elevator.

His heavy build coupled with his rheumatism in later life made the act of rising a somewhat painful exertion but he had a way of half rising which in most cases proved sufficient to indicate to visitors that the interview was over. All and sundry must have carried away with them from his office a highly agreeable impression. It grew to be his nature to radiate graciousness.

Inevitably some queer sticks would from time to time find their way to him.

One poor woman brought him the information that her daughter-in-law had bribed a witch to put a spell on her. Would *The Times* do anything about it? Mr. Miller explained to the harassed soul that the paper could hardly enter into such a private matter but he undertook personally to rationalize her fears. He embarked learnedly, eloquently on such a blasting exorcism of witches, witchcraft and all its works, that before it even she of Endor would have taken flight. But to no avail. His caller's perturbed spirit would not rest. Finally, finding that reason failed with all its powers, he gave advice sufficiently inspired to end the awkward interlude.

"My good woman," he suggested, "go and tell all this to your priest."

In his relationship with his staff his graciousness flowered. He was all consideration and thoughtfulness for the men who wrote for him. Despite the fact that in later years he walked with some difficulty, he never sent for an editorial writer to come to see him. Mr. Miller chose to go himself to the writer's office with any fresh information or word of advice he might have.

One question will very naturally arise just here. "Did Mr. Miller ever consciously exert the power of his position to gain ends which he may have had at heart?" Apparently not. None except publisher and editor knew what *The Times* would say until *The Times* had seen fit actually to say it in print. The record of correspondence holds but one instance where the editor chose in advance to indicate the paper's attitude, and in that all the semblance of threatening found must be nosed out gratuitously from the simple phrase, "*The Times* will advise."

It occurred during the Democratic Convention at St. Louis in 1904. In nominating Judge Parker, the Southern and Western delegates would not consent to repudiate William Jennings Bryan. The compromise arrived at was the leaving out of all references to the gold standard in the platform.

This Mr. Miller regarded as a fallacy so serious that he sent the following messages to Louis Wiley, the paper's business manager, a visitor at the convention, and to the Honorable David B. Hill. These telegrams remain as the unique instance in which the editor sought to bring pressure through the paper's influence to the extent of foreshadowing its comment. Judge Parker, as it transpired, subsequently took Mr. Miller's advice and came out for the gold standard.

New York, July 8, 1904.
To LOUIS P. WILEY, St. Louis, Mo.

If the Convention fails to adopt the Gold Standard plank *The Times* will demand that Judge Parker promptly make an equivocal statement recognizing wisdom of established Gold Standard. It will tell him that he must do this in order to put the party in a sound position so far as its candidate is concerned, but will frankly warn him that the convention by its stupid refusal to recognize an existing fact and abjure an exploded heresy has probably doomed him to defeat. If he cannot do this *The Times* will advise him to decline the nomination since Eastern sound money Democrats would refuse to support him on a Bryanized platform.

C. R. MILLER.

New York, July 8, 1904.

To Hon. David B. Hill.

Surely after your magnificent and successful work of reorganization and with a majority of the Convention behind you, you will not let Judge Parker go before the country on a Bryanized platform now that issue has been raised and made acute by Bryan's fight. If the Convention fails to adopt a gold standard plank the party will neither win nor deserve confidence of the people. It would be a confession that the democracy is not aware of the free silver error. Better fight in the convention a month.

C. R. Miller.

July 8th, 1904.

To Charles R. Miller,
The New York *Times,* New York.

Your telegrams delayed in delivery. Before their receipt, I had strongly urged upon Senator Hill and others wisdom and necessity of declaration for gold standard, in view of discussion that has arisen. Hill agreed plank was extremely important and fought strongly for it. He secured favorable report from sub-committee but found strong and unexpected opposition in general committee on resolutions. He believed fight on Convention floor would be dangerous and believed temper of Convention would result in defeat of gold standard, thereby emphasizing to the country repudiation of sound money and defeat chance of nominee's election. He also thought this step might put Parker nomination in unnecessary peril. Judge Parker will be advised by Hill and Sheehan to explicitly declare at once for the existing gold standard. His own desire is undoubtedly to take this course. Synopses of your telegrams have been forwarded to him. Since the follies of the last two campaigns are distinctly repudiated by absence of re-affirmation, I hope and urge *Times* will abate no effort in behalf of ticket. There will be ample opportunity on the part of the candidate to reassure and hold conservative Democratic sentiment of East, and to indicate party's emancipation from dead issues of the past. I am confident he will avail himself of it.

Louis Wiley.

VII

OUT OF OFFICE HOURS

Mr. Miller never got over being a student. Side by side with his busy professional life he kept on at an almost equally busy career of studious pursuits. Where he found the time remains a mystery. His friends found him always available; his family rejoiced in his ready comradeship. The truth is that he knew few idle moments. The minute he felt free he would turn to those old loves of his, the classic writers, or embark on linguistic delights in the fresher fields of French, German, Spanish, Italian, and later on, Russian.

One of his earliest ambitions—that of becoming a professor of Latin and Greek—got sidetracked early in his career. Nor did he ever get out his own edition of the Odes of Horace. But at one time late in 1881, he came near to placing on permanent record in book form something of his zest for the Ancients. The firm of G. P. Putnam's Sons desired him to furnish them with a history of Greece for boy readers to form part of their series, "The Story of the Nations." The idea appealed to him strongly, but his accession to *The Times's* editorial chair necessitated that he lay it aside. This he did with keen regret. Something of the scope of the proposed work can be gauged from the cautiously worded letter to him from the prospective publishers:

82 Fifth Avenue near 23d Street.
New York, Nov. 29, 1881.

Mr. C. R. Miller,
The Times,
City.
Dear Sir:
    We shall be interested in having you undertake, as suggested, the preparation of "A History of Greece for Young People." The book would be

planned to serve as a companion volume to the "History of Rome" now being prepared by Mr. Alden. We have told him that Higginson's "Boys' History of the United States" could be taken as a desirable model for size, general style, proportion, and comprehensiveness.

We have also suggested to him that while the history ought to be made a thoroughly trustworthy guide and a complete narrative (within the scope fixed upon) for use as a *textbook,* it would be important to put it in such shape that it would be thoroughly readable as a dramatic story or series of stories.

With this end in view, we suggested that special emphasis and space should be given to the "epoch-making" events, the point being that the things which boys most easily remember, can, if properly treated, be made the things most serviceable for them to remember.

Mr. Alden agreed with us as to the desirability and practicability of this plan, and we should wish to repeat the suggestion for the volume on Greece.

It would of course not be practicable for us to bind ourselves to accept the work the preparation for which we here suggest, but it is our understanding that we shall make use of it, unless there is good reason to be disappointed with the manner in which the undertaking has been carried out. We would suggest that it may be desirable for you to submit, when in readiness, a synopsis of your plan of the volume which shall indicate, approximately, the proportion of space to be allotted to the different periods and events; and to accompany this synopsis with a specimen chapter. We shall propose to illustrate the volume, though not extensively.

We should say a copyright of ten per cent. of the retail price of the copies sold (other than as remainders) after the first 1,000, and when 2,500 had been sold, to pay also on the first 1,000.

Yours truly,
G. P. Putnam's Sons.

Fortunately the laying to one side of these ambitions never dampened his ardor for the old tales. On occasion he would sit for hours puzzling over difficult passages with the zest of one keen on the track of a solution to a mystery. Indeed this almost sleuth-like attitude of mind which he brought to study caused him mental stimulation rather than fatigue; it braced him with a fresh exhilaration and buoyancy. Much the same release which the intelligentsia occasionally find in detective fiction, and the unintelligentsia in cross-word puzzles, Mr. Miller obtained in unsnarling some involved piece of translation.

As his son, Hoyt Miller, recalls, he had slight use for dictionaries and sometimes would scorn them altogether.

"He liked best to worry out the meaning of a word without consulting dictionaries; he liked to get at it from the roots or by comparing it with similar words in other languages."

Toward the same end though less for mental stimulation than for the utilitarian purposes served, he kept up his reading of the European press. It was his firm grasp of foreign affairs obtained in this way which had singled him out in the first place as the logical chief editor for *The Times*. Throughout the early years of storm and stress in that position he never relaxed in his comprehensive and up-to-the-minute study of overseas conditions. Mr. Flint holds to the opinion that during Mr. Miller's years as editor, "there was no man in New York so well-informed on international affairs."

All this took constant reading of periodicals and the attempt at least to keep up with the even then rapidly increasing stream of books from the publishers.

For his insight into British affairs, Mr. Miller relied to a great extent on the voluminous correspondence he received from Harold Frederick. Mr. Frederick had enjoyed what Bostonians would refer to as a "full life." He had edited the Albany *Journal;* he had turned out a novel or two dealing with western New York. But one of his chief assets lay in his flair for society. He enjoyed meeting people and people enjoyed meeting him. Mr. Miller felt that this talent for the amenities would make Mr. Frederick a valuable ally of the New York *Times* in London. And so it turned out. He persuaded Frederick to go to the British metropolis as *The Times's* correspondent.

With the urbane London of the early 'nineties Frederick found himself in complete accord. He revelled in the hot-house perfection of the then fashionable decadents. He was at his ease in the exclusive clubs to which his personal charm as much as his influential backing won him an entry. At the Savage, then in its supreme period, he felt particularly in harmony with his surroundings. And there he acquired a wide acquaintance with literary and artistic London and won a real place in the regard of his English friends.

This relationship which *The Times* established with the capital of the Empire brought all the benefits which Mr. Miller had hoped. Frederick wrote interesting, suave and well-informed "copy" for the paper's columns and furnished to his editor confidential sidelights on English public life. This enabled Mr. Miller to write with a real grasp of the situation overseas and an understanding of British political trends and of the personalities that lay behind them. These editorials established the prestige of *The Times* abroad.

When he had time to turn from scanning the foreign press to reading Continental novels for sheer relaxation, he found his chief delight in the romances of Alexandre Dumas. In fact he seldom embarked on even a short trip without tucking a volume or two of that prolific historical novelist in his kit. He had a graphic analysis of his favorite's style which he felt hit off the Dumas père's technique.

"Let us consider history as a straight line. Now Dumas had a way of writing round the facts of history in a spiral, which every now and then would cross the straight line. Each junction would be a fact to give verisimilitude to the tale. The curves of course are the novelist's own fabrications."

Fishing remained a passion with him throughout life. From his early days angling in the Hanover creeks to his septuagenarian years nothing delighted him so much as the chance to match his wits and skill with trout. During his early married life he took the opportunity more than once to answer the call of the wild. Mrs. Miller shared his keenness. Together they would go to the then almost inaccessible Lake St. John country, engage Indian guides and have several weeks of sheer enjoyment, "the world forgetting" in the excellent sport of virgin lakes and streams. Mrs. Miller was one of the first white women ever to camp and fish in this district. Later on, Mr. Miller joined the Blooming

OUT OF OFFICE HOURS

Grove Fishing Club. Thither he hurried each season when the fish were biting if it so happened that there was a lull in important news. As he jokingly wrote in the following letter to George Fred Williams: "I never leave the cosmos when it is in peril."

June 1, 1915.

DEAR TED:

Your uncle Von Tirpitz is responsible for our not going to Blooming Grove. You will remember I planned to go up about the middle of May. When the rolling stars brought the middle of May around, the Lusitania was at the bottom of the sea, our note to Germany was in preparation, and the mechanical and spiritual adjustments of the cosmos were in a state of high instability. I never leave the cosmos when it is in peril. Therefore Blooming Grove was dismissed from my mind; perhaps it is just as well, for the weather has been inhuman. George Greene and I were up there a couple of days the week after you were here, but the sport was not good. The bait fishermen had ravished the streams for two weeks from the opening, April 15, taking some 5,000 trout, and restocking for the later Spring and Summer had not begun. However, they have been taking big trout since then. One member caught eight weighing 12¾, and Mr. Haddon, the president of the club, took one in the meadows weighing 2¼. Possibly I might be able to arrange a trip for June, but I am not confident of it. Things are too mighty uncertain. If I do see an interval of diminished disturbance, I will let you know, and if you are free we will try it. But I fear it cannot be counted on.

Again to Mr. Williams under date of April 2, 1917, we find this paragraph:

I wish you would advise your German friends to scrap the Kaiser and so end the war. So protracted a performance gets tiresome and I should like to feel a little freer to get away now and then and play. For instance there will be trout at Blooming Grove this Spring. You and I ought to go up and slay them. If it should appear feasible toward the end of this month or early in May, would you be open to sealed proposals for such a joint excursion?

And again:

THE NEW YORK TIMES
TIMES SQUARE

August 11th, 1917.

MY DEAR TED:

In compensation for the himmel-schreiendes Unrecht of being cut off from trout at Blooming Grove this year, you and I must catch several important sharks at Woods Hole. Madge, I believe, has written Frances that we shall be there Friday night. If we carry out our present plans you may look for us Thursday night of next week, the sixteenth. We expect to leave Great Neck Wednesday morning and proceed by the way of Greenport and New London to Watch Hill, staying there that night at Elizabeth Belknap's. The next day we shall go by the way of Newport to Woods Hole, reaching there, I suppose, toward evening. I believe Madge wrote Frances to look out for our accommodations at a hotel, but only from Friday night to Monday morning. I wish you would advise Frances that we now intend to arrive there on Thursday. I am having the car overhauled and there is a possibility of delay, but I hope not. The party will consist of Madge, Major and myself, and some other person as yet undetermined. We are trying hard for Betty MacGeorge, but she may not be able to come.

We shall go to Boston Monday morning, staying there Monday night, then to Manchester Tuesday, staying over night with the Straws, and from there to the White Mountains for a day or two, across Vermont to Burlington, over the lake to Plattsburg, down through the Adirondacks to Lake George, spending a day or two at Mr. Ochs's house, then home somewhere around the first of September. I wish you and Frances would get a "flivver" and go along with us.

Do you observe how the price of silver has gone up? It is too bad that we cannot kill off two or three thousand Mexicans and get Tragar to working the mine again. Do you hear anything from him?

I enjoin you to suggest to the amiable lady who runs the hotel at Woods Hole that provisions should be made for a considerable increase in the average daily consumption of lobsters after my arrival.

Yours very truly,
C. R. MILLER.

Hon. George Fred Williams,
Boston, Mass.

Although Mr. Miller enjoyed travel his particular branch of the profession allowed him slight opportunity for it. He made his first trip to Europe in 1899, but the occasion was business rather than pleasure. He crossed as Mr. Ochs's personal representative to confer with James Gordon Bennett the younger, then in the most dazzling period of his electric and erratic career.

Mr. Bennett with thunderbolt abruptness had announced that he intended to kill off the New York *Telegram*.

The thought came to Mr. Ochs as he read that paper's antemortem obituary which followed the printing of the death sentence, that here might be a chance not only to prevent wilful slaughter but to obtain an established evening newspaper. He felt that the evening field might have a place for a paper of like character to *The Times*. Perhaps Mr. Bennett would be willing to sell.

Cables back and forth and negotiations with Mr. Bennett's New York representatives progressed to a point that encouraged Mr. Ochs to send Mr. Miller to Paris to complete the transaction.

James Gordon Bennett received Charles Ransom Miller with all that decorative courtesy he had lived abroad to acquire. In the back of his mind stayed some of the popular misconceptions regarding *The Times's* financial control, and he announced to his visitor that the New York *Times* could never be a success.

Mr. Miller then begged to point out that *The Times* was doing nicely.

"Oh that's just temporary," Mr. Bennett replied. "*The Times* can never be really successful until it frees itself of the Wall Street influence."

Not having a free year in which to trace this mythical "influence," Mr. Miller asked the question that had brought him to Paris. Would Mr. Bennett sell *The Telegram?* Mr. Miller mentioned the price which he understood Mr. Bennett would consider. Mr. Bennett was not one to haggle. Yes, he would sell *The Telegram* at the price offered, but on one condition.

And the condition . . .?

"I will sell *The Telegram* to Mr. Ochs, *but I will take my payment only in shares of the stock of The New York Times Company.*"

In the light of the foregoing let the italics stand as ample and adequate comment.

The immediate negotiations fell through as Mr. Ochs declined to part with any *Times* shares. However in this connection it is interesting to note that later only Mr. Bennett's untimely death prevented the sale of the New York *Herald* and *The Telegram* to Mr. Ochs. Actual terms had been agreed on which only needed

Mr. Bennett's formal acceptance. Before the papers to be signed could reach him, Mr. Bennett took suddenly ill and died.

As on this occasion Mr. Miller crossed at the instance of *The Times,* he kept a detailed expense account. He travelled as befitted his position as editor-in-chief of one of America's leading papers and while his early New England training would see to it that he indulged in no wasteful expenditures, we may be sure that no comfort was lacking. Yet in these days of inflated prices that 1899 expense account appears almost unbelievably meagre. His total budget for six weeks abroad amounted to but $525. The looming item in that grand total was of course the cost of steamship transportation; his stateroom cost him $75 each way.

He enjoyed a longer trip abroad in 1907 when he took over his son and daughter and his daughter's friend, Miss Betty MacGeorge. While in Europe he decided he would like to visit the Russian Duma and set machinery in motion for the necessary visas. After some delay and a certain amount of uncertainty the required permission arrived suddenly while they were sojourning in Berlin. As the time was quite limited all the attachés of the American Embassy scurried over the capital in the effort to round up the Miller party.

It so happened that he was to learn of German efficiency at first hand. Mr. Miller had an old pair of shoes which he no longer had any use for and which he wished to throw away. But he found the wish hard to gratify. He tried in vain to throw them away. Each time some alert hotel flunkey would retrieve them and bear them back to the abashed Mr. Miller with an air denoting the expectance of a gratuity. Several times he just left them in his room on leaving a hotel for another city. At the last moment a panting doorman would catch up with the conveyance and proffer the deserted footwear. More tipping. In the sudden departure from Berlin, Mr. Miller felt sure he had now got rid of the old shoes and the constant expense of his attempts to lose them. It was not to be. They were thrust at him through his railway-carriage window as he pulled out from the station. By this time he had made up his mind that they could not possibly stay lost in Germany. He kept them by his side till they crossed the frontier. Then he solemnly opened the compartment window and dropped them into some Russian river as the train bore them across it and on to St. Petersburg.

Society and its claims held small charm for him. An innate shyness frankly disliked the crowds incident to the wholesale type of entertainment to which New York grew increasingly partial. He was sociable by nature but it was a sociability that flowered chiefly for individuals or at the small dinner parties of his intimates which he loved to attend. Invitations to large official banquets which came to him through the mail in droves left him cold. He accepted the imperative few. As he grew older his rule was to decline them all.

George Haven Putnam tells of a conversation he had with Mr. Miller which illustrates this attitude. He was urging Mr. Miller to go with him to a certain big reception.

"What is the good?" Mr. Miller replied. "It will be a case of standing on one foot after the other when one prefers to sit, of talking to people one has no interest in, and of eating ice-cream one doesn't want to eat. What's the use?"

Social as he was and yet without much use for society, he very naturally found club life his delight. He thoroughly enjoyed his clubs. He liked the informal meeting with men of somewhat the same tastes and background as himself, men many of them like him of New England stock and prospering in the great metropolis which had drawn them to it. And of his clubs, the Century with its quiet dignity, its air of calm assurance, most attracted him. He made a point of attending and taking part in its entertainments and for years frequented it almost daily. The following amusing paragraph indicates the zest with which even on the threshold of three score years and ten, he could enter into a club revel. Unfortunately no pictorial record remains of the editor-in-chief of the New York *Times* garbed in the prophetic robes of Rabindranath Tagore addressing his fellow Centurians in "fluent and competent Russian," as the following letter records:

Dear Ted: January 11, 1917.

I went to our last Century Club Twelfth Night Monday evening in the character of our old friend, Bindy, otherwise Rabindranath Tagore. I addressed everybody in fluent and competent Russian and not a soul knew me, even after I had talked some time. George Greene refused to know me and said I didn't know him. Wyman Drummond wore a splendid Chinese Mandarin costume with, I should say, about a ton of jade ornaments dingling around him, and he was quite unrecognized. This is my night to dine with him and spend the evening, while the children go to the opera, but I have the Entente reply to the President's note to deal with, so I shall sit at home. . . .

Yours very truly,

C. R. Miller.

The Metropolitan Club also held his regard, and it was the Metropolitan that he made the scene of his annual banquets to celebrate each succeeding birthday. In due course he found himself on various club committees and took hold with interest in the work which each appointment involved. When it came his turn to serve on the House Committee of the Century, he found Mrs. Miller an invaluable ally. She relieved him of practically all his duties in that sphere and would herself ring up the chef and suggest menus or make the necessary criticisms.

During the spring, summer and autumn he often took advantage of his membership in the Piping Rock Club to get some fresh air and recreation near home. From youth onward he enjoyed exercise but his naturally muscular build grew heavy as the years passed because of his lack of time for regular play. He used to get considerable fun out of tennis. As *The Times* prospered and he prospered with the paper he leased a country home at Great Neck, Long Island. There he spent most pleasurably the long evenings of each summer. He had a tennis court near the house and would play frequently with his family and his guests. During the war, in fact, when the nature of the news and the hour of its arrival at the office made it imperative that he write a number of his editorials in the evening, he would often turn to tennis in the middle of his writing, play a set or so and then go back to work on the "leaders" before telephoning them in to *The Times.*

While he took a certain pride and drew a real æsthetic pleasure from his Great Neck garden, he had slight knowledge of and little real interest in horticulture. Likely as not he associated it in his mind with those pursuits of the farm which were the bugbear of his boyhood. But casual visitors at Great Neck unless they were corrected by an amused family would carry away with them a contrary impression. They would swear that the great editor's knowledge of gardening ranged from its choicest blooms to its minutest parasites. The reason lay in Mr. Miller's love of preposterous mischief. If asked if he knew the name of a particular flower, he would gravely answer in the affirmative and then draw on his classical background and roll out upon his astonished listeners some high-sounding but quite outlandish Latin tag. If Juliet-like they wondered what was in a name, the Miller family would come to the rescue and inform them that father couldn't tell the difference between a crocus and a cornflower.

Mr. Miller spent few of his off hours in correspondence. If a fear of some future biographer ever crossed his mind probably it soon passed in the assurance that no very personal letters existed. How could they? He declined to write them. Certainly in his practice he seemed to appreciate the sentiment of Dean Inge's famous parody:

> Lives of great men all remind us
> As we o'er their pages turn
> We should never leave behind us
> Letters that we ought to burn.

Fortunately he made one exception in the case of his old college friend George Fred Williams of Boston. To him Mr. Miller would delight in sending notes of gay badinage containing his informal comments on the affairs of the moment. Fully appreciative of this unique honor Mr. Williams kept them and filed them away as they came. The friendship between these two, which had its beginnings when they were freshmen together in Hanover, fell off slightly during the busy middle period of both, only to wax with the growing years. Mr. Miller loved to journey to Boston to celebrate Thanksgiving and sometimes Christmas.

Mr. Miller's relationship to the Columbia University School of Journalism, the chief pioneer in academic training for prospective newspaper men, interested him greatly. While the school was still in the blue-print stage of organization, Joseph Pulitzer its founder had suggested to President Nicholas Murray Butler what a fine thing it would be to secure Mr. Miller's co-operation in some advisory capacity. With this suggestion Doctor Butler was in full accord. He found Mr. Miller eager to help the new school in any way he could, and accordingly appointed him as a member of the institution's initial Advisory Board.

In addition to keeping a perfunctory eye on the school's schedule and courses, the board's most spectacular duty consists in awarding the annual prizes which Mr. Pulitzer established for journalistic and literary attainment, prizes which have grown in public interest with the years.

Mr. Miller took his relationship with Columbia most seriously and proved as expected an influential member of the board. In fact his colleagues on it chose him each year to preside. The board met then as it continues to do in Doctor Butler's office in the Library Building, a room approached by a long flight of granite steps from 116th Street. Mr. Miller's increasing gout and rheumatism made this climb as severe a penance as that imposed by any Scala Sancta. He would greet the notice of each annual meeting with an anticipatory twinge: "Oh, those steps, those steps." But with one exception he attended regularly up to the year of his final illness. As it happened, in the year he was kept from attending, the board awarded the Pulitzer medal to *The*

Times for its publication verbatim of the important war documents—the white papers and others quite as appropriately colored.

Mr. Miller acted as chairman of this board up to the year of his death. With the passing of Samuel Bowles 3d, of Springfield, Solomon Bulkley Griffin, Mr. Miller's old friend of *The Republican,* joined the board to fill the vacancy. On the occasion of his first meeting with them, E. P. Mitchell proposed Mr. Griffin as chairman for the year, but Mr. Griffin withdrew his name and the duty went to Mr. Miller as heretofore.

Mr. Miller's early delight in the classic language and history of the Isles of Greece lay no doubt at the back of the very real admiration he held for certain quickenings in the modern Hellas. He had a firm faith in the soundness of the political theories of the modern Greek movement led by Eleutherios Venizelos and gave both the movement and its leader a steady editorial support. Due to this interest and support was the prominent position he held in the American-Hellenic Society in which he served on the Executive Council.

In 1917 in the midst of strenuous editorial work occasioned by the war, he decided to add to his linguistic achievements. Latin and Greek had been early loves. French, mastered in youth, he spoke with great fluency and a correctness of accent which made visiting diplomats more superlative than ever in their compliments. German, he both read and spoke with equal ease, and while Spanish and Italian were later additions, he had come to use both with a fluent competence. But at the age of sixty-eight, he felt he must know Russian. That nation's literary achievements had fascinated him in translation; he was sensitive to the intensely modern spirit in Slavic culture manifested in so many of the arts; he wanted to appreciate it all at first hand.

Having slight time during these busy war days for this extra task, he devised means by which he could utilize his few unfilled moments. He had large cards prepared, on which were written the letters of the Russian alphabet. These he would put at the foot of his bed at night so that they would be the first objects his eyes would light on in the morning. Before he rose he would get in some intensive study. Then on getting up he would take the alphabet cards with him to his bathroom and attach them around his shaving mirror. In this way, constantly keeping at it with his native doggedness, he came eventually to the point where he could read Russian with facility and was able actually to converse to some extent in it. He took advantage of every occasion to gain an oral mastery of the language. Baron Rosen, an old friend of Mr. Miller's, would drop in at the office occasionally to be greeted by a Slavic outpouring from the veteran editor. The baron had formerly been connected with the Russian Embassy at Washington, but after the revolution took up his residence in New York till fatally injured in a taxi accident. Mr. Miller visited the old diplomat on his death bed and comforted him in his native tongue.

Mr. Miller thoroughly enjoyed some of the advantages incident to living in the metropolis. For years he delighted in the opera. His subscription called for well-placed orchestra seats each Thursday evening of the season, and thither he would go almost weekly with his son or daughter. He welcomed particularly the favorites of the old school and was glad when one of these time-honored pieces formed the Thursday night's bill. He enjoyed Caruso's personality almost as much as he did the great Italian's glorious tenor, and was keen to note the star's generosity to his fellow-singers, and his desire to bring them before the curtain with him to share in the applause.

In 1906 his alma mater, Dartmouth, conferred upon him the degree of Doctor of Laws. Nine years later Columbia added a Doctorate of Letters. On that occasion, Doctor Nicholas Murray Butler, with his customary grace and aptness in introduction, presented Mr. Miller as "for forty years a potent force in expressing, in guiding and in uplifting the public opinion of the American people; never more cogent, more wise or more eloquent than when voicing their moral purpose and their righteous judgment in these latter days when all the forces of evil and destruction are let loose to do rapine and slaughter among men."

A characteristic comment on the foregoing occurs in a paragraph in a letter to George Fred Williams on June 1, 1915.

> The Trustees of Columbia University bid me appear before them tomorrow to receive the degree of Doctor of Letters. Probably you will be as much surprised as I was. Madge and Major are coming in to see the punishment inflicted, and then I have to attend the Alumni luncheon in the afternoon and dine at President Butler's house in the evening, making a day of it in learned society.

This Columbia honor had a certain twice-blessed quality; it inspired compliments and congratulations to both the university and the new Doctor of Letters. Friends and critics alike recognized the appropriateness of the academic gesture. Something of this is voiced in the following letter—one of the many sent to Doctor Miller:

52 & 54 William Street
New York, June 3, 1915.

Charles R. Miller, Esq., Lit.D.,
Times Square, City.
MY DEAR MR. MILLER:

Will you permit me to express my gratification and to tender you my sincere congratulations upon the honor Columbia University has just bestowed upon you, and which is indeed greatly deserved.

Even if for the time being I am not in accord with everything the New York *Times* says in its editorial columns, I freely bear testimony that no-one has done more for clean and high-minded American journalism than you have in your long and honorable career.

Because of this, I rejoice that for this you have now received such high recognition, and wishing you many years yet of undiminished powers, I am, with assurance of friendship,

Most faithfully yours,

JACOB SCHIFF.

VIII

TIMES OFFICE AND WHITE HOUSE

When in 1884 Mr. Miller took his pen in hand to support Grover Cleveland as Democratic candidate for the presidency he had no inkling of the fact that in this Mr. Cleveland he was about to discover a kindred soul. But it soon became evident to both that they had much in common; acquaintanceship ripened into intimacy and intimacy into a lasting friendship. For one thing they shared a real kinship temperamentally; both had been blessed with judicial minds. A certain mental detachment which this implied had long been detected in Mr. Miller by some of his friends; they grew dissatisfied with it; they grew to dislike it and to refer at times to the editor as "cold."

The truth that lies behind the casual anecdote invariably shows that Grover Cleveland shared the same trait. Tim Campbell's story will serve. A proposal made to Mr. Cleveland caused him to reply: "Why, that is against the Constitution." Then the proposer's comment: "But what is the Constitution between friends?" Both Mr. Cleveland and Mr. Miller were on the side of the Constitution to such an extent that friends were apt to feel they were too much that way. Probably it was this mental similarity which drew them together, the bent for logical thinking which pointed out the one and only path for any action to follow.

That something of the New Hampshire granite which had developed in the Miller character as its birthright made him cleave to the man who hearing that a bill was all right but that it was not good politics to sign it replied: "If the bill is all right then it *is* good politics to sign it." Small wonder that the two men stood together; small wonder that the two stood out—the one as editor, the other as statesman.

During President Cleveland's occupancy of the White House, Mr. Miller made frequent trips to Washington. He used to like as he jokingly said to keep his eye on things. President Cleveland welcomed the chance which the Miller visits gave to talk over projects in the Administration's ken, submit them to the scrutiny of Mr. Miller's analytical eye, and sense from his comments thereon what the viewpoint of the sober-minded section of the populace would be.

A man who knew the editor well once described him as "not sweet natured, but calm natured." It was this calmness, derived partly from native Yankee shrewdness, partly from the detachment and the philosophic poise so fundamentally ingrained in his disposition that attracted and made confident those who sought his advice. In the case of Cleveland, the President early appreciated the similarity of Mr. Miller's outlook and mental processes to his own, and more often than not the President rose from an interview ramified in his own opinion by that satisfactory reinforcement that comes to one's ideas when we find they are shared by those whose judgment we respect.

Another trait which the two held in common was a thorough distaste for writing letters. If a letter to *The Times* office had to be written President Cleveland relegated the job to his secretary, Colonel Lamont. But the more satisfactory practice gradually instituted itself—that of sending a personal messenger and a word of mouth correspondence.

Mr. Miller delighted in the pleasant atmosphere which the Clevelands brought to the White House—an atmosphere less of a formal mansion than of a cultured home. He developed a real admiration and enthusiasm for the part taken by Mrs. Cleveland. As he and a friend stood watching her one evening as she received with a winning graciousness, Mr. Miller as he indicated her remarked: "There is one who fills magnificently the rôle of First Lady of the Land."

Mrs. Cleveland at this time was keenly interested in securing satisfactory legislation on the question of International Copyright.

This was a literary project in which she easily interested her friend, the editor-in-chief of *The Times,* and Mr. Miller gladly became a member of the committee.

But *The Times* had an even closer contact with the White House during President Cleveland's occupancy than that of Mr. Miller. The President and Edward Cary of the editorial staff had been intimate friends for years.

With President McKinley's inauguration the friendliness between the paper and the Executive Mansion continued though without the closeness implicit in a political eye-to-eye viewpoint. For years Mr. Ochs and Mr. McKinley had been on the most amiable terms, and the President's friendliness flowered in pleasant courtesies to both publisher and paper.

During this Administration Mr. Ochs through his editor and the editorial staff evolved the policy which has come to be regarded as perhaps the distinctive tenet of *The Times's* editorial credo. This policy maintains that while the paper is an independent Democrat journal it recognizes that the Government of the country while in power is entitled to the support of the country's press. This policy does not of course mean any waiving of the right of criticism, but it tends to direct this criticism along channels definitely helpful and constructive.

Mr. Miller adhered consistently to this policy and from this adherence *The Times's* prestige grew as a *national* newspaper. At home, the national-paper idea was taken with sundry reservations which modified the implication of the phrase to read—as national as any single newspaper can ever hope to be in a nation of such geographic expanses, but abroad the national idea took hold and has remained.

An earlier parallel to this exists in the case of *The Times's* namesake in London. Regardless of the party in power "the thunderer" would back up the Government and voice a national viewpoint in the ears of a puzzled and bewildered Continent.

Mr. Miller's public relationship with Theodore Roosevelt dated from the days in the '90's when they both served as members on the New York Committee advocating Civil Service reform. In those days Roosevelt began to exhibit his characteristic blend of activity and pugnacity which later assumed the proportions of a cult.

With them on this body served G. W. Curtis, Horace White of the New York *Evening Post,* Francis B. Barlow, George Haven Putnam, and Anson Phelps Stokes. Into this assembled group, Mr. Roosevelt came bursting one evening some time overdue.

"Any reporters present?" he asked.

"No," answered Mr. Putnam. "Only two editors."

"Well, then," said Roosevelt, "I'll say what I came to say—damn John Wanamaker."

He thereupon expatiated on this anathema by elaborating the iniquities of the great merchant in his capacity as Postmaster-General in blocking the work of Civil Service reform. He told them of his coup which hadn't come off: how he had collected information from employes of the Post Office who had been influenced politically.

"I took it to John Wanamaker," said Roosevelt, "he glanced at it and then handed it back to me with the comment: 'This is all second-hand evidence, Mr. Roosevelt.' "

There and then he vowed that he would get first-hand stuff.

He went to Baltimore, found a staunch ally in Bonaparte and there secured direct and duly signed and attested statements from employes who had been bullied into Republican allegiance.

Mr. Roosevelt hurried back to Washington, swore himself in as witness before himself as Commissioner and made out a detailed report. This he submitted to Wanamaker and to President Harrison.

For a time he waited patiently for some word from the White House. But not a syllable came and waiting patiently was hardly his long suit. The convention in the case of course required that no matter tabled with the President be referred to until released from the White House. He felt that to abide by this convention would result in frustration and he sought out two of his editorial friends, Carl Schurz and Mr. Miller, to see if they could devise ways how to get around it. He put the case up to them and the necessary detour was soon forthcoming.

Miller and Schurz agreed to call a meeting of the committee and then summon Mr. Roosevelt as a witness. The material could then be brought in as news matter.

"We will see that it's printed," said Schurz.

"More than that," promised Miller, "we'll see that it's referred to and distributed."

From committee work together and occasional meetings in town, Mr. Roosevelt developed an intense admiration for Mr. Miller's excellent judgment as well as his ready-to-hand information on the current world. During his years as Chief Executive of the State of New York this attitude increased and he took it with him to Washington when he went there as Vice-President. But at no time were their relations sufficiently close to lead anyone to foretell the very great compliment which T. R. was about to pay the editor of *The Times*.

When the assassin's bullet at the Pan-American Exposition in Buffalo sent the nation into mourning and Mr. Roosevelt hastening from a late summer holiday to the capital as President, he showed on how high a pinnacle he had placed Mr. Miller's good counsel. He wired him to join the presidential train at New York and proceed with him to Washington. The two spent the hours of travel together and upon arrival, Mr. Miller drove to the White House with the new President as his first luncheon guest.

When the meal was served the two men, hungry after their trip and talk, sat down to a lamb chop each. These they quickly demolished and the President ordered more to be brought. But it turned out that the White House ménage had not expected a guest the first day and had prepared but one order of chops for the President alone. Similarly with the desserts. These the President divided when they came and the demi-lunch progressed.

Inevitably this love-feast relationship had to end. For a while, the new President's dominant personality carried all before it, but he soon found that *The Times* had a personality too. On minor issues at first and then on more pertinent ones, the paper through its publisher and editor begged to differ. Naturally so frank an expressor of opinion as Mr. Roosevelt could not object to frank expression even of contrary opinion by others. His first disagreement with *The Times* centred on its news columns rather than its editorial page. He felt that through its special Washington correspondent at the time, the paper day in and day out misrepresented him. Accordingly he wrote a series of letters from the White House to Mr. Miller which claimed that *The Times* man either wilfully or temperamentally failed to grasp the presidential meaning in the daily press interviews. Realizing that a paper defeats its own ends which keeps as its Washington representative a correspondent persona non grata with the Executive, *The Times* withdrew its man but preserved its own ideas as to his integrity and intelligence.

The successor at the Washington bureau proved only slightly more to Mr. Roosevelt's taste, and the publisher and editor presumed what they had suspected right along that it was the paper rather than any individual which was persona non grata with the President.

Fortunately *The Times* maintained mutually profitable relations with the other Government Departments. John Hay had long had a genuine respect and admiration for *The Times*. In fact, with the assent of publisher and editor, Mr. Hay would from time to time send up "trial balloons" in *The Times's* columns to ascertain the public's reaction to State Department policies.

Here are the two chief letters which President Roosevelt wrote to express his dissatisfaction with *The Times's* man at Washington. The first merely registers the complaint on the ground "that he deliberately misstates facts." The second goes quite fully into the pre-campaign gossip of the day and illustrates one of Mr. Roosevelt's most ingratiating traits—his respect for foemen worthy of his steel. In discussing an appointee mentioned in the letter, the President goes on to say: "I was glad to appoint him, *for I grew to like the man during the period I was fighting him hardest when I was in the Civil Service Committee.*"

WHITE HOUSE
WASHINGTON

Personal

MY DEAR MR. MILLER: June 14, 1902.

Your correspondent has repeatedly, indeed habitually, misrepresented my position on certain matters. My belief is that he utterly misrepresents the attitude of many of the party leaders towards me; but with that I am not concerned. For instance, this morning he states that I "had repeatedly assured senators and representatives that he (I) had no objection to a rebate." This statement is a simple untruth, which if he had taken the slightest pains to find out the facts, he would have known to be an untruth. I have never to any human being said that I had no objection to a rebate, and on two or three occasions, of which your correspondent either did know or should have known, after it had been asserted that I had made this statement, I authorized its immediate and public denial.

I do not suppose there is anything that you care to do, or anything that you can do in this matter, but I wanted you to understand why it was that of late I have felt unable to see Mr. —— or to tell him, as I do certain other newspaper men, what are the inside facts as regards pending matters; for I have grown to feel that he deliberately misstates facts. He certainly suppresses a great part of the truth in this Cuban reciprocity business; his course is precisely that of a man desirous by any means to help the anti-Cuban side.

With regard,
Sincerely yours,
THEODORE ROOSEVELT.

Mr. Charles R. Miller,
New York *Times,*
New York, N. Y.

Personal

WHITE HOUSE
WASHINGTON

MY DEAR MR. MILLER: Oyster Bay, N. Y., July 10, 1902.

Your very kind editorial in today's issue of *The Times* impels me, with some hesitation, to write a line to you. In it you quote from your Washington correspondent as to the proposition to "form a Roosevelt party in Congress under leaders inspired from and in a manner responsible to the White House." After your kind last letter I do not feel like again mentioning the subject of Mr. ——, and all the less so because of your great personal courtesy and kindness. But I really wish I could make you understand that his statements in reference to me have not one particle of foundation, and that as a matter of fact I am inclined to think they are deliberate and wilful falsehoods. No responsible man has ever dreamed of making a Roosevelt party in Congress, for I could not have failed to hear about it had any human being of the least account ever thought of such a thing. Certainly no one whom I have seen ever thought of it until they saw it suggested by Mr. ——, and it was then alluded to merely as a matter of amusement.

He has recently been stating, not once but again and again, that Mr. Clarkson is to try to control the southern delegations and that he was appointed for that purpose. Mr. Clarkson has never spoken to me or to anyone else whom I know one word about a southern delegate. On his recent visit to Washington he never treated of the matter at all. He lunched with me, as did Mr. Payne, and had there been any such conversations as that of which your correspondent spoke, I could not have failed to hear it. In direct contravention of the case as stated by Mr. ——, Mr. Clarkson's appointment was earnestly and repeatedly urged by Senators Allison and Bolivar, and then asked for by Senator Platt. I was glad to appoint him, for I grew to like the man during the period I was fighting him hardest when I was in the Civil Service Committee, and he has up to this time justified the appointment by making an admirable official. As far as I know, he has confined himself strictly to his official duties.

If Mr. —— cared to find out the facts—and I beg you to believe that the reason I do not try to show him the facts as I would like to in the case of your correspondent is because I am convinced that he deliberately intends to falsify—he would know from Mr. Payne or from Mr. Booker Washington or from Judge Jones, of Alabama, or from Judge Brawley, of South Carolina, or from Judge Henry Clay McDowell, of Virginia, that nothing whatever has been done on the lines he suggested in reference to the southern delegations. On the contrary, in certain states—Louisiana and Mississippi, for example—after careful consideration I have deliberately adopted a course which will in all probability insure hostile delegations to me, if there is any serious opposition to my nomination. I adopted such a course because the character of the Republican organization was such that after patient and careful investigation and effort I found myself unable to get from among its members men for the responsible offices whom I regarded as of sufficient character and standing.

I understand entirely that if I am to be nominated in 1904 it must be because there is a strong and active sentiment among the Republicans of the Republican States to the effect that I represent the policy and principles in which they believe, and that if I am to be elected it must be because various other Republican leaders and I working together are, should fortune favor us, able to convince the bulk of the honest and intelligent voters that it is for the best interests of the country to continue for the time being the Republican Party in power.

Faithfully yours,
THEODORE ROOSEVELT.

Mr. Charles R. Miller,
Editor, New York *Times,*
New York, N. Y.

P. S. I have just received a note from Mr. Payne reading in part as follows: "As to the story about Mr. Clarkson, it was made up out of the whole cloth, and he has never discussed with me or even spoken to me regarding the Southern delegate question, as would be inferred from the correspondence in *The Times.*"

Despite official differences the President and Mr. Miller kept up a working personal entente and Mr. Miller took occasion to attend most of the President's public appearances in New York. He took in among others the famous Gridiron Club dinner in 1906. At this season the President was reading lessons to financial magnates and to captains of industry and took occasion at this dinner, which had as guests Pierpont Morgan and H. H. Rogers among other kindred gentlemen, to throw out one of his verbal bombshells.

The bomb exploded in the midst of the assembly with stunning detonations, but in the news reports the public could grasp but inadequately the extent of the sensation caused. Readers of the speech as published in the papers could see in it slight cause for such a commotion.

At the Century Club the next day, George W. Wickersham in conversation with Mr. Miller voiced the general query of all those who had not actually heard the speech. Feeling that something must have been left out of the reports Mr. Wickersham asked the editor:

"Now just what did he really say?"

Mr. Miller's answer cut directly to the point:

"It was not so much what he said. It was the *manner.*"

Apocryphal stories persist that the President went out of his way to show his displeasure at *The Times's* criticism of several of his pet projects by deliberately cutting Mr. Miller on one of the editor's visits to Washington, but there exists little to disprove that the two men, despite inevitable differences, kept a mutual regard for each other to the end.

Coincident with Mr. Taft's advent at the White House was the departure of Mr. Miller's club-mate, George W. Wickersham, to Washington to become Attorney-General in the Taft Cabinet. Mr. Wickersham's many friends turned out to do him honor at the congratulatory dinner tendered him on his appointment. Although the bouquets have long withered and the pleasant words of eulogy and compliment have ceased to echo, Mr. Wickersham still recalls with amusement an example of Mr. Miller's "realism" on that occasion.

As the two men shook hands after the banquet, the editor's comment ran something like this:

"I'm just wondering what the reaction in Wyoming and Nebraska will be to this appointment of a Wall Street lawyer as Attorney-General."

During the campaign which resulted in Mr. Taft's victory, *The Times* gave him its editorial support, for it would not and could not support Mr. Bryan, the Democratic candidate. Mr. Miller's relationships with the new President were pleasant but never in any sense close. But Mr. Ochs and Mr. Taft had enjoyed a personal friendship over a long period.

All contacts between the editor and the President kept on a formal plane which needs no better illustration than the tenor of the President's letter to Mr. Miller on the occasion of the celebration of the sixtieth anniversary of the establishment of *The Times*.

WHITE HOUSE
WASHINGTON

Beverley, Massachusetts,
August 29, 1911.

TO THE EDITOR OF THE NEW YORK "TIMES":

I congratulate you on celebrating the Sixtieth Anniversary of the establishment of your paper. There is no instrument in society more powerful for good than a clean, clear-thinking, truth-loving newspaper which minimizes the details of crime and prurient scandal and gives accurate account of the doings of the day that people of intelligence ought to know and remember.

In your editorial columns you have disagreed with me on many issues and have agreed with me on others. But the standard you have maintained in your editorial columns and in your news columns since the days of Raymond have always commended my admiration.

I sincerely congratulate you on the Sixtieth Anniversary of the paper.

Sincerely yours,

WM. H. TAFT.

No comment on this period should ignore the strong friendship which existed between Mr. Miller and Elihu Root. This relationship had its genesis in the turbulent days of the old New York Times Publishing Company. Mr. Root acted as chief legal advisor to that ill-fated concern and Mr. Miller found in him a tower of strength when everything and everyone around seemed to crumble and fall. Mr. Root's advice continued in the transition period and their uninterrupted friendship grew in strength with the years.

We reprint Mr. Root's most readable letter apropos of his election to the Senate:

DEPARTMENT OF STATE
WASHINGTON

Personal

January 23, 1909.

MY DEAR MILLER:

I am much obliged to you for your congratulations on my election to the Senate. It has been indeed a most extraordinary proceeding. I had no real faith in any such thing ever happening in the State of New York and I am now studying the cause of it with much interest as a matter of political psychology. Certainly one great element was the kindly and vigorous treatment of the subject which your friendship has brought about in *The Times.*

It is rather a tradition of *The World* to regard me as a monster of iniquity. I preserve myself from all injurious effects by never reading the paper, and I doubtless receive great benefit from it, for, it is necessary to have enemies and to be attacked in order not to be hated. One amusing thing about it is that on such casual inquiry as I have made from time to time I have become satisfied that *The World* is really sincere in its views of me and perhaps they are right. Who knows!

Always faithfully yours, ELIHU ROOT.

C. R. Miller, Esquire,
The Times,
New York, N. Y.

In the pre-convention campaign of 1912, *The Times* had no favorite candidate. But when the tumult and the shouting of the actual convention itself centred around the heads of Woodrow Wilson and Champ Clark, the paper in no uncertain voice threw its editorial support in favor of the Governor of New Jersey. Wilson, Mr. Miller felt, had attributes for the presidency that should not be overlooked and he underlined them editorially for the guidance of the wavering delegates. His strongest editorial appeared during the lull in the deadlock necessitated by the arrival of the Sabbath, and in Mr. Wilson's own opinion this editorial worked potently in turning the tide in his favor. In a telegram addressed to the publisher of *The Times,* the Democratic candidate for the presidency wired that the paper's support had been of incalculable value.

With Mr. Wilson's inauguration in 1913, *The Times* began an editorial support as loyal and as consistent as an independent paper could well give, but Mr. Wilson's first Cabinet was hardly one to arouse Mr. Miller's editorial enthusiasm.

Speaking with the voice of *The Times* he pointed out its virtues and its defects. To his one regular and intimate correspondent, the Honorable Geo. Fred Williams of Boston, he wrote much the same thing if somewhat more informally.

March 1, 1913.

DEAR TED:

The tidings you give of a probable visit to New York before long are most encouraging. We shall have to talk over the new Administration and perhaps arrange for its proper guidance. I learned today that Brandeis is not to go in the Commerce and Labor Department, but that Redfield, the Brooklyn Congressman, will have that post. That is a very wise change, for Brandeis would have been continually under attack. Redfield is a strong and competent man. The general average of the Cabinet, as it is now believed to be made up, will not be one of great ability, but I am inclined to think that it will be fairly well received by the country. Bryan will be a shock to the East but that will be in a very large measure offset by McAdoo, who is a business man and is not at all of the Bryan persuasion. Indeed, the West will probably say that he has been plucked right out of the heart of the money trust. Josephus Daniels for the Navy Department has a very jocose sound. It looks as if Wilson wanted to treat that Department with contempt. But on this and other matters we will hold discourse when you appear.

A few days later when the Cabinet's complete personnel became known, he wrote to Mr. Williams again in much the same strain.

DEAR TED: March 6, 1913.
The appointment of Bryan has created no excitement here. They had all expected it. Beside it is more than counterbalanced by McAdoo. If McAdoo should meet the money trust in the street he would invite it in to have a highball. But he is an able and a very sound man, who has won favor here by the principle of "the public be pleased" which he has applied in the operation of his tunnels. I am hopeful he will do well. But it is not a very powerful Cabinet it strikes me.

It was not long before Mr. Miller became aware of the now well-known Wilson traits. By Election Day of the same year he had seen signs of "cephalic enlargement" at the White House, and hoped on the sly, as he put it to his friend, that New Jersey would go agin the Government and act as "a useful corrective."

DEAR TED: Nov. 4, 1913.
Now that some 600,000 gallant gentlemen who have been in the polling booths alone with their God and their lead pencils today trying to follow the advice *The Times* has given them have nearly completed their labors, I will take a few moments to acknowledge the receipt of the stated tribute which arrived the other day and was put to its destined use. . . .
I am hoping on the sly that New Jersey will go agin the Government today. There are some signs of cephalic enlargement at Washington, and a defeat in the home state would be a useful corrective. I have heard of no intelligent guess as to how your Commonwealth is going. Here we expect to down Tammany.

Although no paper ever gave to any Administration more loyal and continued support than *The Times* gave to that of President Wilson, through fair weather and foul, the relations between Mr. Miller and the President and between the President and *The Times* were so slight as to be practically non-existent. What contacts occurred remained purely surface contacts. Mr. Miller never penetrated the presidential hard shell; Mr. Wilson never took advantage as his predecessors had done of Mr. Miller's well of wisdom.

For one thing actual meetings between the two men were few. But on one occasion it did look as if a happy intimacy would ripen but it was a case of surface amenity only. The world to-day might have been a different place if mind had met with mind and deep called unto deep. This occasion consisted of an extremely felicitous luncheon party during the Shadow Lawn summer. The President invited Mr. Ochs and his editor to spend the day with him. The two New Yorkers arrived at the President's summer home shortly before lunch. A lackadaisical sentry let their car through the front gate with little more than a passing glance. A younger and brighter boy on the porch intimated that they had been expected and they were shown in to await the President. To Mr. Miller the luncheon itself remained in his memory as a happy and pleasant hour. Everywhere those formalities which at Washington hedge the Chief Executive were relaxed. The two visitors from New York found themselves seated at no official board but taking part in a simple family meal. With the President were Mrs. Wilson, her mother and several members of her family and the lunch itself was served by one old Southern man-servant. Everyone seemed at his best and the conversation sparkled. After the ladies had left the table both Mr. Ochs and Mr. Miller stood aside for the Chief Executive to pass out first. But he motioned them to precede him.

"I am not in Washington now but in my own home—so please go out first."

The trio spent the rest of the afternoon deep in conversation. The President discussed unreservedly with his guests the problems which at the moment perplexed and worried him. Naturally those springing from the war came uppermost. The three went into the difficulties arising from the British insistence on searching American shipping for contraband with its inevitable interference with neutral trade. Apparently only the expert statesmanship of

Sir Edward Grey and Walter H. Page kept this friction from starting a blaze, for Mr. Wilson's comment on this situation was: "Personally I make no difference between imperialism on land and imperialism on the high seas."

Oddly enough Mr. Wilson's first communications to the paper closely resembled in subject matter those of Mr. Roosevelt. Like "T. R.," Mr. Wilson took occasion to suggest that *The Times* man "covering" him be removed. His chief complaint came in a note to Louis Wiley, the paper's business manager. Mr. Wilson it appeared liked the reporter personally and found him a very likeable, honorable ingenuous fellow, but he considered him singularly unable to see a thing simply and as it was. A certain whimsical fancy, he complained, gave this reporter's stories from the Governor's Cottage at Seagirt both a color and a squint that often proved embarrassing. Mr. Wilson admitted that the reporter's stories had "human interest." What he objected to was that they put the human of whom he was writing in a very false light.

As in the case of the Washington correspondent in President Roosevelt's day, *The Times* transferred its man.

But this minute attention to the quality of the press reports concerning him which the foregoing complaint implies seemed to disappear from Mr. Wilson's regimen as he grew into his rôle as Chief Executive. He came to treat *The Times* with aloofness, but in this connection it is only fair to call attention to the seldom noted fact that he came to treat the press as a whole in exactly the same way.

This complete detachment from newspaper comment stands unique in a public man of prominence. One of his few real intimates recalls that during the most important years of his Executive career, the President neither read the papers nor cared what they said. He would scan the news dispatches and augment them from his private and official sources of information, but to the carefully clipped and ordered columns of editorial comment placed in his way by an attentive staff, he seldom gave a glance.

Only three editorial writers, apparently, held any interest for him. He often turned to the leaders of the Springfield *Republican;* he cherished the writings of a small-town Southern editor of a paper whose name the late President's intimates no longer remember; and he read with care the editorials of his chief newspaper friend, the late Frank Cobb, in *The World*. For the rest, newspapers and newspaper men hardly existed for him. Once his advisors thought it expedient that the President meet Mr. Hearst, but the President had no intention of meeting Mr. Hearst just then, nor did he.

But to say that in his habitual disregard of newspapers, the President remained oblivious to *The Times's* editorial utterances is to say too much. Mr. Miller's editorial opinions did reach him from time to time. H. H. Kohlsaat saw to it that salient clippings from *The Times* went off to his friend, Colonel House, and Colonel House saw to it that President Wilson got wind of their contents in conversation if not by actual reading. During the Paris Peace Conference for instance, Mr. Kohlsaat kept up a constant correspondence with Colonel House and seldom did a letter leave him without its quota of clippings. Something of their import stayed in Mr. Wilson's mind and was doubtless fresh in his memory when in November, 1920, he intimated to a friend with reference to *The Times* that "it was fine to have at least one such paper in the country that can see straight and talk straight."

As one can judge from the foregoing, nothing remotely approaching intimacy ever existed between Editor and President. But Mr. Miller made himself fully intimate with every detail of the Wilson Administration and on the whole held both the man and his works in high esteem. His personal viewpoint is best summed up in a remark which he addressed to a member of his family.

"In order to be fair to President Wilson, one must separate him into two people—an idealist and a schoolmaster."

His public viewpoint he placed on record at the end of the

Wilson period when in a lengthy editorial he set down his candid appreciation of the President's achievements. This editorial has a place in the appendix to this book.

With the coming of President Harding came, oddly enough, an era of much friendlier co-operation. For one thing both Mr. Ochs and Mr. Miller found themselves in hearty accord with the aims of the Conference for the Limitation of Armaments which the new President sponsored. Mr. Ochs and Mr. Miller in fact were fully cognizant of the conference's ideas and ideals from their genesis, and much that Mr. Miller wrote in connection with it had a basis in inside official information.

As it happened, President Harding and Mr. Miller never met but they had a cheery intermediary in H. H. Kohlsaat. Mr. Kohlsaat was one of those rare human beings whom people instinctively trust and love. At this time his active journalistic career in Chicago had ended, and he found himself free to go about doing good.

He had known Mr. Ochs and Mr. Miller for years, and nothing more natural than for him to become an almost daily luncheon guest of *The Times* while he stayed in New York. His genial charm and his genuinely sweet nature were open sesame everywhere and leading men of all parties made him their confidant. From President McKinley's day on, the latch string of the White House had always been out to him, and President Harding followed his predecessors in welcoming "H. H." as an advisor and friend.

Mr. Kohlsaat delighted to visit between New York and Washington and from this penchant of his there came into being an informal "ambassadorship." Official circles in Washington knew Mr. Kohlsaat to have friendly associations with *The Times; The Times* realized the extent of his entrée at Washington. Almost spontaneously the idea occurred to both parties to utilize for mutual benefit Mr. Kohlsaat's good offices. Accordingly, and with the consent of everyone, he would repeat at *The Times* office conversations he had had at the White House and State Department, and, returning to Washington, he would bring to President Harding and to Secretary Hughes the comments which Mr. Miller and his associates had made on the disclosures.

All concerned soon found this word-of-mouth communication important and useful. Washington realized that here lay the chance to secure expert editorial opinion on prospective undertakings before an inkling of them reached the public as "pronouncements," or "attitudes," or "policies," and Mr. Ochs and Mr. Miller welcomed the advance information. It resulted in a clearer perspective all around.

For Mr. Miller's editorial writings Mr. Kohlsaat's mission proved of real advantage. It enabled him to write in a number of instances as wise before rather than after the event. In the case of the Pensions bill which bothered the Harding Administration in its early months, Mr. Miller knew perfectly well as he dictated his editorials against the measure that President Harding had made up his mind to veto it.

Of course both parties recognized their good fortune in having a man of Mr. Kohlsaat's tact, discretion and charm as "ambassador." For years the desire for such a sounding out of editorial approval or dissent had bothered the White House. One President would try one way, his successor would try another.

Oddly enough, Mr. Kohlsaat in his own book, "From McKinley to Harding," makes this exposition of the Rooseveltian method:

> Frequently the President would make suggestions of some course he might take in public questions or legislation, and then he would watch for the public reaction. If it was favorable he would proceed in accordance with his suggestion, and if unfavorable, he would reject it absolutely.

It was for Mr. Kohlsaat to devise the pleasanter technique. Unfortunately its success rested on that happy blend of gifts unique in his own personality, and with his passing, one might apply appropriately to "H. H.'s" informal ambassadorship, Garrick's tragic lament: A common grave holds both the actor and his art.

During this period Mr. Kohlsaat received a regular retainer from *The Times,* and was attached to the editorial staff as an advisor and an informer. His death in Washington while a guest at the home of Herbert Hoover inspired on the paper's editorial page two notable tributes—an editorial full of deep feeling written by Rollo Ogden, and the following quatrain from the pen of the associate editor, Doctor John H. Finley:

H. H.
Sought by the greatest and the least as friend,
He gave himself unsparing to the end;
He even kept death waiting at the door
Till he could do a friend one kindness more.
F.

IX

THE SENATE INQUISITION

On March 15, 1915, Mr. Miller became at one and the same time a defender of the freedom of the press and a professor of journalism to the United States Senate. In both rôles he acquitted himself in a way to win nation-wide applause. Ostensibly the occasion was a Senate Committee's investigation of allegations that "influence had been exerted" against the then pending Ship Purchase bill. In reality the session consisted of a lengthy airing of a succession of innuendoes against the paper, its proprietors, and its practices. Tongues had wagged; senatorial ears had buzzed.

The Times had opposed the Ship Purchase measure for the simple reason that it did not approve of it. But simple reasons fail frequently of simple acceptance. Certainly the committee, headed by Senator T. J. Walsh of Montana, then in the first flush of inquisitorial ardor, had no inhibitions on the score of curiosity. What it itched to know it asked about without regard as to whether its queries were pertinent or impertinent.

The investigation may not have satisfied the investigators but it accomplished results important in the world of journalism. It showed that even in days of mass production with the emphasis accordingly put on newspapers as vast commercial enterprises, the press has still a soul and the desire to call that soul its own. More particularly it cleared up the persistent rumors that *The Times* was backed by "British gold."

This idea died hard. It was this allegation that lay back of the whole inquiry, and although a certain humming and hawing about the Ship Purchase bill formed a necessary preamble, the committee's curiosity would out. Carr V. Van Anda, managing editor of *The Times,* instructed by Mr. Ochs with complete information, furnished a list of all persons owning more than one per cent of the capital stock and produced a table showing how much each one of them owned. The table proclaimed the fact that Mr. Ochs held 62 per cent of *The Times* and Mr. Miller, over 14 per cent. It showed that most of the remaining 20 odd per cent belonged to individuals connected with the paper,—the sum total of it all in American hands. This left no chink or cranny for the insertion of the thin edge of the British golden wedge, nor did it leave any need for it. But the legend persisted.

The next day it cropped out again. Mr. Miller on the stand was his usual calm, urbane self. Inwardly he resented the whole business. He resented what he considered the unwarranted prying into the private affairs of his publisher, but most of all he disliked proceedings which tended as he said "to repress freedom of utterance and to put newspapers under a sort of duress." "Inquisitorial proceedings of this kind," he frankly told them, "if continued and adopted as a policy" would reduce the American press to the level of certain degenerate mid-European journals, "the press that has been known as the reptile press, that crawls on its belly every day to the Foreign Office or to the Government officials and Ministers to know what it may say or shall say—to receive its orders."

Finally the cause of the Senate Committee's distress came to the fore. The name of Lord Northcliffe was mentioned. Elmer Davis in his "History of the New York *Times*" has shown how the whole fuss originated in a series of anonymous letters. True they bore signatures. Putting their heads together, Senator Walsh and *The Times's* staff deciphered some name that might be "A. M. Abbey" or might just as well be "G. M. Hubbell," but no individual arose in the land to claim either cognomen when their contents were made public. These notes alleged that a "well-known Englishman has been backing Mr. Ochs with money to get control of *The Times*." The writer added as a further indictment: "I understand that Mr. Miller is also mixed up in some way with this Englishman."

But the chief value of Mr. Miller's appearance at Washington did not lie in his setting the Senatorial Committee's mind at rest. It lay as previously indicated in his steadfast championship of untrammelled editorial utterance, and in his terse exposition of editorial procedure. Throughout the affair, *The Times* maintained the position that it represented the American press at large:

> This is not a personal issue. It is a question of the extent to which a government's machinery may be privately misused to annoy and attempt to discredit a newspaper whose editorial attitude has become distasteful and embarrassing.

Teachers of journalism all over the country welcomed the trip behind the editorial scenes on which this skilled practitioner personally conducted Senator Walsh and his colleagues. In fact Professors Cunliffe and Lomer in their journalistic text book, "Writing of Today," use an excerpt from Mr. Miller's testimony as a preface to the department of their book which deals with editorial writing:

> Every newspaper that enjoys continuity of existence and management has a certain body of principles. They are called the policy of the paper. Those are the principles and beliefs that guide its expressions and opinions. The men who express those opinions are the editorial writers. . . . They are men. They wear neither halos nor horns. They form their opinions just as other men form their opinions, by observation and reflection and information. . . . But each paper has a body of principles that guide its utterances, and the men who write those principles believe them. Nobody in *The Times* office is ever asked to write what he does not believe.

On the question of the responsibility for editorial utterance, Mr. Miller pointed out that editorial writers "appear before the jury every day."

> We appear before the grand inquisition, one of the largest courts in history; we are judged at the breakfast table. We feel that, if we were improperly influenced by anybody outside of the office, there is none so quick to discover that as the reader of the paper.

MR. MILLER OF "THE TIMES"

Chiefly because it makes good reading, we reprint here the verbatim account of the Senatorial inquisition as it appeared in the daily press of the time. But it belongs by divine right to any complete record of Mr. Miller's career, for in his succinct way it sums up his observations of his craft arrived at over a full lifetime spent in its service:

The Chairman: A part of the duties of this Committee is to ascertain what truth there is in the suggestion that certain individuals holding official relations with the Government of the United States or others closely related to them, have secured options upon belligerent ships interned, as it is said, in our ports, with a view to acquiring them, eventually to be transferred to the Government in case the Ship Purchase Bill should pass. In an editorial appearing in *The Times,* under the date, Dec. 18, 1914, is found the following:
There are signs that somebody knows what ships are to be bought and who is to buy them from the Government.

Q.: Can you enlighten the committee as to what the signs are, and who the somebody is, referred to in that sentence?

A.: There is no knowledge there derived from any sources except such as are open to everybody. It is what was in public discussion and in the atmosphere, in the newspapers and technical journals, trade journals, and the general sources of information. There is no hidden or private knowledge back of that suggestion.

The Chairman: Now, that is just what the Committee was appointed for, Mr. Miller. There was a great deal of the kind of comment that you speak of. Of course it attains some degree of respectability by reason of being thus incorporated in your editorial. You are not able to give us any more definite information than that?

Mr. Miller: No more definite information than that it was derived from sources open to everybody, just as I might say now that there are signs that the *Eitel Friedrich* will never take to the seas again for her cruising; that there are signs that there are going to be lively times in Constantinople; that there are signs that the English and French have resumed their pressure on the German lines—sources that are open to everyone, the general knowledge and talk of the community, of the country.

Q.: You could specifically tell us to this extent. Doubtless you could tell us what the signs were?

A.: When the Government is in the market as a buyer, the sellers usually come forward. That was practically all that was meant. If it were known that the Government was going to be a purchaser of ships, people who had ships to sell would naturally be somewhat in evidence.

Q.: Do you recall any owners of ships that thus did come forward?

A.: It is impossible at this distance of time to recall any specific instance.

THE SENATE INQUISITION

It was the general discussion in the newspapers. There might have been something in the trade papers about it. There was nothing specific, so far as I can say. There is no allegation of any impropriety or any improper act. That certainly was not the intention.

Q.: Of course it is conceivable that some officer of the Government, acting with exceeding prudence and foresight, might have taken some options?

A.: There is not the slightest shade of that suggestion in that sentence, so far as I can see, and certainly there is no intention to convey any such impression. It was an allusion to common reports that were open to everybody.

Chairman Walsh here produced a clipping from the New York *Times* of Sept. 8, headed, "Norway To Sell Ships—Anxious for America to Get Her Old Ones and Build a New Fleet," which he read. This quoted a dispatch from Copenhagen to the London *Daily News*, which spoke of the United States as proposing to buy a fleet of ships for $400,000,000. It was the $400,000,000 that interested Senator Walsh. It was explained to him by the witness that this was probably a typographical error for $40,000,000.

Chairman Walsh passed on to an editorial in *The Times* of January 20. This expression interested him:

Those who have our moral approval of their contentions are in control of the seas and can get all the contrabrand they need.

Who was meant by the expression, "those who have our moral approval"?

Mr. Miller: "The Allies."

Q.: And the pronoun, "our" refers to whom?

A.: The American people.

Q.: That was intended as a declaration that the cause of the Allies has the general moral approval of the American people?

A.: We have often said that.

Q.: That is the position which *The Times* has taken?

A.: Repeatedly.

Q.: Has *The Times* any business connections of any character in England?

A.: None whatever, except that we maintain an office there and have our own employees there; our own correspondents. There is no business connection with anybody in England.

Q.: Mr. Ochs appears to be the largest stockholder of the New York *Times* according to the testimony of Mr. Van Anda?

A.: Yes.

Q.: Are you able to tell us whether he has any financial support of any kind in England?

A.: I can tell you that he has none. So far as any one man who is in daily association with another, in confidential relations with him, knows his business affairs, I can tell you positively that he has not.

Q.: I asked because I was informed that that was the case.

A.: He has none whatever. I suppose I know the rumor to which you allude. It is absolutely false.

Q.: What is the rumor?

A.: It is one that has been circulated by persons who are not in sympathy with our course, that the London *Times* has some relation with us. It has none whatever.

Turning to another subject, Chairman Walsh called the attention of the witness to a report of a meeting of the United States Chamber of Commerce in Washington, in *The Times* of February 5, and raised again the questions presented at the examination of the managing editor of *The Times*. Whether the headline correctly represented the dispatch. Mr. Miller thought it did.

Chairman Walsh next read from an editorial of *The Times* of Feb. 5, the following:

When conditions are normally competitive American boats cannot live upon the seas. But when the rates are such that anything afloat can make profits, then even American shipping can fly the flag under the handicap of our laws.

The Chairman: Is it your understanding that at the time that was written, under the rates prevailing, anything afloat could make profits?

The Witness: The rates were higher. I should say any ship, properly conducted, could have made a profit at that time.

Q.: Even under the handicap of our laws as they existed at that time?

A.: I am unable to say. I am not an experienced shipping man.

Q.: What is the particular handicap of our laws to which you there refer?

A.: The navigation laws in general, and, for one thing, the much higher wages that are paid to American seamen. It has been a general contention for many years that our navigation laws have been an impediment and a detriment to the building of American ships.

Q.: Yes, but you know we have removed all those we could think of?

A.: In admitting foreign ships to registry?

Q.: Yes, the complaint was made that foreign built ships could not obtain registry under the American laws, and we removed that difficulty. The complaint was made that it became necessary to man the ship with American officers exclusively, and we removed that. Now, what specific handicap of our laws was there upon American shipping upon Feb. 5?

A.: No specific impost or burden, but the general conditions.

Q.: Yes; but, Mr. Miller, this is a complaint you made against our laws. What I should like to know is what specific provision of the laws was left that handicapped our commerce and shipping, and which you think ought to be removed?

A.: I think of nothing at the present moment except the general conditions under our laws. It is more expensive to build and man and operate our ships.

THE SENATE INQUISITION

The Chairman: Yes; that is why I interrogate you about this. A great deal of the opposition to the Ship Purchase bill is that we are told that we cannot operate ships under our laws. We are told that we cannot develop our merchant marine under private ownership. We are told that neither the one nor the other plan will work because of the handicap of our laws. I am anxious to learn, if I can, what those handicaps are, that, if possible, they may be removed.

The Witness: The evidence of their existence is in the fact that so few American merchant ships have been sailing the seas.

Q.: You think that is due to evils in our laws?

A.: Not wholly. I think it is due very largely to the fact that American capital can be more profitably employed than in shipping.

The Chairman: Of course that, perhaps, we could not remove very well.

Senator Sutherland: It is a fact, is it not, that every other considerable maritime power except our own has by some affirmative legislation encouraged shipping?

A.: Yes.

Senator Sutherland: That we have neglected to do. My question is whether that was in the mind of the editorial writer?

A.: I do not think so.

The Chairman: I thought of the same thing, that possibly, it was because we did not have some laws that in your judgment we ought——

The Witness: No, sir. We have always been opposed to subsidies. If the Committee will permit me, here, I would say we have felt that in passing the law permitting foreign ships to register with us and be operated under our flag, and in enacting the Ship Purchase bill, the Government would be inconsistent. It would be inviting with one hand and slaying with the other. They are not logical parts of Administration policy, to invite private capital to enter into the shipping business, and then set up a Government competition against it; and we have felt that the inevitable result of that would be, that when you had taken away the profits from private ships, they would come to you for subsidies, and it would be impossible for you to resist their appeal. Logically, you would have to give it. Having taken away their opportunity, you would have to give them another out of the public treasury. That is one reason why we have opposed the Shipping bill.

The Chairman: However persuasive that might be, it appeals to me as a perfectly illegitimate line of argument.

The Witness: Perhaps so, if you believe in subsidies, which we do not happen to. Would you be patient with me if I should give you a general explanation of the policy we adopted toward this bill? The policy we adopted toward that measure is one that *The Times* has consistently pursued for certainly more than twenty-five years, and I suppose for thirty years. Every newspaper that enjoys continuity of existence and management has a certain body of principles. They are called the policy of the paper. Those are the principles and beliefs that guide its expressions of opinion. The men who express those opinions are the editorial writers.

The managers and the editorial writers are the persons responsible for the expressions of opinion. They are men. They wear neither halos nor horns. They form their opinions just as other men form their opinions by observation and reflection and information. When it comes to a specific public measure they express in their own opinions, which they write, the opinions of the paper. The opinion and policy of one paper differ from those of another. Some are for high tariff and some are for low tariff. Some papers are radical and some are conservative. But each paper has a body of principles that guides its utterances, and the men who write those opinions believe them. Nobody in *The Times* office is ever asked to write what he does not believe.

In the case of the Shipping bill, when that came up it was studied and information was obtained, and then the principles were applied that *The Times* has long maintained to it. I should say for thirty years, certainly ever since the matter came up for public discussion, *The Times* has opposed Government ownership and Government operation of industries and enterprises. It has opposed them because it believes that the Government is a poor manager; that the Government is expensive because the Government does not operate under the restraints of a balance sheet as private enterprises must. It is very costly and *The Times* does not believe, and has never believed that it is right to take the money of the whole people to provide advantages for some of the people. It believes Government ownership, Government operation, to be inefficient. There are abundant evidences of that.

Moreover, *The Times* believes that it is not right for the Government to set up, with its immense, boundless resources, competition with private capital, private brains, and energy in concerns where private enterprise has shown itself to be efficient. As I said a moment ago, it seemed to us that the Shipping bill led inevitably to subsidies, an entire reversal of the policy of the Democratic Party. It seemed to us that it was an improper venture for the Government, and we opposed it, not from anything we heard as to who was opposing or who was supporting this bill, but in pursuance of what practically to me has been a life-long policy, a life-long belief, that it involves an enterprise in State Socialism, to which we have always been opposed. So far as anything in this bill was concerned, nobody in *The Times* office ever talked to anybody outside the office on the subject until I came down here, or until Mr. Van Anda, the managing editor, came here. It was the application, the general policy, that *The Times* has persistently pursued ever since I have had anything to do with it.

The Chairman: That is to say, *The Times* has pursued such a policy that everybody connected with it knew in advance that in view of the general policy of the paper, it would not be able to support this particular measure?

The Witness: Anybody could have foretold that who knew the history of the paper.

THE SENATE INQUISITION

Q.: So that really this was only an incident of the general antagonism of *The Times* to public ownership generally?
A.: Yes.
Q.: Do you recall what attitude *The Times* took on the bill to construct Government railroads in Alaska?
A.: I opposed it.

Chairman Walsh next read from an editorial in *The Times* of Dec. 3 as follows:

It is necessary to believe either that he (the President) has other sources of information than those with which he cannot afford to co-operate, or that he is proceeding as a volunteer in the public service. Volunteers of unasked service get scant thanks. The sort of service the people appreciate is response to their appeals, and the appeals worthy of consideration are all to the contrary of the President's proposal. For example, the greatest foreign shippers are the trusts who are defendants in prosecutions permitted by the President. He allows his officials to proceed against these great shippers, often furnishing their own shipping, even after the courts have given them a clean bill of mercantile good conduct.

The Chairman: What were the shippers there referred to?
The Witness: In the District Court in New York a clean bill of mercantile good conduct had been given to the North Atlantic conference, to what is called the Brazilian conference and the Far Eastern conference. The allusion was to those combinations specifically. As a connotation there I should say also, the Harvester Company, which had a clean bill of health in the Missouri courts, the court saying that although the operations of the company had been beneficial to the farmers of the State, yet under the law it would have to be ousted; possibly to the Steel Corporation.
Q.: Are we to understand that it is the attitude of *The Times* that the Administration is open to criticism for prosecution of the Harvester Trust and the United States Steel Corporation?
Mr. Miller: I think I stated a moment ago that we do not see the public benefit of proceeding against corporations that have done no public harm. Wrongful acts of trusts and combinations should be punished, and there are plenty of laws for their punishment, but here harassment because of size is not the policy that we approve.
Q.: You refer specifically to the Harvester, and Steel Trusts?
A.: I do not think so, specifically, but they are included in the thought of the writer. Take the Harvester case for example. The Harvester Company got a clean bill of health in the District Court in Missouri.
Q.: We are to understand then that *The Times* condemns the prosecution of those guilty of violation of the law, but not guilty of good mercantile practice?
A.: Oh, no. We would not condemn a prosecution for violation of the law. If the law is on the statute books suit must be brought, but why a policy of that kind should be continued after corporations had been

once pronounced guiltless of wrong is what we do not understand or approve.

This line of examination was continued at great length, the Chairman seeking to discover the witness's attitude in detail to the various trust prosecutions, after which he passed to an editorial statement in *The Times* criticising the Government for the amount paid to the railways for carrying the mails and parcel post. On this point also the examination was long and discursive. Chairman Walsh asking questions apparently intended to show that by comparison with express rates, the railroads were well paid for carrying the parcel post; and Mr. Miller taking the ground that the railroads had made out a very plausible case of underpayment. It was in the course of this branch of the examination that Senator Sutherland made the remark, quoted above, that he could not, for the life of him, see what this line of inquiry had to do with the Ship Purchase bill.

Turning to another subject, the Chairman then called attention to the item in a recent issue of *The Times* showing that there would be no ship leaving New York for English ports for a week, pointing out that three newspapers other than *The Times* gave it prominent headlines upon their first pages, and adding: "The incident was calculated to impress forcibly on the public mind the embarrassment in which we find ourselves by reason of the want of shipping facilities."

Mr. Miller: It impressed upon the public mind the fact that there was a war.

The Chairman: I call your attention to mention in *The Times* of the same incident. It was scarcely a very prominent notice.

The Witness: I should not say that it was either very prominent in *The World* or in *The American*. However, I cannot possibly see what relevancy the exigency of the makeup of *The Times* has to the question under consideration here. There are many accidents, material and mechanical, aside from those of having a gnarled and a crooked soul, which might possibly account for that story having been published at the bottom of the page instead of at the top. What I want to convey is that there is no possible implication there that we intended to use that method of printing that item as an argument against the Ship Purchase bill or otherwise, or that we wanted to minimize its importance.

The Chairman: The position in the paper you gave it was not particularly calculated to invite attention to it.

Mr. Miller: I think it was decidedly. It is on the first page of the paper, and we assume that everything in the paper is read.

Q.: The item in *The Times* appears at the bottom of the second column of the first page, does it not?

A.: Yes, from which I would draw no inference, whatever, as any attempt to minimize its importance, or otherwise.

Q.: Have you followed the news columns sufficiently to tell us whether the proceedings of this committee have been noted from day to day in *The Times?*

A.: I have not observed specifically; no.

Q.: My attention is called to the fact that no mention was made, whatever, in the paper of the examination of Mr. Franklin, who testified before the committee. Mr. Franklin is the Vice President of the International Mercantile Marine. Could you tell us how that omission occurred?

Mr. Miller: I could not possibly explain what never happened. If it was not published in *The Times* I am sure I do not know the reason.

(In spite of Chairman Walsh's statement, Mr. Franklin's testimony was printed in *The Times*.)

The Chairman: That is all.

At this point Mr. Miller entered the protest already referred to. He said:

Mr. Chairman, I do not know that it is proper for me to ask a question, but I should like to protest against any attempt on the part of this committee to intimate or insinuate either by what I say or by what I do not say, that there has been any effort on the part of the New York *Times* to suppress news or to pervert news or to shape its policy in that respect to accord with its opposition to the Ship Purchase bill. I want to make that as plain and as positive as possible. The nature of your questions seems to intimate or indicate to me that you have a suspicion that we shaped the physical appearance of *The Times* in accordance with its editorial policy, in suppressing and minimizing news. There is nothing more erroneous, nothing more absolutely contrary to the fact. We attempt to make the news columns of *The Times* fairly reflect the news of the day without any bias or prejudice one way or the other. The editorial page goes its way and the news columns go their way. We print impartially both sides of the question so far as information proper to print comes to us.

I want to make that very plain, and, again, I would like to say, and I say it with entire courtesy and with the utmost respect for this committee, that I can see no ethical, moral, or legal right that you have to put many of the questions that you have asked me today. I do not acknowledge your right to inquire into the way in which we conduct our business any more than you would have the right to inquire into the way in which a public speaker addressing an audience had formed his opinion. I think you have a right to ask me if I had any knowledge of improper influences used for or against the Ship Purchase bill. I have told you frankly that I have not. There, it seems to me, the privilege of the committee in reference to me and the New York *Times* stops. However, without acknowledging the right, I have been entirely free to answer so far as I could all of your questions. I am very sorry that I have not been able to answer them more fully and explicitly and satisfactorily.

The Chairman: You will understand, as a matter of course, that this committee has a public duty to perform.

Mr. Miller: Yes.

The Chairman: It is charged by the Senate of the United States to investigate these matters, and it seems quite reasonable that differences of opinion should arise as to just exactly what are the limits within which that inquiry should proceed. As far as the chairman is concerned he has been guided by such little judgment and wisdom as he possesses, and he has no desire to go outside the matter entrusted to him.

Mr. Miller: I understand. I feel, however, that inquisitorial proceedings of this kind would have a very marked tendency, if continued and adopted as a policy, to reduce the press of the United States to the level of the press in some of the central European capitals, the press that has been known as the reptile press, that crawls on its belly every day to the foreign Office and to the Government officials and Ministers to know what it may say or shall say—to receive its orders. For that reason I cannot help feeling that a proceeding of this kind and such questions and minute inquiries, and I will not say insinuations, but intimations as you have in the accomplishment of your function felt to be necessary, constitute an invasion of the press. I think they tend to repress freedom of utterance and to put newspapers under a sort of duress, and for that reason I cannot feel I ought to leave this room without in the most courteous manner entering my most vigorous protests against such a procedure.

Senator Sutherland asked further questions in relation to the parcel-post after which Chairman Walsh reverted to the witness's protest saying:

I simply desire to say in this connection, for your own information and enlightenment, in view of the protest that you have made against the examination to which you have been subjected, that the committee feels at liberty also to prosecute these inquiries when they are addressed to a gentleman like yourself, who is the editor of a great and powerful newspaper, which can influence public opinion, in exactly the same way that it would against the humblest individual, and while you may feel that the freedom of the newspaper may be hampered to some extent by an inquiry of this character, you will appreciate likewise, that your protest might be calculated to restrain some legitimate activity on the part of this committee in the enquiry with which it is charged.

Mr. Miller: I would not have the slightest wish to do that.

The Chairman: Nor should you feel that the committee desires in any way to restrain the liberty of the press.

Mr. Miller: My feeling is this, if you will permit me: We appear before the jury every day. We appear before a grand inquisition, one of the largest courts in the country. We are judged at breakfast time.

If the judgment were adverse, the criminal would be dispatched to execution before a great while. This is not his present prospect, it is not his present condition. We feel that if we were improperly influenced by anybody outside of the office, there is none so quick to discover that as the reader of the paper. Your committee would be left far behind in that race, and we should suffer the greatest punishment that could possibly be inflicted upon us, namely the loss of all standing. I wanted to have you feel that the great newspapers—and I speak of *The Times* because I have a personal knowledge of that—are made by self-respecting men, who respect their public, and who respect themselves and the arguments and appeals they make, and that any improper influence could be expected to turn the paper into crooked and devious sources is entirely foreign to the thought of any upright or honest newspaper man.

For instance, you spoke of the railroads and of persons who control the railroads, who are also the persons behind the shipping trust, and you drew the inference that because we had listened to the arguments or had read the arguments of the railroads in behalf of the increased pay for the carrying of the mail and the parcel post, it is possible that the railroads have influenced us and through them the shipping trust. I want to disabuse your mind of that impression, if it exists. Neither the railroads nor the shipping trust nor any one outside of the office of *The Times* has a word to say as to its conduct. You can go there—the poor or the richest can go there—and state your case, and if it appeals to our judgment as being sound and honest, we will say something about it, but our opinions are our own. I want to leave you with that impression in your mind, and I want to protest against any other intimation or insinuation.

The Chairman: I think you can very safely trust to the rectitude of the great jury of which you speak.

Mr. Miller: I think they would find it out sooner than any one else.

The committee then adjourned.

Naturally editorial opinion throughout the country ranged itself on the side of Mr. Miller and *The Times*. It realized that in him it had a shrewd and sterling spokesman. And it was even more outspoken than *The Times* in its criticism of the whole proceeding. *The World* labelled the Senatorial prying "a public inquisition without an arraignment," while to the Baltimore *American* the hearing appeared "the most extraordinary exhibition of bad judgment, peevishness, or evil motives, the country has had from a Senate Committee for years."

On the day following the inquiry, *The Times* came out editorially with this reiteration of its editor's statements as to its policy and proprietorship:

That there may be no cause to believe that Mr. Miller's answer to the pertinent inquiry about Mr. Ochs's private affairs does not fully and satisfactorily end the inquiry, Mr. Ochs wishes to make the assertion as broad and sweeping as language will permit that he is in possession, free and unincumbered, of the controlling and majority interest of the stock of The

New York Times Company, and has no associate in that possession, and is not beholden or accountable to any person or interest in England or anywhere else in the world, nor has he ever been beholden or accountable in any form, shape or fashion, financial or otherwise, for the conduct of the New York *Times,* except to his own conscience and to the respect and confidence of the newspaper-reading public, and particularly the readers of the New York *Times*—and more particularly to the respect and confidence of those who are associated with him in producing the New York *Times* and expressing its opinions.

Mr. Miller's personal view of the affair coincided with his editorial utterances in all save the manner of expression. We find it in a letter addressed to Geo. Fred Williams, dated March 20, 1915:

You may have read in the public prints that I was in Washington the other day. Down there they have got the idea into their heads that they could edit *The Times* through a co-operative arrangement between the Senate and the Treasury Department. In an off-hand and plausible way I tried to disabuse them of that impression. In fact as George Wickersham said to me, I told them to go to hell, but did it in the politest possible way. The whole proceeding was a model of urbanity on both sides.

X

THE WAR AND THE LEAGUE

In these days when "foreign affairs" is a phrase often on the glib tongues of the many, when the fascination of studying how the wheels go round in the Governments of Europe has transcended even Browning in the affections and affectations of Women's Clubs, it seems a far cry to the years before the war in a self-contained and self-satisfied America, when an intelligent understanding and appreciation of the machinations of overseas diplomacy was limited to a select few. Fortunate for both *The Times* and its readers was the fact that when the great war broke out in 1914, there held the editorial helm a man whose qualifications to understand and interpret stood out as unique in the whole United States. Accordingly Mr. Miller's editorial elucidations of war causes and war conduct rank above even the comprehensiveness of his paper's news surveys in point of service to American readers.

So complete indeed was his background, so unstampeded his judgment and so acute and unerring his penetration that Elmer Davis in the paper's official history was able to state without fear of contradiction:

> After the lapse of years, despite all the voluminous publications of secret archives which since the armistice has informed the world of what went on behind the scenes in those days, there is not one line of *The Times* editorial analysis of the responsibility for the war, written in the days when the war was being made, which would have to be retracted today.

In Mr. Miller's mind one idea possessed him as the prime editorial function of the time—the need for careful interpretation and patient exposition for an American public as yet anything but world conscious, of the forces both hidden and patent which had brought on and at the moment were carrying on the nearest approach to Armageddon that the human race had seen.

Mr. Miller saw from the first where the trouble lay and through the columns of *The Times* he daily pointed it out in no uncertain voice. Neutrality, *The Times* felt, should never muzzle truth and commonsense. As early as July 27, 1914, when Austria turned a deaf ear to Serbia's reply to the ultimatum, he wrote:

> It will be freely said that Count Berchtold has seized what seemed to him a most propitious moment for dealing a blow at Pan-Slavism and strengthening Pan-Germanism, and incidentally reviving the German party in Austria. . . . The only hope of peace seems to be in the awakening of the German conscience.

On July 31, the spectacle of a whole nation herded willy-nilly at the instance of its war lords, moved him to comment:

> Now is the very best of all times for taking account of the frightful wrong involved in governmental systems which permit great and prosperous peoples to be dragged into the war without consulting their will and their welfare.

Nor did he like some others let Teuton rhetoric pull the wool over his eyes. In the light of the coolly calculated actions of the German militarists, he viewed the Kaiser's vocal outpourings about the sword which had been forced into his hand as "a piece of pompous humbug." On August 6, he had no hesitation in writing,

> The historian will have no trouble in placing his finger on the cause of the war, and there are men in Vienna today whose descendants for many generations will redden at the verdict.

But of course later events tended to convince him that the Entente had neither shame nor the capacity for reddening in its make-up.

Political forecastings have long proved the most futile of all uses for a paper's editorial columns. But in the case of Mr. Miller's war prophecies—all of which came true in the course of events—there lay more than happy chance. It was not luck but a sound knowledge of historical principles and their inevitable sequences, an understanding of the national psychologies involved which enabled him to foretell the war consequences with an almost uncanny accuracy. As early as August 6, 1914, four days after Great Britain entered the conflict, we find him predicting that the war was very likely to result in revolution in Russia, revolution in Germany, and the break-up of Austria-Hungary.

Naturally this outspoken denunciation of German war guilt together with a steadfast editorial support of the Allied cause quickly roused into antagonism sympathizers of the German persuasion in America and the always vocal Irish. The German secret service in the United States even flattered Mr. Miller to the extent of making him the subject of a *dossier*. He was living at the time at 21 East 9th Street, Manhattan, where he had resided since 1904. As all New Yorkers know, this neighborhood is blessed by old-established French restaurants, The Brevoort and The Lafayette. Accordingly the conscientious but not over-humorous German sleuths represented him as maintaining a pro-Ally home "in the French quarter." But like Mr. Miller the writers of the document were given to prophecy; like him too, their forecastings were to come to pass. Hinting at the even then somewhat hackneyed notion of "British gold" the *dossier* reported that Mr. Miller would soon move to a more desirable neighborhood. So it turned out. In 1920, Mr. Miller rented a large apartment at 635 Park Avenue.

Feeling as Mr. Miller did that the editorial's chief service at the moment was elucidation, it is hardly surprising that he should throw open those columns of the editorial page not used for the paper's expression of its own opinion as a forum for discussion by experts of points raised by the war. On this page that boasts *The Times's* "masthead" appeared an exchange of correspondence between Charles W. Eliot and Jacob H. Schiff, published in December, 1914. Earlier in the fall, Theodore Roosevelt wrote a series of letters on "What America Should Learn From the War," and in 1916, Robert Ludlow Fowler, Surrogate of New York

County, under the pseudonym of "An American Citizen" contributed articles of noteworthy brilliance. In *The Times's* desire that both sides be heard not only these columns of the editorial page but much of the Sunday magazine section was turned weekly into a printed debate.

But in point of view of the interest it aroused, the high peak of Mr. Miller's editorials on the war appeared on December 15, 1914. This article two columns in length bore the heading "For the German People, Peace with Freedom." The editorial commenced with the succinct prophecy: "Germany is doomed to sure defeat." Then it follows that short journalistic sentence with a sonorous period well in line with age-old editorial usage:

> Bankrupt in statesmanship, overmatched in arms, under the moral condemnation of the civilized world, befriended only by the Austrian and the Turk, two backward-looking and dying nations, desperately battling against the hosts of three great Powers to which help and reinforcement from States now neutral will certainly come should the decision be long deferred, she pours out the blood of her heroic subjects and wastes her diminishing substance in a hopeless struggle that postpones but cannot alter the fatal decree.

The editorial based its conclusion on the assumption that at no cost would the neutral world permit a German victory.

Structurally, the writing stands as highly typical of Mr. Miller's later method, of his keenness for a thorough analysis of his subject, his facility for forceful rhetoric, his talent for arranging ideas so that the logic would culminate in *crescendo,* and the sledgehammer directness with which he drove each point home. The article, reprinted in full, has a place in the appendix to this volume.

Its publication caused a stir throughout the world. Many papers on this continent and overseas reprinted it verbatim. Others presented their readers with large portions of it. All paid it the compliment of more comment one way or the other than was inspired by any single American editorial which the war brought forth.

Facsimile of the first page of Mr. Miller's editorial, "For the German People, Peace with Freedom"

Naturally the Allied press hailed it, and naturally they turned its implications to prove their own ends. Although the Washington correspondent of the London *Times,* in submitting it as "the most remarkable individual utterance of American opinion yet published" warned the British readers that no single newspaper in the United States "can be held to represent or mould public thought," yet the English papers hailed it as "the voice of America."

The French press were enthusiastic over its "peace with freedom" advice to the enemy and chose to see in it chiefly the failure and futility of German propaganda in the United States. *The Figaro* devoted a whole column to commenting on this phase of it, and commenced the article with this paragraph:

"Who has written this? It is neither a Frenchman, nor an Englishman, nor a Russian. It is an American. . . . His article is addressed especially to the readers of German origin whom he adjures to yield to the evidence."

Interestingly enough this great editorial of his, "For the German People, Peace with Freedom," a page of which is printed in facsimile herewith, serves as an excellent demonstration of two of his professional traits—his facility in dictation and his lack of it in legible penmanship. Mr. Miller first wrote this editorial with his pen. After discussing it with Mr. Ochs, he added to the article several hundred words which he dictated. Mr. Ochs, who retained the original manuscript as it went to the printer, points out that "you will find in the part written in Mr. Miller's handwriting, many alterations, changes and interlineations, but in the part he dictated, there is only one word changed and three words added, by which I mean that his dictation is so correct as to be almost letter-perfect."

As a preliminary to this editorial, Mr. Miller sent his secretary at the time, H. B. Brougham, to Washington for a confidential interview with the President. This interview stands out as important not only for its amazing grasp of the issues and the succinctness of President Wilson's exposition, but because in it lies the seed of his settlement by arbitration ideals in the flowering of which as the League of Nations the names of both Mr. Wilson and *The Times* are forever linked. "There remains," he says, "the alternative of trying to reason out our differences according to the principles of right and justice."

Now that there no longer remains the need for war secrecy, we give the notes of this interview as Mr. Miller received them. They make interesting reading in their own right. Read in conjunction with "For the German People, Peace with Freedom," the interview may have a certain value to students of the editorial art.

MEMORANDUM OF INTERVIEW WITH THE PRESIDENT, DEC. 14, 1914.

The President hopes for a deadlock in Europe. During the half hour I was with him he talked mainly on this subject. He praised *The Times* for its fair spirit in printing the chief documents of the war, and for its editorial analysis of them. He said he could not foresee what would come of it all, but he thought the greatest advantages for all concerned in the war, including the neutral nations, would accrue from a deadlock that "will show to them the futility of employing force in the attempt to resolve their differences." The rest of what he said I will give as nearly as I can recollect in his own words.

The Powers are making the most tremendous display of force in history. If the result of it all is merely to wear each other down without coming to a decision, the point will at length be reached when they will be glad to say, we have tried both bluff and force, and since neither could avail, there remains the alternative of trying to reason out our differences according to the principles of right and justice. So I think that the chances of a just and equitable peace, and of the only possible peace that will be lasting, will be happiest if no nation gets the decision by arms; and the danger of an unjust peace, one that will be sure to invite further calamities, will be if some one nation or group of nations succeeds in enforcing its will upon the others.

It will be found before long that Germany is not alone responsible for the war, and that some other nations will have to bear a portion of the blame in our eyes. The others will be blamed and it might be well if there were no exemplary triumph and punishment. I believe thoroughly that the settlement should be for the advantage of the European nations regarded as people and not for any nation imposing its governmental will upon alien peoples. Bismarck was longheaded when he urged Germany not to take Alsace and Lorraine.

It seems to me that the Government of Germany must be profoundly changed, and that Austria-Hungary will go to pieces altogether—ought to go to pieces for the welfare of Europe.

As for Russia, I cannot help sympathizing with its aims to secure natural outlets for its trade with the world, and a proper settlement should permit this.

"If the decision is not to be reached wholly by the forces of reason and justice after the trial at arms is found futile, if the decision by arms should be in favor of the nations that are parties of the Triple Entente; I cannot regard this as the ideal solution, at the same time I cannot see now that it would hurt greatly the interests of the United States if either France or Russia or Great Britain should finally dictate the settlement. England has already extended her empire as far as she wants to—in fact she has got more than she wants—and she now wishes to be let alone in order that she may bend all her energies to the task of consolidating the parts of her empire. Russia's ambitions are legitimate, and when she gets the outlets she needs her development will go on and the world will be benefited.

He expressed himself as grateful to *The Times* for its general support of his Administration "even if in the case of certain measures it has not come so far in support of them as I should like." I asked him about the Government shipping bill, and he explained at some length that it was introduced only after he had ascertained that private capital would not go in and accomplish the same thing for which it was intended.

Anyone studying the day in and day out war editorials in *The Times's* files during say the years 1915 and 1916, can hardly help but be struck with Mr. Miller's typification of the genuinely American desire at the period, constantly to seek for some loophole in the trench lines and barricades overseas through which an olive branch could be poked. Always there runs throughout this stream of exposition and argument the deep, steady undercurrent: "Let us have peace."

Taking at random from this period a long editorial with the caption, "Are the Germans Planning to Leave France?" dated September 8, 1916, one finds half way through the peace wish made father to this thought:

Conceivably the Germans have the men to hold on everywhere until the end of the season. It is unlikely, but it is just possible. Then they are bound to make a new bid for peace, which will fill the world and have very interesting echoes here in the United States, where the machinery is being organized at this very moment. Such a peace will not be based on the "war map" of Europe, but on the peace map of July, 1914. We have covered a good deal of ground since last May.

But if Germany cannot hold on until fall on all fronts, then she must shorten her western front, because it is the front from which she can most easily draw men and it is the only front on which she is entirely upon enemy territory. It is small comfort for the Hungarians, for example, when Transylvanian cities are falling rapidly, that Germans still hold Lille and St. Quentin.

Shortly after there creeps into the daily columns the conviction that the desired peace can be hastened only through the active participation of the United States in the conflict. From then onward this idea is taken up again and again and driven home by that most potent of all editorial battering rams—reiteration. *The Times's* editorials throughout these months stand out historic in their significance as moulders of the national thought and inspirers of the national action.

After the entrance of the United States into the war as an "Associated Power," Lord Bryce sent a letter to William Howard Taft, through an English friend of both in New York, urging him to come across and make a series of speeches in England. The aim of the proposed tour as Lord Bryce defined it was to aid the morale of the English people, then sorely tried by the years of strain. Hearing of the letter, Mr. Miller pronounced the proposition an excellent idea and along with others urged the Ex-President, then a professor at Yale, to accept the invitation.

Complying with this general feeling among those who knew of the Bryce letter, Mr. Taft left New Haven for Washington for an interview with President Wilson.

The following conversation as reported privately in New York indicates the temperature of Mr. Wilson's reception of the idea.

The President: What would you go for? Many people do not think that the relations between the two countries should be strengthened.

Mr. Taft: What is your own attitude, Mr. President, toward this request?

The President: I can't say. I am not really interested.

Mr. Taft: Then I won't go.

THE WAR AND THE LEAGUE

Mr. Taft ended the incident by sending a regretful letter to Lord Bryce.

When Mr. Miller heard how this international gesture had been checked by the Wilson coolness, he came out at the Century Club with an emphatic personal judgment:

"Mr. Wilson apparently does not understand the real policy of the nation. It is for us to take leadership with Britain. The President doesn't understand his Europe."

During the last few months of the war an incident occurred that fairly shook *The Times*. To understand why, one must travel back in memory to that period of tense excitement and extreme nationalistic touchiness.

One Sunday evening, September 15, 1918, the news reached *The Times* office of the first tentative bid for peace from the enemy. It came in the form of an invitation from the Austro-Hungarian Government to all the warring Powers to take part in a "non-binding" discussion. Following the usual precedent, the news editors in charge that day telephoned the substance of the report to Mr. Miller, then at his summer home at Great Neck, L. I.

To Mr. Miller the report caused no surprise. The four years of constant study had made him knowingly alert to every move on the tragic chess-board overseas. Information from confidential private sources came to him constantly and placed him in a position readily to grasp the significance and importance of the Vienna dispatch.

He pondered over it for awhile that Sunday evening, called the office and over the phone dictated an editorial bearing the title "The Austrian Peace Overture." It appeared as *The Times's* leader the next morning. After that the deluge. In the office itself, most noisily in rival offices, and from the man in the street, there gathered the roar of a storm of protest. In a moment the crowd stampede showed itself ready to forget all that *The Times* had stood for throughout the conflict. In a flash there passed from the public mind the paper's consistent support of the Allied cause from August, 1914, onward and its steady urgings to a reluctant Government at Washington to throw itself into the conflict as an Associated Power.

The loud-voiced "righteous indignation" waxed strident in corners where *The Times's* growing success had caused irritation and jealousy. Naturally enough too, *The Times's* Irish enemies held a field day. The opportunity safely to malign this consistent friend of Britain, coupled with the traditional Celtic distaste for reticence, assured substantial volume to the swelling chorus of this "Hymn of Hate."

What then caused this spontaneous combustion of public sentiment? Merely the quietly reasoned suggestion that the Allies might "honorably accept" this first "veritable peace offer" and accept it moreover "in the confident belief that it will lead to the end of the war."

We at this date, wise after the event, read the editorial that shook *The Times* and marvel at its words of truth and soberness:

THE AUSTRIAN PEACE OVERTURE
Monday, September 16, 1918

From Vienna, the quarter in which for three years the Allies have felt that the movement for peace would originate, comes the first veritable peace offer, and it comes in a form which the Allies may honorably accept in the confident belief that it will lead to the end of the war. The Austro-Hungarian Government invites all the belligerent Governments to authorize their representatives to attend a conference held on neutral soil with a view to a "non-binding" discussion of the terms of peace. It is the hope of that Government that if, in a confidential exchange of views, the position of the different Governments shall be mutually made known, it may be possible to formulate a statement of terms which, when reported by the delegates to their respective Governments, might be accepted as a reasonable basis of formal peace negotiations.

The custom and practice of nations demand that this invitation to enter upon the preliminaries of peace receive the most serious and respectful attention of the Governments to which it is addressed. It is a very different matter from the long-range peace offers made in speeches and notes, of which there have been so many, all futile. It comes from a Government second only to the chief power of the Teutonic alliance. We are bound to accept it as the sincere expression of a desire for much needed peace, and we may assume with entire confidence that it is issued with the full

THE WAR AND THE LEAGUE 147

knowledge and assent of the Imperial Government of Germany, after conference and deliberation. This assumption finds confirmation in the announcement late last night that Germany has made a definite peace offer to Belgium, an offer hardly made in the expectation that it would be accepted, but rather, perhaps, as notice to the world, in advance of the proposed conference, that Germany is ready to evacuate Belgium.

The immediate preparation for these overtures was made by Baron Burian in his speech last week, when he suggested a confidential exchange of views. For the actual and moving cause of the proposal we must look to the battlefields of France. The French, British, and American troops under the command of Marshal Foch, the advancing and victorious legions directed by Haig, by Petain, and by Pershing, have brought about this complete change in the minds and in the attitude toward the war of Vienna and of Potsdam. The refluent current that began to bear the Germans back from the Marne on July 18 and has never ceased its irresistible sweep extinguished their last hopes of victory; St. Mihiel comes as an admonition of impending and irretrievable disaster. But what fills their souls with deepest disquietude is the failure of their man power and their morale just at the moment when American soldiers literally in millions are moving forward to their places in the vast, unconquerable armies that confront them. The Vienna invitation to conference is not of the kind that victors send forth.

Upon that we need not dwell. All the belligerents desire the end of the war. The stricken world longs for peace. While no armistice precedes the proposed conference, we are justified in entertaining the hope, the belief, even, that fighting will cease this year as the fruit of this "non-binding" discussion of terms. It would be the worst of blunders for us or for any of the Entente Allies to abate war preparations now. But reason and humanity demand that the Austrian invitation be accepted. The case for conference is presented with extraordinary eloquence and force, a convincing argument is made for an exchange of views that may remove old and recent misunderstandings. It is pointed out that Mr. Wilson's four principles of peace have encountered no contradiction in the countries of the Quadruple Alliance; and there is much in the note that indicates a change of heart and of purpose there.

We cannot imagine that the invitation will be declined. When representatives of the belligerents meet at the council table and proceed to their confidential exchange of views, to their respective statements of terms, there is much antecedent probability that after no considerable interval the formal meeting of peace commissioners will follow. The preliminaries of peace have usually led to the conclusion of peace. There are historic exceptions to the rule, but when we consider the deluge of blood that has been poured out in this war, the incalculable waste of treasure, the ruin it has wrought, the grief that wrings millions of hearts because of it, we must conclude that only the madness or the soulless depravity of someone of the belligerent Powers could obstruct and defeat the purpose of the conference.

But "this agony must not be gone through with again." For the Allies that affirmation of President Wilson's will be the foundation principle of the negotiations. The sufficient safeguards are plain to the view of all the world. A peace that left Germany master of the East would be a crime against ourselves and our posterity. Over the lands of the Near East and the whole of the old Empire of the Czars she can be permitted to have no dominion. Control of vast regions where she could renew her now diminished might she must once and for all time renounce. The restorations and reparations to be decreed in the West are equally indispensable, but reiteration has made them familiar. It is in the East that the new danger will arise, there with iron resolution it must be destroyed. Entering a conference with definite instructions to yield no point that would leave Germany in a position to call to her armies and their support the men and the resources of the boundless Eastern lands she now holds in thrall, the delegates of the United States, Great Britain, France, Italy, and their co-belligerents may meet the representatives of the Central Powers without arousing among anxious peoples at home the fear that they are about to barter away the soul of the allied cause.

Probably Mr. Miller never quite recognized the extent of the uproar the editorial caused. In one sense he was too far above the conflict.

Probably too, had he read the editorial in proof, he would have felt inclined to rearrange its contents in a way to avoid crossing public sentiment on its rough edge. Bowing to the psychology of the situation he might have considered placing the last paragraph first. Then the editorial would begin with his ringing declaration of no peace without victory. From this starting point his readers might have followed him without demur to the suggestion that the Vienna offer opened the door to substantial victory as well as to the end of bloodshed. But he never saw the article in either written or printed form, till it appeared in *The Times*.

The amateur philosopher will find much food for thought in the whole occurrence. Chiefly from it there emerges this perplexing question: What after all is a carefully acquired reputation worth if in the twinkling of an eye the public will so readily forget it?

For the student of journalism the editorial and its resulting hullabaloo points to that axiom which Mr. Miller would be the first to lay down: an editor should never be too far in advance of his readers.

Although himself convinced of the editorial's rightness, Mr. Miller felt that he needed the satisfaction of comment and criticism from a source that he revered and respected. Accordingly in the midst of the outcry he wrote to President Eliot of Harvard and asked for his candid opinion of the whole affair.

In reply President Eliot sent back his reassuring o. k. He agreed with both the argument and the sentiment. After intimating that the phrasing here and there might have been happier, he added: "I see nothing wrong with it."

With this endorsement of his viewpoint from the man whom he considered the country's "first citizen," Mr. Miller felt relieved, the more so when other critics whom he respected pointed out that the pilloried editorial merely continued the same quiet line of thought and argument which the unnoticed article of the preceding day had initiated. Beyond this the editorial was never referred to though the memory of it continued to pain him.

An impression persists that Mr. Miller "crawled" the next day; that he and his paper ate humble pie by taking back holus-bolus the unpopular opinions expressed in "The Austrian Peace Overture." In fairness to both editor and paper we reprint that next day's editorial. Readers will find that its flavor scarcely suggests humble pie.

Despite the clamor the article was never retracted but a certain amount of editorial oil did pour on the troubled waters. For the next few weeks the subject was soft-pedalled and it gradually dropped from the public mind. The second day's editorial follows:

NOT ACCEPTED
Tuesday, September 17, 1918

In the name of the President, Secretary Lansing announces that the invitation of the Austro-Hungarian Government for a preliminary non-binding discussion of peace terms is rejected. It is true that Mr. Wilson has many times set forth the conditions indispensable to peace, the principles upon which we would be willing to make peace, conditions and principles which have the unanimous, the determined, support of the people of the United States. It may be that nothing would be gained by a formal restatement of these conditions and principles in a conference. Nevertheless, we had hoped that the Allied Governments would make a different reply to the Austrian invitation, a reply that would have been by no millionth part of a hair less conclusive of our unshakable resolve to enforce a peace on our own terms, a peace that would have had the important advantage of disclosing to us the motive that prompted the invitation.

The primary question is whether this proposal was made in sincerity or in hypocrisy. That is a question of fact to be best determined by a scrutiny of the terms the Central Powers would consent to accept. The Allies would have had the right to demand an unequivocal assurance that the Austrian note was sent in good faith. They are much occupied with the affairs of war. They could not reasonably be expected to turn their attention even briefly from that engrossing subject to a discussion of peace terms unless it were made clear to them that the issue might be fruitful. To that end, with entire propriety and in conformity with usage, they might have demanded of the Central Powers as a guarantee of good faith and serious purpose that they forthwith withdraw their troops from the occupied territory of France, from Belgium, and from Alsace-Lorraine.

At the beginning of the war Germany had it in mind to demand of France as the guarantee of her neutrality permission to occupy two French fortresses with German troops. We might have demanded the right to hold in pledge German fortresses on the Rhine, but that would have been beyond the pale of reason, for we have no intention of seizing and holding German cities or forts. We do intend to restore Belgium to its people, to enforce the retirement of enemy troops from France, and to restore to her the stolen provinces. These being peace terms that we shall never consent to modify, Germany and Austria knowing that they must accept them in the end, we could have put them to the test by demanding that they accept them now. The rejection of the demands would have disclosed the perfidy of the invitation, it would have exhibited the Teutonic powers as still unwilling to acknowledge that they are beaten, not yet ready to discuss peace on the only basis that would insure its permanence. Then the Allies, not having slackened their efforts, would have continued them with ever-increasing energy and determination to a successful issue.

The demand as a proof of good faith for the retirement of the German armies would very likely have ended the matter, but it would have proved to all the world that the Central Powers, so manifestly defeated, are not cured of their insolence, that they are still bent upon retaining in their hands enough of the spoils of war to enable them to wage another war in their own good time. Still, there are in the Austrian invitation signs of change of heart. It is declared in the note that further discussion of peace terms in speeches of statesmen would be futile. They are aimed at the masses and publicity destroys them as overtures. This is a pretty plain intimation that in a confidential conference Austria and Germany would be prepared to accept the Allies' terms.

Mr. Wilson has made known the foundation principles, which will not be modified or withdrawn. The Allies are one in the resolve that Germany must give up the land she has despoiled in the West, she must relinquish her control in the East. The publication of the proof that at Brest-Litovsk she caused bribed Russian traitors to sign a treaty she had herself drawn up has made it impossible for her to pretend that that instrument is binding on anybody. In the Balkans her dominance depends on the collusion of Austria, and that empire will be dismembered. We have recognized the Czechoslovaks as a nation, the ending of the war will end their bondage. With these purposes embodied in our terms there could not have been the slightest danger of falling into a German "trap." The representatives of the Allies would have been grown men, not to be hoodwinked.

The proposal is rejected, it remains for the Allies to carry on the war with the utmost vigor. The enemy grows weaker, his resistance fails. The invitation sent forth by Austria is virtually a confession of defeat. Had the Allies consented to a conference they would have proposed their own terms. They will now impose terms by forcing the foe openly to acknowledge the defeat to which he indirectly confesses. This country will support every endeavor of the President to make our strength felt at the front, where we have already done so much to turn the tide of battle. All our resources are pledged to the cause and to victory.

During these years of war, the editor kept at his work without holiday or let up. What relief he got he found in the hours at his country home, Great Neck, Long Island. Out there, in fact, he planned and wrote many of his chief war editorials. Often he would add stimulus to their composition by playing a set or so of tennis between paragraphs.

The Times would phone out to him during each evening the news of all important developments, and his fellow residents came to look upon him as the chief source of all reliable war information.

Finally when on that November morning the news of the actual Armistice reached Great Neck, the central of the local telephone office would not announce it to the community before she had received Mr. Miller's personal "o. k." on the dispatches' authenticity. When she did announce it the town celebrated with a vengeance. Not only did church bells peal and whistles blow but an enthusiast turned on the town's fire alarm siren and then promptly lost the key. The siren accordingly continued to celebrate for the space of eight hours. By the time the key was found to stop its screeching, Mr. Miller and the Long Island townsmen would almost have welcomed the resumption of hostilities.

As gracious expressions of their appreciation of Mr. Miller's work in their cause, the Allied Governments conferred upon him their highest honors. France made him a Chevalier of the Legion of Honor; Belgium decorated him with the Order of Leopold; and Greece created him a Knight Commander of the Order of King George I. And one of the few letters which he could ever have been said to treasure was that from Sir Cecil Spring-Rice, the then dying British Ambassador at Washington, who wrote in his own hand:

BRITISH EMBASSY
WASHINGTON

Jan. 11, 1918.

MY DEAR MR. MILLER:

May I take this opportunity (on my official death bed) of expressing to you in the warmest way my sense of the great help and sympathy which you gave me on several critical occasions? I needn't mention the help given the Allies by the brave and constant friendship of *The Times*—and its steadfast upholding of the cause of freedom and righteousness.

I don't know what other diplomatists would do without *The Times*, but I know it has been absolutely essential to the conduct of our Embassy business and I fear if our correspondence ever comes to light you will recognize your own thoughts and words pretty often.

Please excuse the haste with which in the last day of my official stay here, I venture to express, most inadequately, my deep, my very deep feeling of obligation and gratitude to your great journal and to you.

Yours,

CECIL SPRING-RICE.

But peace had her labors no less pronounced than war, and the editor found slight let up in the arduousness of his routine. His private and public convictions as to the need of some international tribunal to arbitrate national differences and so outlaw war ran parallel with those of the President and found daily expression in the editorials which pre-dated the Paris Peace Conference. In this series, two of his chief editorial assets came to the fore—his detailed and exact knowledge of international law and his ready familiarity with the classics. In his "leader" which said farewell to President Wilson as he set sail in December, 1918, for Paris, Mr. Miller recalled Horace's Ode to the ship which bore Virgil to Athens.

His private view always favored this personal participation of President Wilson's in the formation of the Treaty of Versailles and in substantiation of its wisdom he loved to quote an anecdote which alleged that on one occasion while the Big Three were in conclave and disagreeing over sundry points, the President turned to the British Premier with the comment:

"Mr. Lloyd George, you make me sick."

And Mr. Miller would always end this story's retelling with the remark:

"No mere Secretary of State could ever have said that."

With the President's actual methods, however, he had private as well as public disagreement. He regretted from the first that the President did not see fit to take with him a party of outstanding Republicans which would have included Elihu Root and Ex-President Taft. At the Century he referred to the entourage that did sail as "a right smart, colorful, weak group." But with the main contentions of Mr. Wilson overseas both Mr. Miller and *The Times* remained in hearty accord.

Something of the editor's personal attitude may have reached the President. This is mere surmise. But certain it is that shortly after Mr. Wilson's return from Versailles, an atmosphere developed in his relationship with *The Times*. The cause remains a mystery; what happened stays as a fact—the President lowered his invisible but impenetrable curtain between the White House and Times Square. Even later in his retirement at S Street, he seemed to forget the support of the paper in days past and ignore the continued backing which *The Times* continued for his ideals and principles. On the occasion of the twenty-first anniversary of the paper under its present management—an occasion of which men of all parties and indeed the outstanding representatives of all nations vied in lauding a great journalistic achievement—no word direct or indirect came from Mr. Wilson.

The Times's consistent and constant support of the League of Nations is too widely known to need stressing. The chances are that it will shine out from the long scroll of history as the paper's most glittering achievement.

XI

THE EDITOR TALKS SHOP

The working newspaperman has scant time to dilate on the principles of his craft. He finds his zest in the practice, and, contentedly enough, leaves to others the theory. Dates of newspaper conventions, meetings of committees for the formulation of journalistic "ethics" and the like, seldom go down on the calendars of metropolitan editors. Invariably when pressing invitations arrived urging Mr. Miller's attendance at some such journalistic get-together in Chicago, St. Louis, and points West, they went into the waste-paper basket. He would pause for a moment to wonder where on earth these people found the time to gad about the country and talk, and then he would pick up at once the work in hand, the focusing of his editorial attention upon the dominant public issues of that day.

Indeed, he prided himself on his abstention from all journalistic jamborees and with characteristic conciseness he noted on the biographical sheet sent him by the Secretary of his old Dartmouth Class of 1872:

"Have never been a member of any 'organization of editors' and never travelled with an 'editorial excursion.'"

Fortunately, however, he did find time while engrossed with the practice of his profession, occasionally to talk and occasionally to write on subjects closely appertaining to it.

The first of these occasions came on February 24, 1890, when he delivered an address on "Demand and Supply in Literature," before the Goethe Society of New York. This address is given in full, in the appendix to this book.

In May, 1890, Mr. Miller travelled up to Hanover to make a speech. Dartmouth men turned out in force to welcome, honor, and listen to one of their college's most distinguished alumni.

But beyond a copy of the poster which heralded his talk on the Hanoverian hoardings, no echo of that oratory remains.

On the invitation of *The Youth's Companion,* Mr. Miller compiled some advice and suggestions for those young readers of that magazine who cherished journalistic ambitions. The article came out on February 23, 1893, with the title, "Training for Journalism," and stressed directness of style and a breadth of academic background. "For newspaper-writing that style is best that is most direct. The spoken style of plain minds is a good model."

Despite the advances in the newspaper, Mr. Miller could make no truer comment to-day, for the short declarative sentence used conversationally, when transferred by printer's ink to the columns of the paper, aids substantially in that "easy readability" for which the expert editor continually strives.

Those Dartmouth classmates of his who read the article must have chuckled as they noted the insistence placed on a college education. Here is the man who deliberately scamped through the collegiate curriculum sagely informing his young readers that "the old-fashioned college education will do very well." Let us hope that the whirligig of time has a sense of humor!

TRAINING FOR JOURNALISM
The Youth's Companion, February 23, 1893

The editor of *The Youth's Companion* asks me to write a short article on training for newspaper work. If we are to go about the matter logically we shall want to begin with a definition. Let us understand just what newspaper work is, what faculties of the newspaper worker's mind are specially called into play, and then we can more readily determine how to train them for the service.

To put it in the briefest way, newspaper work consists of impression and expression; the art of taking in and giving forth. My young readers will most likely think that if that is all there is to it, the art of making a newspaper must be an absurdly simple thing. So it is.

Like music and painting and architecture, newspaper-making is a simple art. The artist and the architect record in visible or audible form their impressions; that is all the newspaper man is called upon to do.

For the most part he records impressions received from external sources, with very little admixture of his own opinions, or none at all. That is news-reporting—the work of the reporter and the correspondent.

If he expresses views and opinions largely or wholly originating in his own mind, then he becomes an editorial writer. But for news report or editorial article the phrase opinion and expression defines the process and nature of the work. And inasmuch as the newspaper man must get his impression before he can give his expression, we ought to consider first how that side of his mind may be trained. We must first train him to learn things, then to say things.

Here again the matter becomes absurdly simple. The reporter has merely to see and hear things as they are; then to write down correctly the things seen and heard. That must be the easiest thing in the world. Any boy can see and hear things as they are if he has eyes and ears, and with a little practice any fairly bright boy ought to be able to write correctly. Hence any boy can become a good newspaper reporter.

Let us see about that. Will you lads who happen to be in the country tell me offhand, or write down for me on a slip of paper, the order in which the leaves will put forth this spring upon the trees about your father's house, or in the woods at the top of the hill?

You are fifteen, eighteen years old, perhaps, and for ten years you have known the trees by their names, so that you could tell the beech from the maples and the birches from the oaks. Every spring you have watched with eager interest the coming of the buds and the leaves. Surely you can all tell me whether the birch first leaves out, or the beech or the maple?

But I am not so sure that you can tell me. In fact, I feel sure that not one in fifty of you knows in what order the leaves come out in the spring.

But if you cannot report correctly an event so beautiful and interesting, that you have witnessed say ten times, how can you expect ever to report correctly events neither beautiful nor interesting, that you will see but once?

So I might call you up for examination about the birds—which among them build their nests on the ground and which in tree-tops; whether the robin loves best the recesses of the woods or the vicinity of the farm-house; and whether the crow really deserves his very bad reputation. These questions are easy, but I fear that many of you would fail to pass the examination.

Still there is nothing in all this that need put you out of heart. I suppose the animals are quick and perfectly accurate in observation. The wild animals which have to look out for themselves undoubtedly are so. But civilized man has only a very imperfect notion of what is going on around him.

His eyes do not see things as they are; his ears do not hear things as they are. He must take thought about his senses, and diligently school them before they will become good reporters, or enable him to become one.

I have used the leaves and the birds as illustrations because the naturalist's work is so much like the reporter's. The naturalist must see accurately the color of the bird, even in rapid flight. The reporter must see or hear accurately what is done or said, even if quickly said or done.

If the naturalist's notes give the bird a red breast when only his wings are red, his readers, if he have any, will be misled. If the reporter's notes declare that the meeting was adjourned for two weeks, when in fact the adjournment was for one week, he will have a bad quarter of an hour with his city editor.

First and foremost, then, the youth who wants to go into training for newspaper work must train his senses. He must drill all his faculties of perception and observation until they become trustworthy instruments. Severe discipline will make them alert and obedient to his will.

I need hardly add that in the process of training the senses the mind in all its departments will necessarily be made a vastly better and more useful organ. When our young friend has once gained what a scientific friend of mine, in the expressive language of his kind, calls a highly-trained sensorium, he is ready to concern himself with the next step in his newspaper education, the art of expression.

I heartily wish that every American boy who aspires to write for the newspapers might reasonably hope, in time, to write good English. Every French boy who becomes a newspaper worker seems to write his language with purity and correctness from the very beginning. Whether the secret of this excellence is in the boy, in the language, in the training of the French schools, or in the severe traditions of the French newspaper offices, I do not know.

I am equally unable to say why so much American newspaper-writing is deplorably bad. The schools and colleges, I fear, must bear most of the blame.

At the risk of being deemed impertinent I will permit myself to say, quite bluntly, that if teachers and professors would give their pupils a little less trigonometry and a good deal more English composition and English literature, they would do better for their pupils.

Of course nobody can lay down a working rule for acquiring a good style. The best that can be done is to put before the pupil good models, indicating their excellences, and bad models, pointing out their faults.

For newspaper-writing that style is best that is most direct. The spoken style of plain minds is a good model.

How does William tell neighbor John that neighbor Thomas's house was burned? Why, he cries out, "Tom's house was burnt up last night!" That is the whole story; and the vital points of the story occur in the actual order of their importance. First, it was Tom's house; second, it was burnt up; third, it was last night.

How does a badly trained reporter write the story? Like this: "Shortly after midnight last night, a fire was discovered in the house of Mr. Thomas Blank, and before the flames could be extinguished the unfortunate structure was burnt to the ground." That is the same story, wrong end foremost.

A good news report never begins with "yesterday," or with any words expressing date or time, or with any subordinate detail or statement; and the best news reports usually give the pith of their story in the first ten lines.

Beyond a few hints like these there is not much that can profitably be said on the subject of newspaper style.

A good style for newspaper-writing differs in no respect from a good style for histories, novels, essays and sermons. In the old days the solemn admonition to read Addison was given to every youthful seeker after the treasure of a good style. If I had the training of a lad I would tell him to let Addison alone until he had read Thackeray and Robert Louis Stevenson.

Thackeray was the master of an unequalled narrative style, and Stevenson's English is about the best and purest in contemporaneous English and American literature. The ability to write good English comes in part from native gifts of mind, but chiefly from practice and the appreciative reading of good English books.

The actual training and storing of the mind for newspaper work, it has generally been held, is best attended to in a newspaper office; and in proof of this theory examples are cited of boys who have risen from the printer's case to the editor's chair. It will be found, I think, that most great editors who have come up in that way were men of extraordinary powers.

At any rate, I am pretty sure that the average boy will have a better chance of rising if he takes the trouble to get the best education he can before he begins newspaper work.

What we call a college education is undoubtedly the best foundation. It is not absolutely necessary. But it helps in so many ways, is such a very great advantage, that I should advise every boy who wants to become a newspaper writer to get a college education if he can.

The old-fashioned college education will do very well—Greek, Latin, and mathematics, only not too much mathematics. If you can get to know something of French, German and Spanish, it will help you. If you can get to know a good deal about them it will help you more.

You cannot learn too much history and politics. The politics of your own state and of other states, and of the whole country, must be studied with unflagging zeal and minutely, if you would equip yourself in a way that will make you immediately useful when you enter a newspaper office. I know nothing more likely to commend an applicant for work to the attention and favor of a managing editor than a knowledge of politics and politicians. It is so rare in men under twenty-five or thirty.

But the young man who has the means and the time to "go through college" is a pretty independent fellow, and can get on very well without my advice. Let me point out a way in which the lad on a farm or in a country village, who does not see his way clear to a college education, can get another kind of education that will serve him about as well, and in some things better, when he begins to do newspaper work.

Remember that education has generally two purposes—to train the mind and to store it with knowledge. My plan for the country boys does both. Here it is:

Think of yourself as standing on one side of an imaginary line, and the great world, with all its men and women, and governments and institutions, on the other. Cross the line and find out in what way and through what things you come in contact with the world. Then study those ways and those things until you know as much as you can find out about them. This is what a sociologist would call determining the relation of the individual to the aggregate, or the relation of man to society. Let us explain the process a little.

You will be pretty sure to discover that you have relations with the great world through the school, the church, the government, through trade or business, and socially through your friends and companions. That is not all, but that will do very well to begin with.

First get all the information you can about the school system of your state. Ask the teacher all the questions you can think of. If you are a country boy there is probably a prudential committeeman in your district. Ask him what he has to do. Then get at the superintending committeeman, and ask him questions.

Find out where the money comes from to build schoolhouses and pay the teacher. If you live in a village large enough to have graded schools, find out how the system is organized, from the primary grade up to the high school. Let nothing escape you that you can possibly learn.

Then the churches in your town—study them. You may not find it easy to get at the differences of belief that separate the Methodists from the Baptists, and the Congregationalists from the Presbyterians, but your minister or any minister will probably lend you books that will tell something about creeds and faiths.

Then make yourself a master of the system of government or control in the various churches. Inquire what churches have bishops, what ones elders, what ones deacons, and what the powers and duties of these church officers are. In short, learn in how many ways, and go as far as you can, why one church organization is different from another.

Next comes government. It is a big subject—take it up in detail. Your father is a county commissioner or a selectman or a town clerk. That is a capital opportunity. Get him to tell you all he knows about the duties of town and county officers—who lays out new roads and closes old ones, who sees to it that the paupers are housed and fed, who determines how large a sum shall be raised by taxes in the town, how much each tax-payer's share shall be, and what shall be done with the money.

If one of your father's neighbors is a member of the legislature, persuade him to tell you how bills are introduced, referred to committees, reported, discussed, amended and passed or enacted as laws. He will tell you that bills, after they have been passed by the Assembly or House of Representatives, must be passed also by the Senate and signed by the governor; but that only opens up new fields for your investigation.

If, perchance, another neighbor is to go as a delegate to the Republican or the Democratic convention to help nominate his party's candidate for the Presidency, get him to tell you all about the party machinery by which conventions are assembled and candidates named; about the town caucuses, the county or district convention, the state convention, the national convention and the delegates to it, their number and their duties; also about the electoral college and its work.

This will lead you into inquiries and studies in respect to parties and politics, and state and federal governments, that will be in the degree interesting and profitable.

So in regard to business. Ask the village storekeeper where he buys his cloths, his crockery, his molasses and his hardware, and where they were got by the man of whom he bought them, and so on until you have traced them to their origin. You will in this way learn something of wholesale trade and manufacturing, something about notes, credits, insurance, transportation by rail and water, and quite likely something about the tariff.

Opportunities for this kind of home study and training will multiply as you follow them up, until the field of research broadens out surprisingly. Your mind will broaden with it, and in following out these pleasant paths of common knowledge you will acquire a fund of information that will be constantly useful to you in future years of newspaper work.

CHARLES R. MILLER.

The next year, 1893, for the August issue of *The Forum,* Mr. Miller wrote "A Word to the Critics of Newspapers." This article is as timely now as when written, for the old bogey of unenlightened censorship will not down.

A WORD TO THE CRITICS OF NEWSPAPERS
The Forum, August, 1893

"I am not in politics—I am in morals," said Charles Sumner once, in that sententious, complacent way of his. If the modern censors of the press could have their wish, the newspapers would not be in the business of printing news, but in morals. Somewhere between the Church and the political reformer, I judge, the newspaper would take its stand. Martin Luther on the one hand and Cavour on the other would be its models; but those who hold that a newspaper should always be scolding at something or somebody set up John Knox as the editor's great exemplar. It is conceded, I believe, that the Christian religion shall still be ranked as the greatest regenerating force at work in human society, but the press must come next, and not far behind. It has not yet been proposed that newspaper editors shall take orders or vows, but it is insisted that they shall have no knowledge of the ways of this wicked world, or if they have such knowledge they shall scrupulously hide it from their readers. Sin and crime will continue their ravages, of course, and the presumably righteous will now and then slip or fall, but the newspapers must look the other way. And there must be nothing trivial or frivolous in the newspaper. This is, or is supposed by the critics of the press to be, a very serious world, a sad and quite unhappy world, indeed. Therefore the newspapers should concern themselves only with large and solemn matters. A newspaper must not make mistakes. This rule is a major canon, and as mistakes are assumed to be needless, they are to be attributed to the editor's malice or to his ignorance. Finally, there must be no pictures, for pictures are an abomination in the sight of the censors, and that settles the case against them.

When in some remote era the press shall pass all the challenges of its critics, when the newspaper shall be a potent agency of righteousness, irreproachable in matter, exalted, inerrant, and unillustrated, this world will doubtless have made great millennial advancement. In the present age, however, a journal of this ideal perfection would find itself in such incongruous surroundings that its editor, unless he were devoid of the "news sense," would be made miserable in the struggle between his moral duty and his carnal opportunities, its publisher would be in continual pain, and its cashier in continual idleness. In every period in the history of journalism some newspapers have made a heroic effort to "leave all meaner things" and soar against the sun, or at least have talked much and loudly of the effort they were making. But it makes the feeling heart sick to note the variance between their practice and their profession. I apprehend, therefore, that the castigators of the newspaper press have set up standards that are either wrong or untimely. They would make the newspapers what no considerable or controlling number of their readers want them to be, and what they cannot be until society has become something very different from what it is now. For my part, I have always believed the professional railers against the press to be very bad judges of what a newspaper ought to be, and they are too frequently guilty of the injustice of judging the entire newspaper press by its worst examples, and of denouncing the whole for the vices practised by a few.

These undiscriminating censors are without authority or credentials. They do not represent—in fact, they directly misrepresent—the opinions of the great body of intelligent men and women who read newspapers. Among the mass of newspaper readers I do not find any warrant for the assertions made with such flippancy by those reckless critics that newspapers are everywhere regarded as untrustworthy and debasing. The statement is not true, nor does it approximate the truth. The "average reader" is not at all of the censor's mind. The "old subscriber" regards his newspaper with a feeling of affection and almost of reverence. He has taken it from its first issue. Every day or every week through the long years it has brought to him the news of the world. It has gladdened his heart with eloquent praise of the leaders and the candidates of his own party, and has delighted him by the sound drubbings it has administered to the leaders and the candidates of the other party. Upon most public matters he has accepted its admonitions as a son accepts the words of a father. He owes countless pleasant hours to the literary charm or graceful fancy of some favorite writer or correspondent, many a hearty laugh to the humorist's column, and to the teeming pages he has faithfully read a growing store of information that could have come to him in no other way. It has even, upon occasion, printed his "letters to the editor," and so won a new title to his esteem. Through all these years his newspaper has been an intimate part of his life. He knows all its views, its every peculiarity, and he admires and loves them all. And now in his old age, by the evening lamp in his country home or at the breakfast table in his city house, he unfolds with ever fresh eagerness and reads with undiminished respect the newspaper that all his life has been his guide, counsellor, and friend. Let one of the chronic railers against the press lift up his plaint in the hearing of such a loyal newspaper reader and he would fare as the scolding Thersites fared when the staff of Ulysses smote upon his back and shoulders.

No doubt the newspapers ought to be a great deal wiser and better than they are. I hasten to make this declaration of doctrine lest some press censor should conclude that I am quite content with the press as it is and that I am contending for its exemption from moral obligation—that is, that, while it may not be immoral, it may lawfully be unmoral, not caring particularly whether society goes to the dogs or not. That is not my purpose, and I hope I have not given any one reason for supposing that it was my purpose. I should be glad to see the newspapers win and hold a title to higher public respect and confidence. I should be glad to see them, within the limits of reasonable possibility, rid of their blemishes and blunders. At the same time, I should like to see great lawyers lose fewer cases and great doctors fewer patients, great judges less frequently reverse each other's decisions and experienced business men less commonly make erroneous prognostications concerning profit and loss. Being a member of the craft, I dislike to think myself engaged in an ignoble and vicious calling. It comforts me, therefore, firmly to believe that the press is as virtuous and commendable as most other institutions set up by peccant and fallible man. The newspapers are as good as the age and the world in which they are published. It would be a monstrous breach of the law of evolution if they were much better. Nevertheless, the berating and denunciation of the press has become a sort of cult in this country, having its prelates and its preachers, self-ordained and very earnest, and its sectaries, not numerous, but faithful as an echo. The thing is a schism in its origin and nature, I think, and will die out, unity being restored by the return of the schismatics into the great body of men and women who refuse to believe that editors are rogues and newspapers a pestilence. Lowell said of Burke that "no man who ever wrote English, except perhaps Mr. Ruskin, more habitually mistook his own personal likes and dislikes, tastes and distastes for general principles." In a critic this is a serious, I may say a disqualifying, fault. If the gentlemen who see no good thing in the press have this defect, it explains why the world pays so little heed to them.

Some years ago a clerical critic of the press declared from the pulpit that "it has a short root and no accumulations." I never could guess his meaning, but it seems probable that he meant to say that the press has no record of achievements. That is not the view held by the public in general, and it is not the true view. The daily publication of the news is the greatest, the incomparable service of the press; but aside from that, the achievements of newspapers by which men and communities and nations have been made better and happier seem to me to constitute a record as worthy as it is incontestable. To consider the record of only one city, the successful search for Livingstone must surely be reckoned an "accumulation" for Mr. Bennett's newspaper. Everybody is tired of hearing about the assault upon and overthrow of the Tweed ring. The illustration is trite, but the achievement gave the newspaper that overthrew the ring the right to say, with Othello: "I've done the State some service." Twenty years later the same newspaper took by the throat a man who was squandering the resources and mismanaging the affairs of the great life insurance company of which he was President, and dragged him from his seat, though under peril of two libel suits for damages aggregating $1,750,000. These public services may safely be called "accumulations." *The Tribune's* fresh-air-fund labors constitute a continuing beneficence of the highest and most useful type. I should be glad to know that any of the gentlemen who say such unkind things about the newspapers have done as much good to their kind. *The Sun's* attack on the Washington ring, recalled to memory by the recent death of the judge who shielded its editor from the lawless vengeance of the ring, was a service to the country and, though unacknowledged and doubtless unwelcome, to the party then in power, which was in peril of complete demoralization.

A more recent instance of the power of the press to do great public service is afforded by the New York *Times's* telegraphic canvass of the Senate and House of Representatives upon the proposed repeal of the Sherman act. The results of that canvass, showing a large majority for the repeal, were cabled to London, and their publication in the London *Times* of June 19 and in the other London papers greatly facilitated the obtaining of sterling loans here and gave relief to New York merchants at a time when the rates for money ranged from ten to seventy per cent. In countless strifes against municipal corruptions and against political bosses and party machines, in exposures of official malfeasance, in prophetic warnings of evils to come from unwise executive or legislative acts, in unwearying exhortation against political and financial follies, and in the promotion of public or charitable undertakings, the press has demonstrated its high utility and put its title to the possession of "accumulations" beyond all contest.

The bitterness of some of the assailants of the press is due probably to a misconception of the province of a newspaper. If there were in the world no persons save those whose minds dwell constantly upon the loftier problems of society and the finer truths of philosophy, the newspaper would be very different from what it is now. But taking the world as it is, which is the way editors have to take it, the publication of a newspaper devoted entirely to exalted themes is commercially impossible. Personally I am glad of it, for such a newspaper would be tough reading, and its writers would be the most miserable of men. Let me say, however, that a newspaper that intentionally and as a matter of policy purveys matter acceptable to low and vulgar tastes, a newspaper that is habitually unclean, sensational, untrustworthy, and ill-bred, deserves all the denunciations that the most violent critics of the press may visit upon it. Lay on, gentlemen, and spare not. But pray discriminate. Don't accuse a newspaper of pandering to low tastes because it prints matter intended for the edification of persons not in your set. There are hundreds of persons in this city to whom tennis is a bore, baseball a weariness, yachting an unknown realm, and horse-racing a gateway to the bottomless pit. But there are hundreds of thousands to whom all these or some of them are agreeable pastimes.

Healthy Americans for the most part are interested in sports. A newspaper must take account of this great portion of the population who demand sporting news, and whose demand is so reasonable and innocent that every newspaper now prints this information fully and carefully. Yet this is one of the offences that glare in the eyes of the critics. Moreover, every newspaper that has or aspires to any considerable circulation must print every day a great multitude of items of news that for many of its readers have little or no interest and to some seem quite unworthy the space they occupy. The number of men and women who take no interest in the proceedings of Congress, who don't care to know what the Legislature may be at, who find the tariff an intolerable nuisance, and the silver question a bore, and who can get along comfortably without knowing anything about great public affairs, is much larger than their highly-educated fellow mortals suspect. Yet these persons are mostly of orderly lives, simple tastes, and innocent minds. They have their pursuits and their pleasures, and they want to read about their pursuits and their pleasures in the newspapers. They have an appetite, also, for almost any gossip or happening that is of contemporaneous human interest and not beyond their range of sympathy and understanding. Is it sinful, is it debasing, is it vulgar, to print news readable and acceptable to this audience, provided the matter printed is not immoral or improper? I do not think so. This class of persons constitutes a very large proportion of the population of every town or city. They are entitled to consideration from the newspapers. They are respectable, and the news that interests them is respectable news, though in point of historical importance it usually ranks some distance below announcements of the abdication of sovereigns and the discovery of new and valuable laws governing the action of tides and the behavior of planets. But for printing such news the press is denounced for giving up so much space to "trash."

Newspaper men are not wiser than other men of similar training and powers. But some newspaper men know their own business well enough to know that a newspaper managed to please the more unreasonable members of the priesthood of critics would be a ghastly failure. Fair, reasonable, constructive criticism is welcome and suggestions made in a friendly and helpful spirit. If he is a serious man and conscientious, he will heed well all criticism that brings more plainly into his view the great responsibility that his office puts upon him. But he may exact of his critics human sympathy, breadth of view, and some little knowledge of the conditions under which newspapers are made.

C. R. MILLER.

For the next decade and a half, Mr. Miller found himself too busy with his profession to have time to write or to talk about it. But in 1912, on a visit to Morningside Heights, he broke this long silence. In that year his chief public address dealt with editorial writing and the prerequisites of the editorial writer. It formed his personal message to the would-be newspapermen and newspaperwomen of the Columbia University School of Journalism. Not only the few first students enrolled in that newly established Faculty, but a throng from the other schools of the university turned out to hear him. He faced a crowded auditorium.

The message he brought was thoroughly characteristic. He who had exemplified by his writings that an editor might well take all knowledge for his province, chose to speak on cultural equipment. His advice was to read much, talk much, think much, and travel whenever possible. He set no boundaries to the fields which students should more or less explore before hoping to write with any insight or weight for the editorial columns of a newspaper. As a partial directory of "sources" Mr. Miller suggested comprehensive readings in law, politics, the philosophy and the interpretation of history, social problems and the habitual study of the daily newspaper.

If the classic gentlemen who statuesquely adorn the alcoves of Earl Hall could have peered that day through their plaster-of-Paris eyes, they would have seen that student audience sit up and take notice and take notes. For that Morningside throng was not slow to realize that it was getting the real thing. Here was a man who spoke as one having authority, and not as—a sophomore.

Falling back on the shorthand of *The Times* reporter of that date, we learn that "Mr. Miller said that he might easily acquit himself of his task by advising the students to read newspapers diligently, since in the nature of the case, the immediate equipment for a great part of the work of the editorial writer was gained by reading the news of current events."

Editorial writing for which preparation is made only by reading newspapers, however, is pretty certain to be without background, without much depth, and in such cases the guidance of fixed principle is too often lacking.

It was doubtless because Joseph Pulitzer perceived that so many newspaper workers were prepared only in this way that by his munificent gift the School of Journalism at Columbia was established. The course of study laid out for the school would supply an admirable equipment for an editorial writer, but there should be something more. The purpose of an editorial article is instruction, admonition and advice; they should be given with authority as by an expert; and a newspaper writer should strive diligently to qualify as an expert upon a wide variety of topics. An editorial writer should read much, talk much, think much and travel when he can. Conversation with those who know a good deal more about the subjects talked of than himself is notably profitable.

The course of study at the school would impart a good working knowledge of history and politics, but for an editorial writer there is great equipment value in the interpretation of history, the philosophy of history, the correlation of events that may be widely separated. The students of the school are giving attention to one of the recurring wars in the Balkans. It would be interesting to know that if the Treaty of Berlin had not deprived Russia of the fruits of her victory a generation ago, there would have been no Russo-Japanese war and why. It is of interest and profitable for comparison to understand why Diaz, whose benevolent despotism had done so much for Mexico, repeated the mistake of Guizot, Louis Philippe's Minister, in refusing to broaden the basis of Government by an extension of the suffrage. Guizot's History of Civilization is a profitable book to read; also Buckle's, which, with all its well-known defects, has many sound chapters upon the philosophy of history. A well-ordered understanding of the nature of institutions and of political causes equips an editorial writer to foresee and foretell the working of statutes, and to show why unwise legislative experiments will fail.

It is vital that writers for the press should have such a general knowledge of law and legal principles as a layman can attain to. Students should read diligently the decisions of John Marshall, the beginning of Constitutional interpretation in the United States, notably the great opinions in which it might almost be said that he established the authority of the Supreme Court and the powers of the Federal Government. Since the law relating to trusts is likely for many years to come to be a frequent subject for editorial writing, it would be a first-rate preparation for a student to make a careful comparison of Justice Peckham's construction of the anti-trust law sixteen years ago, with Chief Justice White's opinion in the oil and tobacco cases. International law, too, should be studied diligently, and for an American writer there is no better source than Professor Moore's "Digest of International Law."

The Columbia course aims to confer a good working knowledge of economics of the tariff, finance, taxation and currency. The closest attention should be given to social movements, to the efforts being made to promote the comfort, the welfare and the happiness of those whose destiny is not fully under their own control, who need help, protection and encouragement. But it is not enough to know of the hardships of the poor and of the working-class; there should be full knowledge of what society and law-makers have done for the poor and for the working-class in the last century, the laws that have been passed bettering the conditions of labor and of living, the continuing and effective influence of public opinion upon Government in giving protection to those who in a former day were defenceless.

The editorial writer should be an optimist; he should not let anyone persuade him that man is desperately wicked and cruel, that society is relentless, for it is not true. He should cultivate, and this is all important, openness of mind, fairness to adversaries in politics and in other strifes. He should equip himself with a body of principles, convictions, reached by candid study and thought. He will find them applicable to practically all his daily tasks, and if they are well-reasoned, sound and enduring, they will invest him with the power to convince others and that is one great aim of editorial writing.

Mr. Miller's next appearance as a speaker on a subject connected with the newspaper came in 1916, when, on a Sunday morning in January, he spoke from a pulpit and gave a history of journalism in a nutshell. To the pastor at that time of the Park Avenue Methodist Church had come with the "laying on of hands" something of the cultural breadth of the great Wesley himself. He chose to devote a series of services to the definite enlightenment of the people on tendencies in contemporary civilization. Accordingly he asked to his pulpit men of distinction in each profession, to talk on the world's work from the worker's standpoint. The idea appealed to the editor of *The Times*. He accepted the minister's invitation and spoke on "How We Got Our Newspapers." He spoke as he was wont to write, with an erudition that never remotely approached academic pomposity and with a conciseness and economy of phrase that scanned centuries in a paragraph.

Let it go into the chronicle as the reporter, assigned that day to "cover" Mr. Miller, recorded it:

"If we are asked where we get our newspapers," Mr. Miller said, "the answer is that we got them from the divine command, 'Let there be light.' " It is certain that darkness would have brooded on the face of the deep for all time if it had not been for the newspapers or something like the newspapers.

The desire to know what is going on is not a modern development. Back in tribal times, primitive man had the same desire for information as we have today. He wanted to know the result of the hunt, the position of the enemy, the gossip current among his fellow tribesmen. As civilization advanced this want became more complex. Paul speaking on Mars Hill mentioned the love of news common among the Athenians.

One of the earliest methods for the dissemination of news was the letter. When Cicero was sent as Governor to Cilicia, he asked a friend to send him the news of Rome. The friend employed scribes—the reporters of that day—to gather the information and prepare the letters. The man who wrote the first letters reported everything from the procedure of the Senate to the result of the latest gladiatorial contest. Cicero objected to his methods and complained that the letters contained items that he would not have bothered with when at home. What he wanted, he explained, was advance information to keep him in touch with the political movements of the time.

Volumes of news letters have come down to us showing that the letter writing continued through the middle ages. The Church and the State both attempted to wipe out the custom. In April, 1572, Pope Pius V issued a bull against the custom. This was a few months before the massacre of St. Bartholomew's Day. His successor issued another bull against them in September, 1572, a few weeks after the massacre, directing that writers should be condemned to the galleys. That was an unpleasant age in which to be engaged in the newspaper business.

The first newspapers made their appearance in Pekin, but the West was not far behind. About 50 B. C., the Roman Government began publishing an official organ. This had to be written by hand so few copies were issued. This paper gave the general news and was not much different from the newspapers of today.

After the invention of the printing press and movable type, in the middle of the fifteenth century, private news letters were printed instead of written but the opposition of the Church and State prevented the appearance of regular newspapers until the beginning of the seventeenth century. A paper began to appear in Holland in 1626. In 1689 the first

American paper began to circulate in Boston. Many of the papers began as Government organs.

Civilization was delayed by the lack of newspapers in the early days, Mr. Miller thought, and he gave it as his opinion that a free press probably would have prevented the French Revolution, as the discussion of the troubles of the people, and of desirable reforms would have resulted in changed conditions.

"Our newspapers," he said in conclusion, "form a great reserve against the growth of evils and at the same time give the discontented a chance to 'blow off steam,' an opportunity similar to that given by the outbursts at Cooper Union in this city, and at Hyde Park in London. Where there is no freedom of the press, as in Russia, we instinctively look for revolution."

The marked material prosperity of the United States in the opening decade of the present century had its inevitable effect on the leading educational centres. Diffidently at first but soon with an unabashed directness they tended to stress the utilitarian studies and soft-pedal those courses which sought merely cultural ends. The humanists intoned their wares to empty classrooms except in instances where such courses still lingered among those "required," and the students herded to hear breezy young instructors exhale the new gospel of "go-getting" and exhibit, by means of elaborate diagrams all over the blackboard, the seductive "psychology of salesmanship." It was not long before this new desire under the collegiate elms had almost turned the old seats of learning into little more than high-grade business schools that the beginnings of reaction set in.

What more natural than that Princeton, with its spiritual kinship to Oxford almost as self-conscious as its architectural, should take the lead in striving to combat this growing utilitarian trend. Accordingly, Dean West of the Graduate School arranged a conference at Princeton on June 2, 1917, to consider the place of "the humanities" in liberal education. In selecting speakers the good dean shrewdly sought out men who had found the said "humanities" of lasting and practical benefit. He made no wiser choice than in calling upon Mr. Miller. The idea appealed to his ardent allegiance to Olympus, and to Princeton he journeyed in com-

THE EDITOR TALKS SHOP 171

pany with his fellow-editor, E. P. Mitchell of *The Sun,* and delivered the following defense of the classical faith. Here is the address in full from the notes he used on that occasion:

A man of my calling, comfortably assiduous and having length of years, puts into print the equivalent of 100 octavo volumes of 350 pages each. Who in the realm of pure literature writes so much? If in Dante's thought, Virgil with the Eclogues, the Georgics and the Aeneid, was the fount of a broad river of speech, then a veritable Amazon of utterance flows forth from the pen that, year after year, contributes a daily column to the press. It is not literature, it would miss the mark if it were, but its object is best attained if it have the form and quality of literature. To the multitude it is the abiding and most familiar example in the use of language in other than spoken form. It is quite unnecessary to argue that a stream from which so many take their fill should be pure at the source. Standards may be kept inviolate by the pen of genius writing for the cloistered few; current speech takes its form very much from the daily newspaper.

It is responsibility not lightly borne by men of conscientious habit. Through what discipline comes fitness to bear it worthily? We must not with too clamorous insistence press the case for Latin and Greek beyond safe limits. Too many men write good English who never read a line of either tongue. Much reading of English gives command of an encompassing vocabulary; good taste and the instinctive sense of language may confer the power to employ it with elegance and propriety. However acquired, there must be instructed discrimination in the use of the elements of the language, a sense always clear and sure of the just word. That discriminating sense comes, if it be unfailing, can come only through knowledge of the origin, history and composition of words. It is my observation and judgment that the surest way, certainly the shortest way to the acquisition of this sense of values leads through the texts of the Greek and Latin authors and the less alluring but indispensable pages of the grammarians. That conviction rests upon a good many years of observation. I should give it much emphasis if I were called upon to advise in this matter young men looking forward to a newspaper career.

This is very familiar ground and I forbear. I mean merely that a newspaper reporter, correspondent, or editorial writer who does not know, citing examples that recently came under my eye, that expurgate does not mean expunge, that egregious is only by custom and not by etymology an epithet of reproach, and that a decimated regiment may still be a force to be reckoned with, has much to learn about the English language. Lord Bryce, in accounting for the new-born interest in this question displayed by "certain sections of the population which were not wont to interest themselves in educational matters," says that "there has been created in the popular mind an association now deeply rooted, between the knowledge of applied science and material prosperity." This is economic determinism applied to education. To the dogs with the higher things of the spirit, youth shall train in branches that will provide the biggest store of bread and butter for the body. For any young man who would become a newspaper writer that is a false deluding doctrine. It is precisely the good old-fashioned classical schooling that gives him command of the higher places, the higher rewards. If he would climb to the high places let him build a stairway during his college years.

I am void of all fear about contradiction when I say that a newspaperman, and particularly an editorial writer, who has missed making the acquaintance of the gods and mortal, speaking men from whom our heritage of civilization has descended, must fail to do justice to his talents, however great they may be. In modern times every unexplored river, every mountain unclimbed, has been a challenge to the daring spirit of man until the secret of all sources has been laid bare, all summits topped, save the very few that Nature reserves for the glory of heroic spirits in later generations. If we strive so unconscionably in these sterile adventures, shall we be incurious about that Roman fountain-head of our laws, our political institutions, and a great part of our language, shall we disdain to climb where through the ages our fathers have climbed, to that Athenian summit whence the light of civilization burst upon the world, where the noblest in art, in poetry, in letters had its birth? For us there is no other source, no other mountain top. Beyond Greece and Rome, saving religion, we trace no line of descent. The Oriental monarchies blazed up and were extinguished. They left us no heritage. Our motherlands are Greece and Rome. There men won deathless fame in works that time has never conquered. Shall we let them die? Shall we undo the Renaissance, and of the coeval printer's art, seemingly born to transmit for our advantage and enjoyment the treasures of Greece and Rome, make a sumpter-mule burdened only with commodities appraisable only in cash?

I think I do not wander from the point, the practical point. Without understanding of the ancient world, our ancient world, there can be no sound understanding of the modern world and its affairs. It is highly desirable that a newspaper man should try to understand the world about him. I know that his effort will be less toilsome, its reward richer and more certain, if the light kindled by classical knowledge burns within his mind. To this mastery and understanding proficiency in science, skill in the mysteries of the external world, no matter in what high degree held, serve no purpose of guidance. What man is doing, singly or associatively, that is the newspaper's province. And for one who has to take thought about the behavior of men and give expression to it, no branch of knowledge is alien, none superfluous. Culture, even if for the pure joy of culture, is of high and constant service. It freshens, stimulates, uplifts, vivifies.

"All the world is sweeter, if the Athenian violet quicken;
All the world is brighter, if the Athenian sun return."

Here follows Mr. Miller's own comment on this academic outpouring:

NEW YORK TIMES

Dec. 20, 1917.

DEAR TED:

Prenk Bib Doda, as his son was about to start for the Palmer and Buckner Convention said to the young man: "Boy, you are no great traveller and you do not know quam parva sapientia mundus regitur." Since your old friend Bib showed this degree of familiarity with the Latin language, I feel that you might be moved to take an interest in the classics, and accordingly, I am sending to you a volume which contains the discourses of a lot of harmless old pokes which were listened to with patience at Princeton last June, by a select audience assembled to sympathize with Dean West's desire to bring about a great, sweeping revival of the classics. I know that this lies wholly outside your sphere of interest. Your lack of interest in the classics dates from the Freshman year, perhaps from an earlier time. But you will frequently meet in society pedantic persons whose allusions to old time things you would quite miss if you did not have some knowledge of the medium by which the Romans communicated their imperfect ideas to each other. In this volume you will find some of my ripened conclusions, also observations by Dana; blacksmiths, storekeepers and trust magnates joined in the symposium, but you need pay no attention to what they say; Dana and I will be sufficient for you.

I am told that you, and . . . will be and appear at our house next Monday morning. I will personally see to it that the dog be tied. Other arrangements which it may be found necessary to make will be in excellent hands. It is proper to warn you that the retail price of liquor has advanced to a degree which puts it beyond the reach of the poor. Therefor, you need expect no provision for the alleviation of thirst other than that made for all in the excellent water supply system of the City of New York.

Yours very truly,
C. R. MILLER.

Hon. Geo. Fred Williams,
Boston, Mass.

Mr. Miller during his years in New York, had watched the metropolitan newspaper so broaden its function as almost entirely to change its reason for existence. He had watched it grow from eight pages daily, and twelve on Sundays, to its present bulky proportions. Looking back, as the vista of years behind him lengthened, he could see to-day in the light of yesterday, and from the general trend thus revealed, predict probable conditions for tomorrow. Fortunately, *The Editor and Publisher,* a trade journal of the craft, caught him in these reflective and prophetic moods, on his seventieth birthday. Turning around in his swivel chair, away from his desk and leaning back as far as the chair permitted, he allowed, what he had rarely allowed before, a formal interview. Punctuating his remarks by hitting the finger tips of one hand against the finger tips of the other as he talked, he briefly reviewed his own swift progress. He spoke of the comparatively meagre news service which the papers of yesterday had given their readers, and then went on:

Today however, the public demands a vast volume of news, international in its scope, and so presented that it will attract the eye. Newspapers have learned how to treat news more intelligently, and that has had the effect of making the readers better informed. This is notably true of women, and their development in this respect has been intensified by the news of the great war. Women are now thoroughly informed on great world events, and they want to get their news at first hand—from the newspapers—and not from the male members of their families as they once did.

Concurrently with a broader and better knowledge of how to handle the news, the editorial columns have changed their character. Of course, my experience does not go back to the days of personal journalism, when men were subjects of editorial attack on strictly personal grounds, but even in my time each paper was a strong aggressive adherent of some political party and conducted both news and editorial pages along lines of service to the one it advocated. The news columns would carry the speeches delivered at meetings of the party of its choice, but the meetings of the opposing party would get brief mention. Editorials supported the chosen political party, being written from chiefly a partisan standpoint.

Then it occurred to newspaper managers that there was no use in sending readers of one paper to whose political predilections it did not subscribe to another paper to get the news about their own party. This led to better treatment of the news, and a presentation of both sides.

It led to political independence, too, for both newspapers and readers. The progress towards political independence really began in 1872, at the time of the Greeley campaign, but got its greatest impetus in the first Cleveland campaign, in 1884. Newspapers had found by that time that political independence was more comfortable and agreeable to operate under. They could criticise both parties, honestly and fairly, and in that way better serve the public. The progress of the editorial page fully kept pace with the development of the treatment of the news. It became the vehicle of a real effort to interpret the news to the readers, gained greater breadth and evolved into a real guiding spirit; one that proved itself worthy of the reader's consideration.

To illustrate. When, in the notable Trent Affair, Mason and Slidell were seized and taken from a British vessel, the action was commended with little consideration of the law of the case, simply because the United States had done it. Mr. Lincoln freed the British Commissioners, of course. Newspapers would not now make such a mistake. Note how clearly and how fairly they set forth the principles of law involved in the recent war. They have been sincere and faithful in the efforts to inform their readers, not only about great events, but also upon the international principles involved in those events.

It must be obvious that the great work along these educational lines could not be done with small papers, nor with the limited circulations of the old days. I know there is a great deal of discussion about cutting down the size of the newspapers, but in my opinion they will never become smaller. A vast volume of news must be presented because an intelligent reading public demands it, and it cannot be presented in smaller newspapers. The field of the newspaper has broadened until it covers the entire world in detail. Less and less attention is being given to the smaller affairs, and more and more attention to the larger interests. Local news comes under this category, and the local matters that some years ago would occupy half a column of the paper, now are told in a few lines. The space can be more profitably used.

XII

THE END OF THE DAY

With the more open-and-above-board phases of the great war ended, Mr. Miller took a holiday. Early in the summer of 1921, he left with his son, his daughter and her friend, Miss Betty MacGeorge, for a visit to Nova Scotia and Newfoundland. The trip was actually his first letting up—the first relaxation he had allowed himself since the war began. His secretary at that time, having social connections with the officialdom of Canada and the Ancient Colony, wrote to the Lieutenant-Governor of Nova Scotia and to His Excellency of Newfoundland, notifying them of Mr. Miller's proposed trip. Both at Halifax and at St. John's, the Representatives of His Majesty received the representative spokesman of American democracy with honors, all the more agreeable to the recipient because unofficial and hearty. At Halifax, Governor MacCallum Grant called at Mr. Miller's hotel on the day he arrived, and later gave a dinner in his honor at Government House. During his entire visit to Halifax, one of that city's first citizens, Colonel F. H. Oxley, acted as Mr. Miller's guide, fellow-philosopher, and friend. At St. John's, Sir William Alexander Harris extended similar courtesies, and Colonel Cluny Macpherson, C. M. G., played a like rôle to Colonel Oxley's. As a tangible souvenir of this British hospitality Mr. Miller brought back a regal treasure—a bottle of three-star whiskey from the "cellars" of the Prince of Wales's cruiser, H. M. S. "Renown"!

While in Nova Scotia, the Miller party motored for several days through the apple orchards and rolling dyked-rimmed pastures of the Annapolis Valley. Looking across that productive panorama, the New Hampshire farmer's son decided: "This is the most beautiful farming country I have even seen."

In Newfoundland, the home of the cod if not of the bean, the excellent angling caused him keen delight. "I can catch trout within ten minutes' drive from my hotel," he wrote back gleefully to New York.

Despite his seventy years, he entered with zest into this phase of his holiday. He fished in Long Pond, and the other waters near St. John's almost daily.

The social fabric of this capital city of Newfoundland interested him immensely. He saw the reproduction there of the English chocolate cake structure of society—without the intermediate layer. To him, St. John's seemed to lack a middle class. He noted the sturdy fisherman element on which the prosperity of the colony rested, the usual artisans, and then the gentry—the Governmental officialdom, the professional men, and the urbane and cosmopolitanly educated scions of the old ruling merchant families. He illustrated all this by the pungent comment:

"In St. John's there are but two makes of cars—Rolls-Royces and Fords." He himself had an amusing experience of this social cleavage. He gave one newspaper interview. It was an interview which he took considerable pains to make interesting, and which in fact the St. John's reporter wrote up with workmanlike skill.

Dining out each day and meeting the city's first citizens at the club, he naturally expected them to make some reference to this article.

But not a word was said. Finally Mr. Miller saw the reason. The interview came out in *The Fisherman's Advocate,* and circulated in the outports and fishing hamlets of the island. Naturally not one of his hosts knew that the interview had been given or printed.

He returned to New York greatly rested and benefited by his trip, and entered upon the enjoyment of a happy and comparatively carefree autumn. To relieve Mr. Miller toward the close of 1920, Mr. Ochs appointed two distinguished additions to the editorial staff. Rollo Ogden, Editor-in-chief of *The Evening Post,* and John H. Finley, Superintendent of Education for the State of New York, joined Mr. Miller's forces as associate editors. Their coming left him freer than he had ever been. Although he kept on advocating the League of Nations and scourging the tariff and all its works, he turned over subjects with which he would normally have dealt, to his able associate editors.

This gave him the opportunity occasionally to relax into a more casual vein. His teasing along of Mr. Edison's questionnaire idea in the following editorial shows the type of thing he loved to dictate when he had the time. The writing of this particular editorial in fact interested him so much that he jotted down a few preparatory pencil notes. This he did only on the rarest occasions. For the most part his articles sprang from his head, full born.

GRADE XYZ

We hope Mr. Thomas A. Edison will not despair of the Republic altogether because so many college graduates flunk in the examinations by which he tests the efficiency and intelligence of young men who aspire to the higher places in his shops and factories. There are eight-score questions on his list. It is not to be wondered at that they are not all answered. Yet Mr. Edison says: "Men who have gone through college I find to be amazingly ignorant. They don't seem to know anything." Why confine the ascription of ignorance to college graduates? How small a part of the total sum of knowledge do the wisest on earth possess. Besides, is Mr. Edison's questionnaire really a conclusive test? "What is copra?" That is one of the questions. Was any man ever kinder to his aged mother because he knew what copra is? How is it important save to grocery clerks? "What is zinc?" Does Mr. Edison himself know what zinc is? Does he cling to the old-fashioned belief that it is a metallic element, fixed, irreducible, not subject to transforming change into two or three new elements for which science will yet have to invent suitable names? It is perilous to be overconfident about zinc.

Mr. Edison's flunking mark is XYZ. He has established that grade for those who fail completely. Dante would have just escaped that rating. He was the most learned man of his time, yet out of six of Mr. Edison's questions prepared to test general information there is but a single one which he could possibly have answered. "How did Cleopatra die?" Dante, who knew his old authors, was familiar with the snakebite tradition:

la trista Cleopatra,
Che, fuggendogli innanzi dal colubro
La morte prese subitana ed atra.

John Milton would have come off no better. Even Henry Ford would be stumped by some of these questions. "Where is Magdalena Bay?" How can anybody answer that question? There are at least three Magdalena

Bays. Does Mr. Edison mean the bay on the west coast of Colombia, the Spitzbergen bay or the Lower California bay? "Which fox?" inquired Mark Twain of the breathless huntsman who asked him if the fox had passed that way within a few minutes. "What is the greatest depth of ocean?" Nobody knows but the sharks and the whales. Man cannot know it until his fathom line has searched every nook and cranny and pocket of ocean's bed. "What are felt hats made of?" and "What fabric is used in auto tires?" "What constitutes the State?" inquired the Sultan of his Grand Vizier. There came the instant reply, "The question is asinine, your Majesty," and so the matter ended.

Can't Mr. Edison understand that the young graduate whose mind is dwelling on the long roll of the hexameter or, more probably, on the uncovenanted caperings of free verse doesn't care to know the ingredients of felt hats or automobile tires? Has it never been brought to his attention that not a few college men who would be entirely willing to be inscribed temporarily upon his payroll nevertheless look upon his shops, his factories, his materials, his processes, as the mere dross and slag of life, not to be compared with the lofty things to which they aspire? Hats and tires and Magdalena Bays—what are they to a young man who feels and knows that some day the public will besiege the book stores for the products of his genius? His XYZ is a meaningless and empty formula. He may enjoy a brief triumph with his catch questions, but he cannot grade the human soul. Mr. Edison should cultivate a little humility. Above all, let him burn his questionnaire and judge the college graduates by their looks or their clothes, by anything so that he may spare himself the mortification of some day seeing some of his XYZ's command the plaudits of an enraptured world.

This era shines out in the annals as one of prosperity and happiness. Pressing cares both professional and private gave place to a letting up in the office routine, and a sharing in and enjoyment of the great affluence which had come to the paper.

About this time he made over to his two children a portion of his large holdings in *The Times*. It was then merely a private transaction and of interest solely to the parties concerned. Later the action became public, for in 1925 at a Washington hearing on the taxes levied on the estate the matter came up. The Court was puzzled as to just why the transfer should have been made at this period. Rulings were quoted which alleged the motive of tax evasion. George Fred Williams, as executor for his old friend, made the whole proceeding clear with documentary proof. The real reason was this: Mr. Miller made the transfer because he had only just then lifted the last of the indebtedness incurred by him in the old ill-fated Times Publishing Company. Now at last he felt himself financially out of the wood. All assets belonged to him to do with as he chose.

Through Mr. Williams's mind there passed as a companion picture the memory of a Dartmouth incident fifty years before. In a room at the top of old Wentworth, a poker party runs its exciting course. "Chuck" Miller sits in at a table where all the players are his creditors. He wins. But in that winning he finds slight joy for his imposing total soon dwindles in paying off the score of past misfortunes.

Uncomplainingly through the years he had borne the burden of this business debt, and all that was New England in him saw to it that he allowed himself no luxury until this adverse score had been wiped completely off the slate.

At Mr. Ochs's wish he sat to Haskell Coffin. The few sittings Mr. Miller had time for proved sufficient for the painter to complete the head, face, and shoulders. Mr. Coffin succeeded in transferring to his canvas much of the dignity and poise of his subject as well as a remarkably accurate likeness.

To the artist, Mr. Miller disclosed his sunny and humorous self.

Unlike his fellow-editor, Joseph Pulitzer, who sat to Rodin in sulky silence, Mr. Miller chatted amiably on this and that, while the artist sketched away.

H. G. Wells, at the time, monopolized the news. Interviews with the novelist, just sailing from American shores after reporting the Arms Congress at Washington, besprinkled the news sheets. Mr. Miller, disliking anything that savored of self-advertising, grew caustic. "The ship with that fellow aboard won't be heard of again," he prophesied. But the ship arrived, and so did another interview.

When the artist came to limn in his sitter's hands he noticed them doubled up with rheumatism. How should he paint them? He was in a quandary. Would Mr. Miller emulate Oliver Cromwell and insist on wart and all? Finally Mr. Coffin asked him.

Mr. Miller decided that he would have his hands in the picture as he preferred to have them in real life—free from pain.

With the beginning of the new year, 1921, he received an invitation to go South for the duck shooting. Having Mr. Ogden and Doctor Finley at the office in addition to the regular staff, he felt free to accept, and tarried in New York only long enough to celebrate his birthday.

From 1911 on he delighted in these annual get-togethers on the evening of January 17. To them he would ask twenty-five or so of his most intimate friends, some of them friends of a lifetime, dating from Dartmouth days or his years as a member of *The Republican's* staff at Springfield. He limited the dinner to these congenial old-timers and for weeks in advance entered with zest in the preparations, personally superintending everything from the menu to the table decorations. The parties became a real institution for host and guests alike. As in previous years, the dinner on January 17, 1921, was served at the Metropolitan Club, and his old Dartmouth classmate, Doctor Charles Loomis Dana, acted as toastmaster.

A few days later he left his office in *The Times* Annex for what he expected would be a ten day vacation. But as it turned out, he was leaving it for the last time. He journeyed to Mulberry Plantation, South Carolina, for the shooting. With his old aim still true, he enjoyed the best of a rather poor bag. The weather was against him. It grew exceedingly damp and raw. He contracted a severe chill and returned to New York to be under the constant care of physicians. While serious from the first, his illness was not depressingly so throughout. He kept a keen interest in public affairs, saw to his more important mail, and radiated good humor when doctors or other callers came. Within a few weeks, he expected to be at his desk in the office. As the few weeks stretched into months, his great ambition was to be well enough to attend the reunion of the Dartmouth Class of 1870 at Hanover on the fiftieth anniversary of graduation. It proved a sore disappointment to him to have to write President Hopkins that it would be impossible for him to be present.

On fine days, however, he went for short drives in Central Park with his daughter, and enjoyed the visits which H. H. Kohlsaat and his co-workers from *The Times* paid him. He read the papers as usual and had a ready comment on the this and that of the daily goings on which interested him. An international lady of great charm was then monopolizing much of the front page, and a caller, knowing Mr. Miller's strong distaste for women in public life, held up the dazzling visitor as an example of feminine success in politics.

"Beautiful, charming, clever, accomplished—" to all these adjectives Mr. Miller gave gallant and genuine assent.

"Yes, she's a great talker, but what has she ever *done*?"

The caller brought into the conversation another international visitor at the time, Madame Curie, then on a mute if far from inglorious tour of American universities and the recipient of several honorary degrees each day.

The old editor took up the challenge. "Ah, yes. Madame Curie, —a man's mind that—a great doer. But what has she ever *said*?"

To his regular physician, Doctor John H. Richards, and to those called in for consultation, Doctor Walter L. Niles, Doctor Warren Coleman, and Doctor T. Wallis Davis, Mr. Miller proved a patient with extraordinary rallying power. Early in June he suffered a recurrence of the complications that followed his chill in January, and successfully withstood it. But the valiant effort weakened his heart and his illness took an acute turn from that time.

During the weeks of constant visitation, Doctor Richards found Mr. Miller the "most remarkable man" he had ever attended.

One morning shortly before the end came, the doctor found his patient propped up reading. He seemed deeply absorbed in the volume. Doctor Richards inquired the title. Mr. Miller held up the book, a novel in the gloomiest Slavic strain and in the original Russian.

"Surely, Mr. Miller, you can find something more cheery than that."

"Very probably," the old editor answered, and added with a certain grim humor, "but I started the book and I thought I'd like to finish it before I died."

The end came, quietly, almost imperceptibly at noon on July 18. Up to within a few hours of his death he was conscious, and as usual interested in the world's happenings; then he seemed to sleep. After it was all over, Doctor Richards said: "He was the most remarkable man I have ever treated. He was always in a good humor, even in the most trying periods of his illness, and his equanimity won the admiration of all the physicians who were called into consultation."

The next issue of *The Times* devoted the whole editorial page to the obituary of its great editor. The reversed leads with which the craft honors its dead bordered each column. Following the one editorial came seven columns of biographical matter which noted the main features of Mr. Miller's career.

Other columns carried the scores of cables and letters which poured in from presidents and potentates and the press of the entire world. Over night, forty years of anonymity flowered into fame.

The Times's own sincere tribute, read:

CHARLES RANSOM MILLER

A great figure is taken from American journalism by the death of Charles Ransom Miller. What his passing means to the newspaper world and to the general public *The Times* would today place before its own grievous loss. The nearly twoscore years of Mr. Miller's editorship, during which he gave direction to American thought and discussion, and furnished watchwords of national debate, won for him a newspaper authority and prestige unsurpassed in his time. His personality he never thrust forward. He was content to do his work through the unsigned article. Few of the large body of his readers knew definitely of the man by whom they had been instructed and led. But they must have been aware that a guiding intelligence, watchful and poised and serene, stood behind the editorial page. If Mr. Miller submitted gladly, as he did, to the limitations of impersonal journalism, he also understood and made use of its full scope and power.

The resources which he brought to his daily task were unrivaled. In addition to his native gifts, special aptitudes and varied training in journalism, he had large stores of learning, of experience and of reflection, on which to draw at need. Deeply read in history, versed in law, steeped in international precedents, at home in all the developments of American politics, with a firm grasp of economic principles, a master of several languages, a lover and cultivator of literature and the fine arts, he possessed an equipment that removed him far from the editorial improviser. Behind his writing lay broad and accurate knowledge which had been caught up by his brooding thought and wrought into a consistent body of opinion and conviction.

It is no exaggeration to say that the labors of such a man in such a position were for years a national asset. His calm and disciplined judgment was, with steadying effect, at the service of his countrymen in crisis after crisis. His prescient sense of the inevitable working of political forces made him a vigilant sentinel to warn the country of coming dangers. His eye was keen to discern the wholesome beginnings of sound reform movements, and he had an anticipatory welcome for new leaders of talent and character. Unsparing in criticism, when the occasion and the offender demanded it, Mr. Miller never failed in generous appreciation of every good word and work. His sympathies flowed freely to every worthy cause. His long-sustained editorship, so wise, so vigorous, so helpful, was an enduring benefit to this country, and his final resting from his labors must be accounted a national loss.

The feelings of his associates in this office at parting with their admired and beloved leader are not for public expression. His spirit, his example, his influence are woven into the very fabric of this newspaper. In the ending of his long and distinguished career there is nothing for tears, nothing to beat the breast. But personal grief at his death will linger in the hearts of all who were close to him. To them his memory will be fragrant, and they will think of him as one of the choir invisible who live again in lives made better by their presence.

To Mr. Ochs and to the editorial staff and council, the death came as a poignant personal sorrow. One and all missed not only the editor; they missed the man. Doctor John Finley caught much of this sense of individual loss in a quatrain which *The Times* published next day.

> "He is mourned at the mill, he is mourned at the mess."
> —Alcman, B. C. 625.

> He is mourned at the mill, he is mourned at the mess,
> The greatest of millers, whose mill was the press;
> The grist it is grinding makes bitter our bread
> For the grist is the news that our Miller is dead.
> One of the Men in the Mill.

The doors of the Annex and the more prominent Times Building in Times Square were heavily draped in black.

A public funeral service in St. James Episcopal Church, at Seventy-first Street and Madison Avenue, gave the employees of *The Times* and representatives from all the city newspapers the opportunity desired to show respect to the dead chief.

Mr. Miller's pallbearers were the sixteen members of the editorial council of *The Times*. Preceding the service they went to the Miller home at 635 Park Avenue and walked beside the hearse which brought the body to the church. These pallbearers were: Adolph S. Ochs, Rollo Ogden, Carr V. Van Anda, Doctor John H. Finley, Louis Wiley, E. A. Bradford, F. T. Birchall, E. M. Kingsbury, O. Phillips, John Corbin, Ralph Graves, F. C. Mortimer, Julius Ochs Adler, H. E. Armstrong, Arthur Hays Sultzberger, and Elmer Davis.

Leading the procession into the church were the honorary pallbearers. They were Doctor Charles L. Dana, John W. Davis, Melville E. Stone, Henry W. Taft, H. H. Kohlsaat, Edward W. Winter, Edward Page Mitchell, Charles R. Crane, Charles R. Flint, John G. Agar, Doctor I. Wyman Drummond and Edward N. Perkins.

As the processional hymn the choir sang "Jerusalem the Golden," a favorite with Mr. Miller since the days of the white-painted meeting house in Hanover Centre.

The Reverend Doctor Frank Warfield Crowder read both the service at the church and the committal prayers at Woodlawn Cemetery. Only his son and daughter, Mr. Ochs, Mr. Kohlsaat, Doctor Dana, Arthur Hays Sultzberger and Mr. Miller's private secretary followed the body to the graveside. There under a bright and cloudless July sky in a bank of living green they laid him down with the words of the beautiful Anglican office for the Burial of the Dead.

The manner of his passing followed close on the pattern of his days. His work at the office ended for the afternoon, he would swing around in his chair from his desk and look out on the darkening sky through the east window of his room which fronted above busy Broadway. He would watch the lights come on, one by one, in office window or on advertising sign, and see on the skyscraper owned by his paper, the large letters spelling " T I M E S " shine out high above the city. There he would sit without a word, except some comment now and then to his secretary, and presently the phone on his desk would ring to tell him that his car had come to take him home.

So it fell out at the last. There came a similar period of relaxation after work. There came the final few months of rest after the busy years, months relieved from routine, labor and worry, and then—the end of the day.

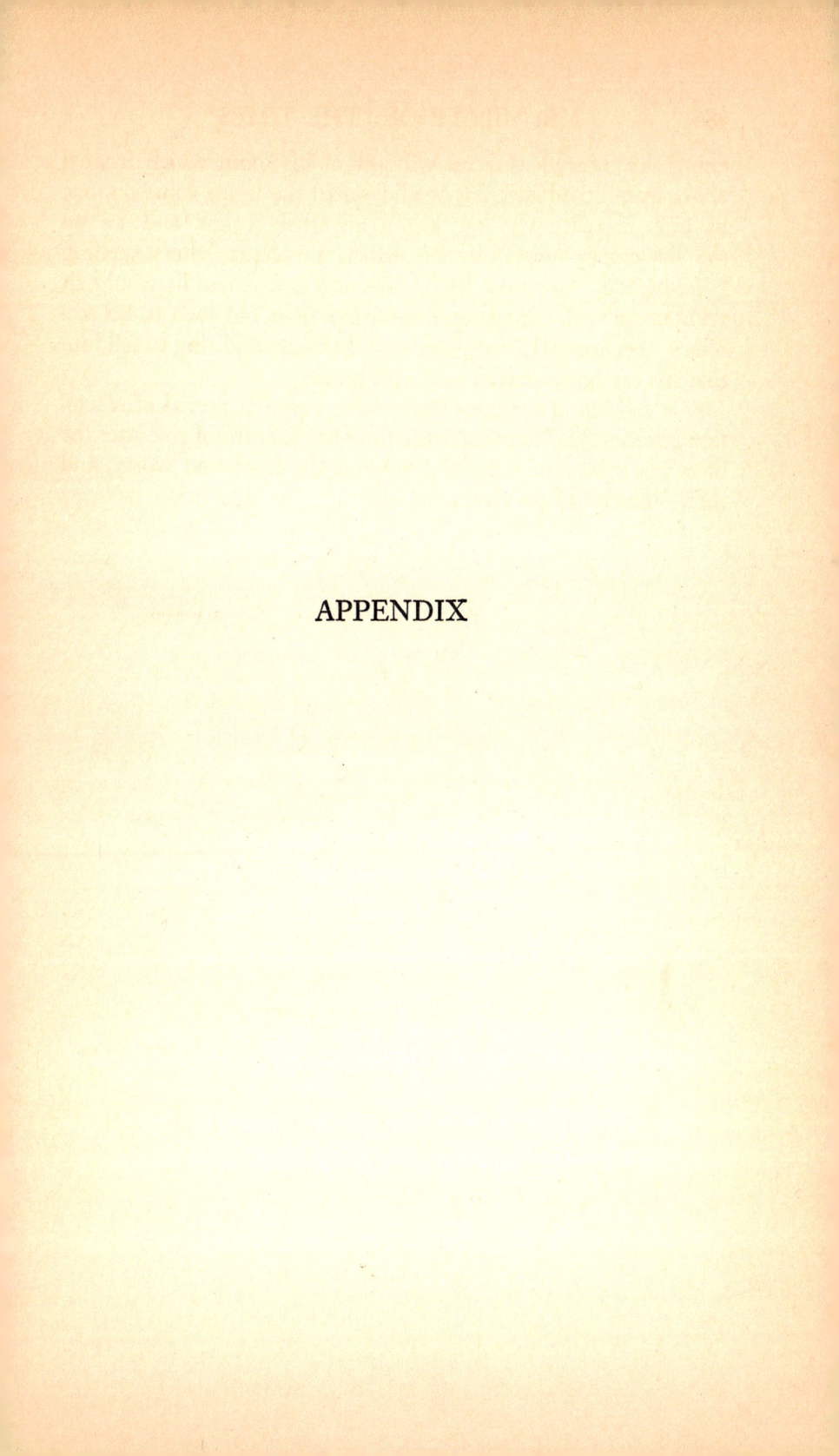

APPENDIX

APPENDIX

The articles selected for this appendix may well stand as a cross section of Mr. Miller's half century as a newspaper writer. Several of them were written in the regular course as editorials for *The Times;* some, like the paper on the Monroe Doctrine, were written at the invitation of other periodicals. Together they give a more adequate sample of Mr. Miller's work than the isolated quotations from his writings found elsewhere in this book.

Those interested primarily in the newspaper and in the editorial will relish the succinctness of his style; the historically minded will find metal more attractive in his handling of the several political themes and personalities; while general readers will turn with relish to find what the great editor had to say on such a topical subject as Socialism.

GROVER CLEVELAND AS PRESIDENT
New York *Times,* Tuesday, March 2, 1897

The best history of Mr. Cleveland's two Administrations is that written by himself. His messages and public papers furnish material for an estimate of his character, an understanding of his principles, and a judgment of the value of his services to the country. I do not propose in this article to review in detail the acts and events of his eight years in the Presidency, but only to consider some matters of public business, not yet out of controversy, in which he took such a part as to win distinguished reputation and the unremitting attention of numerous enemies. The Executive acts and policies which have provoked the bitterest opposition are those which make Mr. Cleveland so great a figure in our gallery of Presidents. They are necessarily the most interesting chapters in the story of his public service.

I

THE COVENANT WITH THE PEOPLE

This is a Government of law. That was the basis of Mr. Cleveland's covenant with the people when he entered their service. It has been the guiding principle of his two Administrations. To read his public papers and to study his acts is to be convinced that the intention to ascertain the law and to be guided by it has been always uppermost in his mind, the controlling force in his career. Fidelity to this supreme duty, as he conceived it, has cost him much. It has caused differences with respected party leaders who were in general sympathy with his purposes. It has completely estranged powerful Democrats who were able to deprive him of the support of great States and to turn against him their Members and Senators. It has provoked implacable enmities potent enough to obstruct or thwart his greatest designs and his highest policies. It defeated him in 1888—perhaps fortunately, for the country had no such need of him in the uneventful four years of Mr. Harrison's term as it has had since March 4, 1893. It has evoked a tireless defamation that has poisoned the minds of multitudes of his countrymen against him. It has separated him from the councils of his party, which presently plunged headlong down to dishonor, disruption, and defeat under the guidance of men who hate him. He might have lived a quieter life in the White House, with fewer troubles and not so many disappointments, had he been facile in compromises and less scrupulous about the exact performance of his covenant. But Mr. Cleveland was never a man who spared himself from love of ease. His stern soul has found a higher joy in writing messages of veto and rebuke in the solitude of the Executive chamber at midnight than in the approbation of politicians. It is a Government of law and he was its chief instrument. That was satisfaction enough for him.

That he should be a sound lawyer was of primary importance. That qualification he possessed. Those who doubted it in the beginning were convinced by the solid reasoning of his early veto messages, and especially by that almost defiant communication in which he denied the Senate's request for papers relating to suspensions of public officers, the famous "innocuous desuetude" message of March 1, 1886. That message showed some other qualities besides his respect for the law that come to the fore in every analysis of his character. It showed the rugged strength of the man, his firm confidence that he understood the people and that they would rightly understand him. "The pledges I have made were to the people," he wrote, "and to them I am responsible. I am not responsible to the Senate, and I am unwilling to submit my actions and official conduct to their judgment." On the part of the Senate this was purely a game of politics. The Republican Senators wished to force the President to admit that he was ordering suspensions and removals for political reasons. Some of the friends of civil service reform had serious misgivings about the President's position. They withheld full faith and credit from his declaration that "not a suspension has been made except it appeared to my satisfaction that the public welfare would be improved thereby." But those critics appeared to forget that in a public service made absolutely partisan by an unbroken Republican sway of twenty-four years a multitude of changes were demanded in the interests of the reform itself. The extensions of the rules made by Mr. Cleveland in his second term would not have been humanly or politically possible if he had not in his first term laid his firm hand upon the party machine which the Republicans had made out of the Federal service.

II

STRICT CONSTRUCTION

The most compact and satisfying exposition of the principles upon which he conducts the public business that I recall in Mr. Cleveland's utterances is to be found in this passage from his message of Feb. 16, 1887, vetoing the Texas Seed bill, authorizing a distribution of seeds in the drought-stricken counties of Texas:

"I can find no warrant for such an appropriation in the Constitution, and I do not believe that the power and duty of the General Government ought to be extended to the relief of individual suffering which is in no manner properly related to the public service or benefit. A prevalent tendency to disregard the limited mission of this power and duty should, I think, be steadfastly resisted to the end that the lesson should be constantly enforced that though the people support the Government, the Government should not support the people."

Protection, pensions, and silver free coinage, the three great domestic questions of policy in respect to which President Cleveland has been conspicuously aggressive, all fall within the scope of this clear pronouncement. Paternalism is the root of them all. The practice of asking the Government to employ its power or its funds for the advantage of individuals who make no return in public benefit or service is the abuse that Mr. Cleveland struck at in his tariff message of 1887, in his innumerable vetoes of pension bills, and in his sturdy and consistent opposition to the demands of the free-silver men.

III

THE TARIFF

The tariff message has been commonly set down as a political mistake. That view is justified, possibly to the understanding of those who still believe that Mr. Harrison was elected because of the American people's devotion to the cause of protection. But the sweeping Democratic victories of 1890 and 1892 disclosed the fatal error of that view. They vindicated Mr. Cleveland's judgment. But whether it was politically expedient or inexpedient, that message was an inevitable outcome of Mr. Cleveland's principles and sense of public duty. On taking office in March, 1885, he had pledged himself "to relieve the people of unnecessary taxation." In December, 1887, he expressed his conviction, ripened and confirmed by close study of the public interests: "Our present tariff laws, the vicious, inequitable, and illogical source of unnecessary taxation, ought to be at once revised and amended." Grover Cleveland was not the man to dodge the main question and appeal to the people on empty issues. The country was overtaxed $55,000,000 a year by its tariff laws that had been shaped by private interests for their own advantage. That was the condition. He and his party were defeated, but the thorough, systematic education of the people during the debate on the Mills bill and throughout the campaign destroyed the foundations of the protectionist temple and made it impossible that that edifice should ever be permanently reconstructed in this country during the lifetime of the voters who then first learned what the doctrine means and how many abuses it shelters. Mr. Dingley and his tariff tinkerers will presently discover how lasting are the teachings of that great campaign of education.

No disappointment of his executive career was so keen and disturbing as the fate of the Wilson bill, smitten by "the deadly blight of treason" in the Senate. Mr. Cleveland was always a Democrat. That party was the party of tariff reform. Every platform recorded its pledges, and these he affirmed by his own repeated promises, born of a deep conviction that protection had exceeded its privilege and become a burden upon the people. "Our abandonment of the cause," he wrote to Mr. Wilson, when the bill was ordered to a committee of conference of the Senate and House, "or of the principles upon which it rests, means party perfidy and party dishonor." "My public life has been so closely related to the subject," he wrote, "I have so longed for its accomplishment, and I have so often promised its realization to my fellow-countrymen as a result of their trust and confidence in the Democratic party, that I hope no excuse is necessary for my earnest appeal to you that in this crisis you strenuously insist upon party honesty and good faith and a sturdy adherence to Democratic principles." It was when the Wilson bill, mauled out of all likeness to its original self by the Senate, acting at the behest of private interests, deformed by over 600 amendments, and saddled with an unconstitutional income tax, had at length reached his desk that his just anger broke forth in the declaration that "the trusts and combinations—the communism of pelf—whose machinations have prevented us from reaching the success we deserved, should not be forgotten nor forgiven." Free wool was about all that was left of the bill. He could not sign it. But as, with many evil features, it promised to work some good, he withheld his veto and suffered it to become a law. Mr. Cleveland wastes no time in punishing his enemies, but he would have been less than human had he not taken a grim satisfaction in observing how Time's revenging cudgel has descended upon the heads of the men who then cheated him out of his triumph.

IV

PENSIONS

Mr. Cleveland ends as he began, by vetoing private pension bills. In his first term he vetoed 253 of these measures, and only the other day he re-

turned one without his approval out of the 700 passed by this Congress.
The unworthiness of the applicant, the want of merit in the case, defects of
proof, previous rejection by the Pension Bureau, and gross blunders of the
lawmakers, undetected in the reckless haste that rushes these bills through,
sometimes at the rate of one every forty seconds, have furnished justifying
reasons for the President's vetoes, but he feels that the immense labors he
has devoted to the faithful examination of pension cases have been substantially wasted, since he has neither checked the waste and misuse of public
funds by a demagogue Congress, nor opened the eyes of the people to the
consequences of this abuse of power. That Congress, like a drunken sailor,
should fling the taxpayers' money into every outstretched palm, and run up an
annual bill of expense for pensions exceeding the cost of maintaining the
standing army of a first-class European power, is a matter of grave concern. The $140,000,000 we pay out every year for pensions empties the
Treasury and deranges our fiscal affairs to a degree that shakes business confidence at home and abroad. It burdens the people with taxes and frightens
them with deficits. Our revenue is ample "for the needs of the Government
economically administered," but it is not equal to the drafts of a prodigal
and irresponsible Congress, and cannot be made so short of virtual confiscation. But the waste of public money is of inferior moment. The major
evil is the demoralization of public sentiment. The one is a surface wound
that time kindly cures. The other is a disease that preys upon the vitals
of the Republic. Nations perish of such corruptions. "The lesson should
be constantly enforced that although the people support the Government,
the Government should not support the people." We come back to the
principle of the immortal veto of the Texas Seed bill. The Government
should not support the people. President Cleveland sees how the obliteration of that principle by laws that extend the support of the Government
to a million pensioners without discrimination between the worthy and
the unworthy has broken down the self-respect and destroyed the self-reliance that have made American citizenship a birthright to be proud of.
Shameless beggary has become a pursuit in prosperous communities and
the auxiliary vice of perjury flourishes by its demand. What sustenance can
civic virtue expect, what permanent support can good government hope
for, from an electorate so largely debauched by the distribution of bounty
notoriously unearned? The greed it engenders but cannot content shows
itself in Ocala platforms, in schemes for loaning Government funds on
farmers' crops, in demands for unlimited paper money, in the appalling
total of six million votes cast for a debased silver dollar, in Bryanism, in
Socialism, and in the thousand hare-brained schemes devised by the vast
army of loafers whom pension extravagance has taught to believe that it is
a function of the Government to support the people. But protection is the
parent vice of all this brood. Before we had a pension list the system of
collecting tribute from the many for the enrichment of a few was in full
and triumphant operation.

APPENDIX

V

SILVER

When this Nation was within a few hours of a silver basis and a dishonorable bankruptcy, President Cleveland made a contract with J. P. Morgan and August Belmont for the purchase of the gold that averted the disaster. That timely measure and the fiscal policy of keeping faith with the Government's creditors, of which it was the most conspicuous act, constitute, in the minds of the business men of the country and of all enlightened patriots, his chief title to grateful remembrance. Detraction has wearied its forked tongue in the utterance of calumnies about the "secret bond contract." It saved the country. It was the only way to save the country. The men with whom the President and his Secretary of the Treasury dealt were the only ones equal to a transaction of that magnitude. There was no time for bond peddling. That was precluded by the suddenness and the alarming volume of the demand upon the Treasury gold. Bad as the actual situation was, a worse situation, the very worst, was to come, and come immediately. They knew that very well in Washington. The contract, or a suspension of payments—that was the choice. Mr. Cleveland chose like a clear-sighted and resolute man. After all, what do the unread slanders of a few newspapers that are malicious without being ignorant, and the echoing abuse of the Populist mob that is ignorant without being malicious, weigh against the President's immensely comforting consciousness that he protected the capital and the industries of this country against a panic and financial convulsion more devastating than any that ever visited it?

Upon the question of silver, the direful spring of unnumbered ills, the views and the policy of Mr. Cleveland have been sound, bold, and absolutely consistent from the first. He declared unequivocally in favor of stopping the coinage of silver dollars under the Bland act in his letter to A. J. Warner and his bimetallist friends, in February, 1885, before he was inaugurated. He repeated and urgently pressed that recommendation in his successive annual messages, up to the message of August, 1893, addressed to the special session convened by him for the repeal of the Sherman Silver Purchase act of 1890. His later efforts to stem the tide of delusion that has swept the Democratic Party far away from its ancient faith might have met with greater success had he been on better terms with the active leaders. Senator Gorman knew in January what Cleveland Democrats did not find out until May, that the Bimetallic League had won, and that the nomination of a free-silver candidate was assured. But there is some personal satisfaction in not being in the political confidence of Senator Gorman.

Mr. Cleveland stopped the purchase of silver, and so removed one menace to financial stability. By repeated sales of bonds he has maintained the gold reserve. He has not been able to break the "endless chain" that bears away the gold reserve whenever confidence is shaken. The retirement of the greenbacks and the creation of a sound currency system not depending on the Government for its working, though urged by him and by Mr. Carlisle, is a constructive task of high necessity which he is forced to leave to the genius of some future Administration, evidently not the one just now about to enter upon its duties.

VI

HAWAII

The Hawaiian monarchy was overthrown, the revolution effected, and the Dole republic set up with the active connivance of the United States Minister and under the protection of United States arms. "The duty of diplomatic representatives of the United States in foreign countries in times of insurrection is scrupulously to avoid interference in the struggle and to refuse to acknowledge insurgent authorities until permanently established." That is the rule and practice of this Government, a caution uniformly embodied in its instructions to its diplomatic agents. Minister John L. Stevens, Mr. Blaine's old friend and neighbor, was not restrained by any such principle. His correspondence with the State Department shows that he was in the secrets of the conspirators more than a year before the revolution. The United States marines from the *Boston* were sent ashore on his demand, at a time when peace prevailed, and no American life or interest was imperilled. The republic was proclaimed under the immediate protection of this armed force, and, disregarding the protests of the lawful Government, Minister Stevens promptly recognized it in the name of the United States. By an abuse of authority, "a great wrong had been done to a feeble but independent State." Ought not this wrong to be undone "by restoring the legitimate Government?" asked Mr. Gresham. The Washington end of the conspiracy was crushed at once by Mr. Cleveland by his withdrawal of the annexation treaty negotiated by President Harrison and sent to the Senate for ratification. In reviewing this disgraceful chapter of our diplomatic history, Mr. Cleveland expressed himself in strong terms:

"The President is satisfied that the movement against the Queen, if not instigated, was encouraged by the representative of this Government at Honolulu; that he promised in advance to aid her enemies in an effort to overthrow the Hawaiian Government and set up by force a new Government in its place, and that he kept this promise by causing a detachment of troops to be landed from the *Boston* on the 16th of January, and by recognizing the Provisional Government the next day, when it was too feeble to defend itself, and the Constitutional Government was able to successfully maintain its authority against any threatening force other than that of the United States already landed."

In private conduct the obligation to repair a wrong done to another is one which every honorable man recognizes and fulfills if reparation be in his power. It was essential to the preservation of our National honor and self-respect and for the overthrow of a dangerous precedent that the irregular proceedings of Minister Stevens be disavowed and their results effaced. Mr. Cleveland was keenly alive to this obligation. The performances of Stevens were lawless. The President was himself a devout respecter of law, and accustomed to exact respect for it of others, even when they did not like it. It was his wish and purpose to undo what Stevens had wrongfully done, to restore the legitimate Government, on condition that it pardon those who had been led into the insurrection by our interference, and to withdraw with honor from the wretched entanglement. But the Dole Government, grown strong and valiant in possession, refused to retire. President Cleveland could not employ force against it except by the authority of Congress empowering him to make war, and the Senate declared that the new republic should be formally recognized. The President's power and responsibility were at an end, and he turned the affair over to Congress, in which the mysterious interests that prompted Stevens's interference and gave such surprising animation to the annexation project have always been powerful.

John L. Stevens sleeps in his grave. But the Hawaiian annexation job lives, and has of late showed signs of fresh vigor and hope renewed. Under the new Administration the union of this remote and unassimilable crazy quilt of nationalities with our Republic may be accomplished. Time may make amends to the Hawaiians for our meddling, but there will be no moral justification of our acts. Meanwhile, the voluble assailants of Mr. Cleveland's Hawaiian policy can find no better defense of their own position than the reiterated assertion that Queen Liluokalani is fat, coffee colored, and not nice.

VII

VENEZUELA

The message of Dec. 17, 1895, asserting the application of the Monroe doctrine to Venezuela's boundary dispute with Great Britain was a peace message. Now that two arbitration treaties have come of it, that statement is easy and safe. But as I said it was a peace message when it was delivered, perhaps the accusation of parading wisdom after the event will not lie against me.

President Cleveland did not send that startling message to Congress on that Tuesday merely because it was a convenient occasion and the message happened to be ready. The time was not of his choosing. It was imperatively appointed for him by swiftly marching events. The boundary dispute was more than three-quarters of a century old. It had been in an active phase for a score of years. It had engaged the attention and enlisted the good offices of every Secretary of State since Mr. Evarts. It had been for months the subject of diplomatic correspondence between Secretary Olney and Lord Salisbury, a correspondence growing out of investigations undertaken in pursuance of Mr. Cleveland's resolve to ascertain what there was in the Monroe doctrine, and what duties it imposed upon this Nation and upon him. A conclusion had been reached, the correspondence had gone on leisurely enough, and the President's brief and calm reference to the subject in his annual message suggested nothing more than that an old international question was still holding to its slow course through the channels of plodding diplomacy.

Two weeks later this serene and academic situation was suddenly and completely altered. So far as the public knowledge goes, Friday, the 13th, and Saturday, the 14th, were marked by no unusual events or excitement in the Department of State. But the President returns in haste from a brief outing. There are conferences with the Secretary of State, prolonged through the entire evening. A syllabus of points and heads of discourse is drawn up and placed upon the President's desk. Mr. Olney retires. At midnight Mr. Cleveland sits down to write the special message. He has completed it at 4 o'clock in the morning. Accustomed as he is to long night labors, these are extraordinary hours. Plainly there is an emergency. The message itself left no doubt about that. The Monroe doctrine, it declared, "was intended to apply to every stage of our National life, and cannot become obsolete while our Republic endures." That was only a restatement of a position taken months before. There was nothing startling in that. But there was new matter in these three concluding paragraphs of the message that instantly arrested the attention of civilized mankind:

"When such report is made and accepted (the report of the commission appointed to determine the true divisional line), it will, in my opinion, be the duty of the United States to resist by every means in its power, as a willful aggression upon its rights and interests the appropriation by Great Britain of any lands or the exercise of governmental jurisdiction over any territory which, after investigation, we have determined of right to belong to Venezuela.

"In making these recommendations, I am fully alive to the responsibility incurred, and keenly realize all the consequences that may follow.

"I am, nevertheless, firm in my conviction that, while it is a grievous thing to contemplate the two great English-speaking peoples of the world as being otherwise than friendly competitors in the onward march of civilization, and strenuous and worthy rivals in all the arts of peace, there is no calamity which a great nation can invite which equals that which follows a supine submission to wrong and injustice and the consequent loss of National self-respect and honor beneath which are shielded and defended a people's safety and greatness."

Those words sound like war, but they insured peace. How can anybody who reads them with his eyes fully open fail to understand what had happened—or rather was about to happen? No gentle and ladylike remonstrance would have changed the course of proximate events. The ponderous executive fist had to come down with a thump that made people leap to their feet, and it did. The blow was heard and heeded. First, there was a British Blue Book, showing a decent respect for the opinions of mankind. Then there were negotiations. Now Venezuela and her powerful co-disputant have honorably come together in a treaty, and the long controversy goes to arbitration.

"But we were in danger of war, there was a panic, and Stock Exchange values shrank four hundred millions." Let the Stock Exchange think on its mercies. A war averted doesn't shrink values a tenth part as much as a war fought.

VIII

ARBITRATION

That the treaty of arbitration is a measure initiated and not achieved during his Administration does not rob Mr. Cleveland of the crowning glory of his career. It is a policy, as applied in this treaty, that originated in the broad and noble mind of Mr. Gresham. He could not have passed it on to an abler or more sympathetic successor than Mr. Olney. Nor have we had since Lincoln a President more heartily in accord with this lofty principle of advancing civilization than Mr. Cleveland. It is a lamentable state of things that has prevented the ratification of the treaty. Partisan jealousy of Mr. Cleveland among the Republicans and the old hates that have long been the sole springs of policy among his Democratic enemies in the Senate have together prevailed over a measure as to which delay was uncalled for and postponement a National disgrace.

IX

CUBA

A President who was seeking a popular party issue, something that would make a campaign "run itself," like a prairie fire, would have been under great temptation last Summer to stir up trouble with Spain as an excuse for giving the Cubans their freedom. Mr. Cleveland's notable lack of interest in the Bryan canvass was not his only shield against this temptation. He is not capable of perpetrating an international wrong to make party capital. At a time when there was much crying out for recognition and intervention, he found sure support for a different policy in law and unbroken National usage. Recognition of Cuban belligerency would have been a popular stroke, but it would have done harm to the insurgent cause and to our own interest. It would have been a reversal of the policy we have invariably pursued in recognizing new nations and changes of Government, since we have always awaited their firm and uncontested accomplishment, and would have been an act of open unfriendliness toward Spain which nothing in her conduct and no consideration of our public interests has justified. Mr. Cleveland deeply sympathizes with the aspirations of the Cubans. What accidents of fortune might befall them if his Administration were prolonged, with the chances of Spanish indiscretions, may be surmised from a careful perusal of his last annual message. But the occasion of just intervention has not presented itself. He has adhered strictly to the obligations of the Nation, and he has earned the grateful esteem of millions of his countrymen by his resistance to the reckless projects of the ferocious warriors of the Senate. As a defense against the Nation's internal enemies, a President with backbone is a boon.

X

THE CIVIL SERVICE

No President will ever become popular by reason of his fidelity to the principles of civil service reform. The brute mass of opposition which so often and so long beat back the pioneers of that cause has been overcome. The principle is established. It will stand. But it has not been set up and it will not be maintained because the politicians like it or because the masses of the people are much interested in it. The evident virtue of the principle and its efficacy as a cure for the spoils evil have put it into the law. Earnest men have worked hard for it, but you could not get a campaign mass meeting to hurrah for it with half the heart they would put into a three times three for a resolution to send warships to Havana. A President who carries the banner of civil service reform far into the enemy's country and plants it there is like a soldier fighting alone and in the dark. He may show great courage, he may achieve precious results, he may do his country rich service, but he will not fire the popular heart nor win plaudits beyond the sympathetic few who know what a brood of mischiefs he stamps out with every extension of the principle. When Mr. Cleveland visited New York shortly after his first election to the Presidency I said to him what was then in everybody's mind, that he had killed the sectional issue between North and South. The Republicans had raised that cry against him in 1884, it had failed, and they would never raise it again. They never have raised it, and it is a boon beyond price that by calling him to the Presidency the country has flung that ugly old bogey into its grave. But the burial of the sectional issue is hardly so great a service as the burial of the spoils system. The spoilsmen have not yet found out, they do not at all understand, how much their pasturage has been abridged by Mr. Cleveland. He has put them out of half their demesne. He has far surpassed the joint achievements of Arthur and Harrison in extending the application of the rules, and there are not enough classifiable places left outside the classified service to give any future Executive a chance to outshine him in this honorable distinction. By the original act 13,924 places were brought within the classification. During President Arthur's term 1,649 were added by natural growth, and in Mr. Harrison's Administration 8,690 places were classified by Executive order and 7,427 were added by natural growth, a total increase of 17,766 for these two Republican Administrations. During Mr. Cleveland's first Administration he added 7,259 places by Executive order, and there was a natural increase of 4,498 places. But since he came for a second time to the White House, on March 4, 1893, he has by a series of Executive orders, made such tremendous additions to the classified service that the approximate total of the places now under the rules is 87,107, against 43,447 four years ago. He has more than doubled the classified service, the increase in his second term being 43,660 places. The crowning act was the order of May 6, 1896, which swept within the protection of the law "every position to which the act of 1883 is applicable, with the exception of the fourth-class Postmasterships and minor positions specifically excluded." Practically "the entire executive civil service throughout the United States" was by that order put beyond the reach of the spoilsmongers. Of the 91,610 places not under the rules, 72,371 are considered classifiable, 66,725 being Postmasterships of the fourth class. A great branch of the public service in which the pay roll expenditure is over $100,000,000 per year has thus come to be administered throughout more than one-half its extent upon business principles, and it is to Grover Cleveland's courage and conscience and persisting fidelity to his strong sense of public duty that this marvelous reformation is chiefly due.

XI

PRIVATE LIFE

In retiring from the Presidency, Mr. Cleveland only nominally retires from the public service. His official example will be a continuing influence. His sense of the obligations of office as a public trust has been higher and more austere than that of any President since Washington. Future Presidents will hesitate to fall visibly below his standards of fidelity. But it is not alone by recorded example that he will continue to serve his countrymen. His great abilities and the wisdom of his long experience will be at their service for counsel. Mr. Cleveland is as young in spirit as when he first entered the White House, as ardent in support of good causes, and as energetic in his disposition to labor for their success. His active career as a patriot, an unselfish toiler for his country's welfare, and as a Democrat is not at an end. He takes his place as a private citizen, respected by every enlightened and unprejudiced American, with a record of public duty performed with conscience and ability that entitles him to recollection as one of the greatest of our Presidents.

C. R. M.

APPENDIX

THE MONROE DOCTRINE IN THE VENEZUELA DISPUTE

BY CHARLES R. MILLER

Century Magazine, September, 1913

Ex-President Harrison was very testy and Sir Richard Webster unmistakeably cross one cool afternoon in September, 1899, when I found a place among the spectators in the Hall of the Ministry of Foreign Affairs in Paris where the Commission of Arbitration in the boundary dispute between Great Britain and Venezuela was in session. General Benjamin F. Tracy was drawn into the area of unpleasantness.

"That is not a way in which I am to be addressed, General Tracy," said Sir Richard to the ex-Secretary of the Navy.

Sir Richard Webster was the chief counsel of Great Britain before the Arbitration Commission; ex-President Harrison was the leading counsel of Venezuela, and General Tracy was his associate. It was about the forty-fourth day of the proceedings. The ill temper of these great men arose from no national antagonism, no professional jealousy, for in that noble strife of minds each had come to hold in high respect the legal attainments of the others. But they had entered upon the eighth week of perhaps the most wearisome and uninteresting trial of an international cause of which the chronicles of diplomacy hold any record, and court and counsel were tired out and bored beyond expression.

Two years earlier I had sat in the President's room at the White House and heard Mr. Cleveland talk of the Venezuela boundary dispute and of his part in forwarding it to a settlement. It was in the month of February, 1897, two weeks before the expiration of President Cleveland's second term. A few days earlier, on February 2, 1897, Sir Julian Pauncefote, on behalf of Great Britain, and José Andradé, representing Venezuela, had signed at Washington a treaty of which this was the first article:

An arbitral tribunal shall be immediately appointed to determine the boundary line between the colony of British Guiana and the United States of Venezuela.

The signing of that treaty, of which ratifications were exchanged on the following fourteenth of June, was a memorable triumph for President Cleveland, for the Monroe Doctrine, and for the principle of arbitration between nations. For it was a message sent to Congress on December 17, 1895—a message which startled two worlds, that had brought about this agreement to arbitrate the questions in dispute.

In a two-hours' talk on that February day Mr. Cleveland had reviewed some of the chief acts of his administration, and I asked him to tell me, as far as he felt free to do so, the reasons that had called forth his Venezuela message. He spoke at length upon the subject, and with much freedom.

APPENDIX

Expressing in substance the impression his words made upon me, I wrote at the time as follows of the message and of Mr. Cleveland's part in bringing the dispute to a settlement:

"These words sounded like war, but they insured peace. How can anybody with his eyes fully open fail to understand what had happened—or rather was about to happen? No gentle and ladylike remonstrance would have changed the course of proximate events. The ponderous Executive fist had to come down with a thump that made people leap to their feet, and it did. The blow was heard and heeded. First there was a British Blue Book, showing a decent respect for the opinions of mankind. Then there were negotiations. Now Venezuela and her powerful co-disputant have honorably come together in a treaty, and the long controversy goes to arbitration.

"'But we were in danger of war, there was a panic, and stock exchange values shrank four hundred millions.' Let the Stock Exchange think on its mercies. A war averted does not shrink values a tenth part as much as a war fought."

It will be well to say in the beginning that the merits of the boundary dispute and the immediate results of the arbitration are not particularly under examination in this article. The finding of the Paris tribunal was a compromise. The extreme contentions of both disputants were denied, although those of Venezuela were abridged much more than the claim of Great Britain. But had England obtained at Paris every square mile of territory to which, in the ultimate stretch of her audacity, she had asserted right and title, the triumph of President Cleveland and of the Monroe Doctrine would have been in no wise dimmed.

The vital essence of that triumph lay in this, that under the constraint laid upon her by Mr. Cleveland's message of December 17, England submitted to a judicial determination of her title to territory which for more than half a century she had sought to wrest without due proof of ownership from a country too weak to resist her continuing encroachments.

"If a European Power by an extension of its boundaries takes possession of the territory of one of our neighboring republics against its will, and in derogation of its rights," said Mr. Cleveland in his message, "it is difficult to see why, to that extent, such European Power does not thereby attempt to extend its system of government to that portion of this continent which is taken," and this, the message continued, "is the precise action which President Monroe declared to be 'dangerous to our peace and safety.'"

For Great Britain to take territory on this continent before proving title was an act of which the United States by its President complained as "a willful aggression upon its rights and interests." Great Britain heeded the protest, yielded to our demand for a judicial examination and finding, and Venezuela had her day in court, and that, not the actual and precise position of the boundary line as finally traced, was the whole point of the

APPENDIX

matter so far as the United States and the Monroe Doctrine were involved in it. That was our triumph.

Historically, the dispute over the boundary between British Guiana and Venezuela dates from the discovery of America and the Spanish occupation. Following in the track of Columbus, who in his third voyage, in 1498, had sailed along the Orinoco delta, his first sight of the mainland of America, the Spaniards, early in the sixteenth century, had explored the country in search of gold. The El Dorado of fable was supposed to lie somewhere in the region between the upper waters of the Orinoco and Essequibo. By right of discovery, exploration, and settlement, for settlements were established later, the Spaniards gained the right to call Guayana their own, for that name was at first given to the South American shore of the Caribbean Sea.

There was in truth a store of gold in the land; the explorers carried stories of their new wealth back to Spain, and before the end of the sixteenth century Sir Walter Raleigh, with a body of English adventurers and certain Dutchmen, visited Guayana in quest of treasure. The Dutch West India Company planted a settlement near the month of the Essequibo about the year 1624, and was strong enough to hold it against the Spaniards, who up to that time had been in undisputed possession. The title of Dutch to the territory upon which they had established themselves was confirmed by the treaty of Munster in 1648, in which Spain recognized the Netherlands as free and independent states. Early in the last century England captured from the Dutch their settlements of Berbice, Demerara, and Essequibo, and in the treaty of 1814 these were formally ceded to her. Thus British Guiana came into being. On the one hand, therefore, Venezuela, when she revolted from Spain in 1811, became vested with the title to all the territory which Spain had held by virtue of discovery and exploration save the districts she had ceded to the Dutch; while, on the other hand, England held British Guiana by cession from the Dutch, who had acquired it from Spain by the treaty of Munster.

In that treaty Spain and Holland had not been at pains to draw the boundary line between Guayana, now British Guiana, and the Captaincy General of Caracas, now Venezuela, and from that act of omission arose all the trouble. For many years after England entered into lawful possession of British Guiana by the treaty of 1814 no dispute over the undefined boundary arose. With the running of what is called the Schomburgk Line in 1849 begins the unbroken chain of events that led to the boundary controversy, brought it to a critical stage, called forth the message of December, 1895, and culminated in the finding and award of the Paris tribunal.

In 1841 the British engineer Sir Robert Schomburgk was commissioned by his Government to ascertain and fix by metes and bounds the line between British Guiana and Venezuela. Then began Venezuela's protest, and then, too, began the singular migrations of the Schomburgk Line.

Lord Aberdeen abandoned it in 1844, but in 1886 it was laid down in British official publications as having a wide detour to the west, the British maps presenting to the eyes of the Venezuelans a startling incursion upon territory they had supposed to be their own by undisputed title. "The Statesman's Year Book" of 1885 stated the area of British Guiana to be 76,000 square miles. In 1887, according to the "Year Book," the area of the colony had expanded to 109,000 square miles. Nor was this the limit of the westward sweep of British pretensions, for in 1890 England obligingly consented to arbitrate her title to a vast tract of territory embracing thousands of square miles wholly outside the Schomburgk Line, and, a circumstance that has oftener explained than excused England's land hunger, including within its boundaries some of Venezuela's richest gold mines.

The protests of Venezuela and her appeals for justice became insistent. She demanded an arbitration of the British claims, and her demands meeting with refusal, in 1887 she broke off diplomatic relations. Our aid was invoked by her, and Secretary Bayard tendered our good offices to promote a friendly settlement. Great Britain firmly refused to arbitrate the question except upon the basis of an antecedent concession to her of a very large part of the territory in dispute, including the mouth of the Orinoco and all territory within the extended Schomburgk Line. Meanwhile the Venezuelans grew more and more uneasy as they observed the behavior of British war-ships in and near the mouth of the Orinoco, and the acts of British subjects asserting and exercising rights of occupation and settlement upon territory they held, and rightly held, to be their own.

This was the situation when Secretary of State Richard Olney addressed to Ambassador Bayard in London, on July 20, 1895, that letter of instructions which the British ambassador at Washington described as a "fiery note." Another British authority called it "Olney's hectoring note." Lord Salisbury, very much at his ease, and taking his time about it, replied to this note on November 26. He explained that "it could not be answered until it had been carefully considered by the law officers of the Crown." It may be recalled that Earl Russell, before making reply to the vigorous protest of our minister, Mr. Charles Francis Adams, against the fitting out of the *Alabama* in a British shipyard, referred the matter to the "law officers of the Crown." One of these learned gentlemen having unfortunately lost his mind, there was a delay of some days, of which the *Alabama* took advantage to escape the jurisdiction by putting out to sea. As the decision of the law officers, when tardily rendered, was that the ship must be seized, it would appear that England should lay the responsibility for the *Alabama* award of $15,500,000 that she paid to us upon the too deliberate working of her legal machinery.

Secretary Olney in his letter, which of course, Mr. Bayard was instructed to lay before Lord Salisbury, had embodied all the substantive declarations of the Monroe Doctrine, and in the very words of Mr. Monroe's message of 1823. The first fruit of the doctrine, he pointed out, was the independence of South America, for it was to the European Powers banded together in the Holy Alliance, and then preparing to assist Spain in the recapture of her revolted colonies, that Monroe addressed his warning message. Every administration since Monroe's had given its sanction and indorsement to the doctrine. It had been successfully invoked to put an end to the empire forced upon the Mexican people by Napoleon II, and now it was upon no general justification of interposing in a controversy between two other nations, but specifically upon the Monroe Doctrine, that we based our remonstrance against Great Britain's high-handed ways with Venezuela.

Great Britain's assertion of title to disputed territory, followed by her refusal to submit her title to investigation, was "a substantial appropriation of the territory to her own use," and we should ignore our established policy if we did not "give warning that the transaction will be regarded as injurious to the people of the United States, as well as oppressive in itself." "While the measures necessary or appropriate for the vindication of that policy are to be determined by another branch of the Government," continued Mr. Olney, "it is clearly for the Executive to leave nothing undone which may tend to render such determination unnecessary." This is the passage, doubtless, which provoked the epithets "fiery" and "hectoring." Those who ponder its meaning may feel that its words were at least ominous.

Lord Salisbury based his reply of November 26 in the main upon the familiar European contention that while the Monroe Doctrine is interesting, and may have had a salutary effect when first promulgated, it has never "been inscribed by competent authority in the code of international law," and that Mr. Olney's principle that "American questions are for American decision . . . cannot be sustained by any reasoning drawn from the law of nations." He reviewed the dispute with Venezuela, defended with many and plausible citations of authority Great Britain's procedure in the territory claimed by her, made a tart reference to "large tracts" of territory once Mexican but now a part of the United States, and firmly declined "to submit to the arbitration of another Power or of foreign jurists, however eminent, claims based upon the extravagant pretensions of Spanish officials in the last century, and involving the transfer of British subjects who have for many years enjoyed the settled rule of a British colony to a nation of different race and language, whose political system is subject to frequent disturbances, and whose institutions as yet offer very inadequate protection to life and property."

The substance and meaning of Lord Salisbury's despatch, and the attitude which Great Britain assumed, were set forth with conspicuous moderation and fairness by Mr. Cleveland in his Princeton lectures:

"These dispatches exhibit a refusal to admit such an interest in the controversy on our part as entitled us to insist upon arbitration for the purpose of having a line between Great Britain and Venezuela established; a denial of such force or meaning to the Monroe Doctrine as made it worthy of the regard of Great Britain in the premises; a fixed and continued determination on the part of Her Majesty's Government to reject arbitrations as to any territory included within the extended Schomburgk Line. They further indicate that the existence of gold within the disputed territory had not been overlooked; and, as was to be expected, they put forward the colonisation and settlement by English subjects in such territory during more than half a century of dispute as creating a claim to dominion and sovereignty, if not strong enough to override all questions of right and title, at least so clear and indisputable as to be properly regarded as above and beyond the contingencies of arbitration."

It was then that President Cleveland, patient, but knowing that patience has its bounds, loving peace, and willing to make the full measure of sacrifice to that high end, but with firm conviction that our interposition in the controversy was necessary and could not longer be delayed, sent to Congress the special message of December 17, 1895. That message fixed the attention of the civilized world upon the Venezuela boundary dispute, a matter which had up to that time held only small place in the thoughts of men other than the immediate official participants; for President Cleveland's plain words brought clearly into view the possibility of war—war between the United States and Great Britain. Christmas was at hand. At that season nobody was thinking of war, and war between the English and ourselves had long been held to be at any and all seasons unthinkable. The civilized world was startled; it is not too much to say that some men of large affairs and international dealings were stunned. "The crime of the century," was the phrase applied to the message by some whose alarm at the possibility of war was equalled by their ignorance of the long series of disturbing events which led Mr. Cleveland to perpetrate that "crime."

It was no crime; it was a saving act, a step that made for peace, and removed a source of long-standing irritation that was a menace to peace. The pen of Richard Olney was the one to set forth the legal basis of our demand —the pen of a great lawyer, not too much cramped by the circumstance that it was also the pen of a diplomat. Mr. Cleveland's strong hand was the one to write the words that proclaimed the Nation's duty. The Monroe Doctrine has never had a sturdier defender or a sounder defense. Lord Salisbury's amusingly English and almost sneering references to the doctrine as one "to be mentioned with respect on account of the distinguished statesman to whom it is due," but having no relation to the affairs of the present day, evoked that memorable sentence in Mr. Cleveland's message, in which he said that the Monroe Doctrine "was intended to apply to every stage of our National life, and cannot become obsolete while our Republic endures."

To the Salisbury argument that the doctrine must be ruled out because it has never been inscribed in the code of international law, "and cannot be sustained by any reasoning drawn from the law of nations," Mr. Cleveland replied that "the Monroe Doctrine finds its recognition in those principles of international law which are based on the theory that every nation shall have its rights protected and its just claims enforced." When we urged upon Great Britain the resort to arbitration, we were "without any conviction as to the final merits of the dispute"; we desired to be informed whether Great Britain sought under a claim of boundary "to extend her possessions on this continent without right, or whether she merely sought possession of territory fairly included within her lines of ownership."

Having been apprised of Great Britain's refusal of an impartial arbitration, "nothing remains," said the President, "but to accept the situation, to recognize its plain requirements, and to deal with it accordingly."

Mr. Cleveland, therefore, suggested to Congress an adequate appropriation for the expenses of a commission appointed by the Executive to "make the necessary investigation and report upon the matter with the least possible delay." Words of grave import followed this recommendation: "When such report is made and accepted, it will, in my opinion, be the duty of the United States to resist by every means in its power, as a willful aggression upon its rights and interests, the appropriation by Great Britain of any lands or the exercise of governmental jurisdiction over any territory which after investigation we have determined of right belongs to Venezuela.

"In making these recommendations I am fully alive to the responsibilities incurred, and keenly realize all the consequences that may follow.

"I am nevertheless firm in my conviction that, while it is a grievous thing to contemplate the two great English-speaking peoples of the world as being otherwise than friendly competitors in the onward march of civilization, and strenuous and worthy rivals in all the arts of peace, there is no calamity which a great nation can invite which equals that which follows a supine submission to wrong and injustice, and the consequent loss of National self-respect and honor, beneath which are shielded and defended a people's safety and greatness."

The commission of inquiry was appointed. It promptly began and industriously pursued its investigations for many months, the governments of Great Britain and Venezuela willingly contributing to the success of the commission's labors by placing at its disposal elaborate statements and all available evidence, while in the archives of Spain and Holland documents were made accessible that threw much light upon the remote origins of the controversy. But before the commission had finished its work, Great Britain and Venezuela, by the treaty of January 2, 1897, agreed to an arbitration. The labors of the commission were not in vain, however. It reached the conclusion that neither the extreme claims of Great Britain nor those of Venezuela were admissible, being unsupported by proofs of title, and the great mass of documentary evidence it had collected was of much use and value for the arbitral tribunal.

By the terms of the Pauncefote-Andradé Treaty, signed at Washington January 2, 1897, Great Britain and Venezuela agreed to the appointment of an arbitral tribunal "to determine the boundary line between the colony of British Guiana and the United States of Venezuela." The tribunal was to "ascertain the extent of the territories belonging to, or that might lawfully be claimed by, the United Netherlands, or by the Kingdom of Spain, respectively, at the time of the acquisition of the colony of British Guiana," in order to establish the chain of lawful title. Rules of procedure were prescribed in the treaty. Adverse holding for fifty years, or exclusive political control, as well as actual settlement of a district was to be considered as making a good title; recognition and effect were to be given to rights and claims resting on other grounds valid in international law; and such effect was to be given to the occupation, at the time of signing the treaty, of the territory of one of the parties by the citizens or subjects of the other, as the equities of the case and the principles of international law should be deemed to require. It was provided in article I that the tribunal should consist of five jurists. Those named on the part of Great Britain were Baron Herschel, and Sir Richard Collins of the Supreme Court of Judicature. Baron Herschel having died before the convening of the tribunal, Lord Chief-Justice Russell was named to fill the vacancy. On the part of Venezuela, Chief-Justice Fuller of the United States Supreme Court, and Associate-Justice David Brewer of that court, were named. The fifth member of the tribunal named by these four was Frederic de Martens, the Russian jurist, who became president of the tribunal.

The tribunal assembled in Paris on January 25, 1899. After various and necessary adjournments, it began the formal consideration of the case on June 15. After seven weeks of painstaking toil, in which the story of Spain's earliest search for the gold of the West, the terms of the treaty of Munster, the law and practice of nations in respect to discovery, occupation, and settlement, and an intolerable mass and multitude of documentary and legal details pertaining to each and all of these matters, had been minutely examined and expounded for the information, but certainly not the edification, of the five learned jurists sitting in judgment in the case, the evidence of nervous strain and irritation to which I have referred in the beginning of this article was apparent. On the forty-seventh day Sir Richard Webster sarcastically invited the attention of ex-President Harrison to certain comments of Sir Travers Twiss on the Oregon case. "I had read Twiss on the Oregon case through long before I had the privilege of seeing you," replied Mr. Harrison. "This investigation has been long and wearisome," said General Tracy, but he reminded the tribunal that it involved the "investigation of four hundred years of history." And on the fiftieth day Mr. Harrison, in closing his argument, said: "Counsel who addresses this tribunal comes to his work in a frame of weariness of mind and body, and he addresses judges who are weary."

It was on the fifty-sixth day that the tribunal announced its award. The true divisional line, as determined by the unanimous decision of the five jurists, gave sanction, as has been said, to the extreme pretensions of neither party. A large area west of the Essequibo River, to which Venezuela, without warrant, had laid claim, was held to be British territory; but, on the other hand, valuable tracts within the Schomburgk Line were awarded to Venezuela, the most important being the region of which the coast-line runs from Barima Point, at the mouth of the Orinoco, to Point Playa. The confirmation of the title to this territory, as to which Great Britain had firmly refused arbitration, gave Venezuela exclusive control of the mouth of her great river and of both its banks. The vast area, including the rich gold-mines, which Great Britain had belted about, by the audacious westward extension of her claims, went altogether to Venezuela.

Of the whole territory in dispute, far the larger portion went to Great Britain, and some few persons who uttered cries of distress over the message of December 17 counted this as a rebuke and rebuff for President Cleveland. That was the very hardihood of perversity in taking a false view. Mr. Cleveland had declared that our Government was "without any convictions as to the final merits of the dispute." The supreme, the vital point is that in the award of the Paris tribunal, accepted by both parties, law triumphed over force. The boundary line was traced, and titles with which Great Britain had vested herself by her own acts, heedless of the protests of Venezuela and rejecting her and our appeals for adjudication, were passed upon by an impartial arbitral tribunal according to evidence and the principles of public law. Whoever gained, whoever lost, that was quite immaterial from our point of view. The process of territorial expansion by stealthy encroachment, by unwarranted shifting of boundaries, and the alteration of maps and statistics, was at an end. The sovereignty of the lawful owner replaced that of the squatter. Venezuela was delivered from duress and from peril, no longer was her soil or her destiny under the menace of foreign control, and the situation created by the attempt of a power over the sea to extend the European system within this hemisphere, which Monroe declared to be dangerous to our peace and safety, and against which Mr. Cleveland had invoked the Monroe Doctrine, no longer existed. Mr. Cleveland had triumphed, the Monroe Doctrine had triumphed, peace had triumphed. General Harrison and Sir Richard Webster parted with expressions of mutual esteem, and the report of the proceedings of the Paris tribunal, in eleven folio parts, now on the shelves of the New York Public Library, was presented by the Marquis of Salisbury, while to Mr. Richard Olney was tendered not long ago the appointment as Ambassador at the Court of St. James's.

The consequences of this successful and momentous assertion of the Monroe Doctrine may now be traced. Three times within the century of its declaration the doctrine was firmly asserted and maintained by the United States as the public system of the Western World, for it may with entire propriety be called our public system, as the concert of Europe is the public system of that continent. First, when President Monroe proclaimed it as a warning to the Holy Alliance, plotting the restoration to Spain of her revolted colonies in Latin America. Second, when Secretary Seward's repeated protests against the establishment of an empire and an emperor, the Austrian Maximilian, in Mexico against the will of the people by French arms, were ominously reinforced by the despatch of General Sheridan to the banks of the Rio Grande with 80,000 disciplined and experienced troops, freed from active service by the ending of the war between the States, the French evacuation of Mexico speedily following. The absence of any mention of the Monroe Doctrine in Secretary Seward's correspondence in respect to the French adventurer in Mexico is without significance. The spirit and the principle of Monroe's declaration were the declared motives of his action. Third, when President Cleveland, by virtue of the doctrine "intended to apply to every stage of our National life," constrained England to submit her boundary dispute with Venezuela to a judicial settlement. The next application of the doctrine, the fourth in this series, all of primary importance, fell within the present century, when the substitution of the Hay-Pauncefote Treaty for the Clayton-Bulwer convention of half a century earlier dissolved our partnership with Great Britain in an agreement to extend a joint protectorship over any transportation route across the isthmus, and so cleared the way for the building and exclusive control by ourselves of the Panama Canal.

The Clayton-Bulwer Treaty was never popular in this country. It was entered into at a time, in 1850, when the discovery of gold in California, and the consequent tide of travel to the land of easily acquired riches, brought into view the need for facilities of transportation across the isthmus; and also, it should be said, when the responsible statesmen of the Nation were perhaps less mindful than at any other time since Monroe's administration of the import and saving force of the doctrine that bears his name. Nevertheless, the Clayton-Bulwer Treaty itself, after a fashion, a most illogical and inconsistent fashion, was on our part an attempt to apply the prohibitions of the doctrine against European colonization in this hemisphere. Great Britain was encroaching upon the territory of Central American States, and she stood in the way of the building of the canal. We negotiated the treaty to free ourselves from this embarrassment, and by that singular bargain, through the waiver of a right, we secured the recognition of a right; that is, we persuaded Great Britain to assent to Monroe Doctrine principles in Central America at the price of taking her as a partner in any undertaking for a transportation route across the isthmus, which was in itself contrary to the spirit of the doctrine.

The treaty of Guadalupe-Hidalgo, ending our war with Mexico, was signed February 2, 1848. By its terms Mexico ceded to us the territory now included within the borders of the States of California, Nevada, Utah, Arizona, and parts of Colorado and New Mexico. Great Britain strenuously opposed the cession to us of any territory on the Pacific Coast. Failing to control the acts of Mexico in that respect, she took measures in her own way to offset our great territorial gain. Six days after signing the treaty she despatched her fleet from Vera Vruz to the coast of Nicaragua, and forcibly took possession of San Juan at the mouth of the river of that name. She set up a governor, erected fortifications, and changed the name of the place to Greytown. This gave her command of the only canal route then under consideration, for it was at a much later time that the Panama route came to the fore as more practicable. The seizure of San Juan was a move so plainly hostile to our interests that our Government at once sent a diplomatic representative to Nicaragua, and a treaty known as the Hise Treaty was negotiated in June, 1849, by which Nicaragua granted to the United States "the exclusive right and privilege" of constructing a canal or railway between the two oceans across Nicaraguan territory. This treaty was not sent to the Senate and was never ratified by either country.

The occupation of San Juan, or Greytown, by the British, and their proceedings upon the Mosquito Coast of Nicaragua, where they had set up a trumpery Indian king, and by virtue of a "treaty" with him assumed a protectorate over the region, were a cause of growing uneasiness at Washington. In pursuance of her age-long policy of insuring her domination of the seas by occupying strategic points giving control of great routes of navigation, Great Britain had with a cool disregard of our rights and interests seized upon vantage-ground in Central America that would make her mistress of interoceanic communication. Holding Greytown, she was in complete control of any Nicaraguan canal, for the only practicable route was that which would make Lake Nicaragua and the San Juan River a part of the canal. Thus upon the one hand, our freedom of action in respect to a canal was hampered, and, upon the other, England, notwithstanding her many excuses and protestations to the contrary, was manifestly establishing a colony in Central America.

With a view to the removal of these sources of embarrassment and of difference between the two countries, Mr. Clayton, Secretary of State, pressed Great Britain to withdraw her pretensions to dominion over the Mosquito Coast. Her reply was a refusal, but an intimation was given that the British Government would be willing to enter into a treaty for a joint protectorate over the proposed canal. This was the germ of the Clayton-Bulwer Treaty, negotiated at Washington between Secretary of State Clayton and Sir Henry Bulwer, the British minister, and signed April 19, 1850. Article I of the treaty, here subjoined, is a declaratory and self-denying ordinance:

"The Governments of the United States and Great Britain hereby declare that neither the one nor the other will ever obtain or maintain for itself any exclusive control over the said ship canal; agreeing that neither will ever erect or maintain any fortifications commanding the same or in the vicinity thereof, or occupy, or fortify, or colonize, or assume, or exercise any domain over Nicaragua, Costa Rica, the Mosquito Coast, or any part of Central America; nor will either make use of any protection which either affords or may afford, or any alliance which either has or may have to or within any State or people, for the purpose of erecting or maintaining any such fortifications, or of occupying, fortifying, or colonizing Nicaragua, Costa Rica, the Mosquito Coast, or any part of Central America, or of assuming or exercising dominion over the same; nor will the United States or Great Britain take advantage of any intimacy, or use any alliance, connection, or influence that either may possess with any State or Government through whose territory the said canal may pass, for the purpose of acquiring or holding, directly or indirectly, for the citizens or subjects of the one, any rights or advantages in regard to commerce or navigation through the said canal which shall not be offered on the same terms to the citizens or subjects of the other."

These stipulations applied only to a canal route across Nicaragua in Central America, not to Panama. But we carried our spirit of complacent self-denial to a further and extraordinary length in article VIII. The first clause of that article is here quoted:

"The Governments of the United States and Great Britain having not only desired, in entering into this convention, to accomplish a particular object, but also to establish a general principle, they hereby agree to extend their protection, by treaty stipulations, to any other practicable communications, whether by canal or railway, across the isthmus which connects North and South America, and especially to the interoceanic communications, should the same prove to be practicable, whether by canal or railway, which are now proposed to be established by the way of Tehuantepec or Panama."

James Buchanan, then our Minister to England, in a memorandum for Lord Clarendon, written on January 6, 1854, referring to the relation of the Clayton-Bulwer Treaty to the Monroe Doctrine, said that while that doctrine would be maintained whenever the peace and safety of the United States made it necessary, "yet to have acted upon it in Central America might have brought us into collision with Great Britain, an event always to be deplored, and if possible avoided"; therefore these "dangerous questions" were settled by a resort to friendly negotiations. In view of the flimsy nature of Great Britain's asserted rights in Central America, and of the manifest unfriendliness of the motives that had prompted her to plant her flag, her colonies, and her forts in the pathway of communication between our Atlantic and Pacific coasts, it must be said that Mr. Buchanan's memorandum could not easily have been outdone in politeness. The sounder opinion, the opinion which the country has held and acted upon, is expressed by Francis Wharton in that edition of the "Digest of International Law of the United States" which he edited:

"For Great Britain to assume in whole or in part a protectorate of the Isthmus or of an interoceanic canal, viewing the term protectorate in the sense in which she viewed it in respect to the Belise and the Mosquito country, would be to antagonize the Monroe Doctrine; and for the United States to unite with her in such a protectorship would be to connive at such antagonism. The Clayton-Bulwer Treaty, if it were to be construed so as to put the Isthmus under the joint protectorate of Great Britain and the United States, would not only conflict with the Monroe Doctrine, by introducing a European Power in the management of the affairs of this continent, but it would be a gross departure from those traditions consecrated by the highest authorities to which we can appeal, by which we are forbidden to enter into 'entangling alliances' with European Powers. No 'alliance' could be more 'entangling' than one with Great Britain to control not only the Isthmus, but the interoceanic trade of this continent. No introduction of a foreign Power could be more fatal to the policy of Mr. Monroe, by which America was to be prevented from being the theatre of new European domination, than that which would give to Great Britain a joint control of the continent in one of its most vital interests."

The appearance of Ferdinand de Lesseps upon the isthmus and the public discussion of his canal project brought the possibilities of foreign control plainly into view, and public opinion in this country ripened into form and expression. "The policy of this country," said President Hayes in his message to Congress on March 8, 1880, "is a canal under American control. The United States cannot consent to the surrender of this control to any European Power or to any combination of European Powers. If existing treaties between the United States and other nations, or if the rights of sovereignty or property of other nations stand in the way of this policy—a contingency which is not apprehended—suitable steps should be taken by just and liberal negotiations to promote and establish the American policy." And Secretary Blaine in 1881 instructed Minister Lowell to let it be known that in the opinion of the President our treaty of 1846 guaranteeing to New Granada, afterward the United States of Colombia, the protection of the projected canal across the Isthmus of Panama, did not require reinforcement or assent from any other Power; and that any attempt to supersede it by an agreement between European Powers would "partake of the nature of an alliance against the United States, and would be regarded by this Government as an indication of an unfriendly feeling."

In a further instruction to Mr. Lowell, on November 19, 1881, Secretary Blaine stated at length the reasons for holding that the Clayton-Bulwer Treaty had become obsolete, or at least inapplicable to the conditions existing thirty years after its ratification, and he expressed the hope of the President that Great Britain would consent to such modifications as would remove every obstacle to our fortification and holding political control of the canal "in conjunction with the country in which it is located."

President Cleveland, in his first administration, did not approve the policy of exclusive American ownership, control, and guaranty, favoring rather a neutralized canal "open to all nations and subject to the ambitions and warlike necessities of none." But Mr. Gresham, Secretary of State in Mr. Cleveland's second term, expressed the "deep conviction" of our Government that the canal should be constructed "under distinctively American auspices." Secretary Olney, who succeeded Mr. Gresham, in a memorable communication rejected the argument frequently heard, that the treaty had been abrogated by Great Britain's persistent violation of the provision relating to her Mosquito Coast colony, and recorded the conclusion that if the treaty had now become inapplicable or injurious, the true remedy was "a direct and straightforward application to Great Britain for a reconsideration of the whole matter."

Thus, in the slow process of time public opinion was prepared and the way cleared for the ending of a joint protectorate agreement with Great Britain by the substitution of the Hay-Pauncefote Treaty for the convention negotiated fifty years before between Mr. Clayton and Sir Henry Bulwer. The time for action had now come. The French company was bankrupt, the commercial demand for a canal had become more pressing, and the voyage of the *Oregon* from the Pacific coast around Cape Horn to take her place with the blockading squadron that encircled the harbor entrance at Santiago brought vividly to the minds of the American people the vital need of a canal as a measure of national defense. Commissions were studying routes and making estimates of cost. There could no longer be any doubt that the two oceans were to be connected, and with all possible speed, by a navigable way. There was an obstacle—the Clayton-Bulwer Treaty. If we built a Nicaragua canal, we must forego "any exclusive control," and we must submit to the engagements of article V, that the United States and Great Britain jointly will "protect it from interruption, seizure, or unjust confiscation, and that they will guarantee the neutrality thereof." We must observe the further stipulation of article VI, requiring us to join Great Britain in inviting other nations to enter into the arrangement for the construction, control, and guaranty of this American canal. If we chose to build at Panama, we were bound by article VIII to make a new treaty with Great Britain for a joint protectorate over that route.

Never for a day after President Cleveland's Venezuela message would the American people have been in a mood to sanction any canal undertaking under these vexatious and impossible conditions. We were quite done with the idea of a joint protectorate over an isthmian canal. The resolve had been taken to build a canal, and the conclusion reached that it must be a canal of our own construction and under our exclusive control.

Most fortunately, we found the Government of Great Britain in an assenting mood. Indeed, the contrast between the rasping quality of Lord Salisbury's notes declining arbitration of the Venezuela boundary dispute and the candid, placable tone of Lord Lansdowne's correspondence in the negotiations that led to the superseding of the Clayton-Bulwer Treaty by the Hay-Pauncefote Treaty silenced, if it did not shame, those half-hearted Americans who had denounced Mr. Cleveland's memorable message of December 17 as "the crime of the century" and a menace to the friendly relations between ourselves and our kinsmen of England. Following President McKinley's message of December, 1898, in which he pointed out that the prospective expansion of American commerce and influence in the Pacific called more imperatively than ever for the control of the projected canal by the United States, Lord Pauncefote was instructed to acquaint himself with our attitude. He was informed that we desired at once to enter upon the necessary pourparlers, with a view to such modifications of the Clayton-Bulwer Treaty as would remove all obstacles to our construction of the canal, which it was evident would not be undertaken by private capital. To this Her Majesty's Government assented, and a draft of the proposed convention was handed to Lord Pauncefote by Secretary Hay on January 11, 1899. This convention her Majesty's Government, after due consideration, "accepted unconditionally as a signal proof," said Lord Lansdowne, "of their friendly disposition and of their desire not to impede the execution of a project declared to be of National importance to the people of the United States."

This was the first form of the Hay-Pauncefote convention, signed at Washington in February, 1900. Consideration by the Senate followed, but it was not ratified until December 20 of that year, and then with three amendments which proved to be unacceptable to Great Britain. As to the first of these amendments, declaring the Clayton-Bulwer Treaty to be "hereby superseded," Lord Lansdowne, in his memorandum of August 3, 1901, objected that no attempt had been made to ascertain the views of his Government upon the entire abrogation of the former treaty, which dealt with several matters for which no provision had been made in the new instrument; and with rather startling frankness he pointed out that if the Clayton-Bulwer Treaty were wholly abrogated, "both Powers would, except in the vicinity of the canal, recover entire freedom of action in Central America, a change which might be of substantial importance." That was enough to make the Senate open its eyes, for it was not exactly the purpose of our Government to confer upon Great Britain entire freedom of action in Central America.

The statesmanship and the diplomacy of John Hay found a way to reconcile these divergences and bring the negotiations to a successful end. He submitted a new draft of the treaty, providing by a separate article that the Clayton-Bulwer Treaty should be superseded, a method of accomplishing that important object more acceptable to Great Britain than procedure by Senate amendment. Lord Lansdowne's comment upon this article of the draft was that "the purpose to abrogate the Clayton-Bulwer convention is not, I think, inadmissible if it can be shown that sufficient provision is made in the new treaty for such portions of the convention as ought, in the interests of this country, to remain in force." The victory for American control and for the Monroe Doctrine was won. From that point the negotiations proceeded smoothly. Lord Lansdowne suggested the article, accepted by Secretary Hay, providing that the general principle of the treaty should not be affected by any change of sovereignty over the territory traversed by the canal. The question of our right to take measures for the defense of the canal presented no great difficulty.

To the first of the rules for the neutralization of the canal, as it appeared in Mr. Hay's draft, Lord Lansdowne suggested an amendment which served to bring into the clear light of day both our purpose to secure exclusively American control over the canal, and Great Britain's willingness to consent thereto. After the words "the canal shall be free and open to the vessels of commerce and of war of all nations," his lordship proposed to add, "which shall agree to observe these rules," and further on the words "so agreeing" after the clause declaring that there should be "no discrimination against any nation," and so forth. To this, Mr. Hay informed him, there would be opposition "because of the strong objection to inviting other Powers to become contract parties to a treaty affecting the canal"; and he suggested as a substitute for Lord Lansdowne's amendment: "the canal shall be free and open to the vessels of commerce and of war of all nations observing these rules," and instead of "any nations so agreeing" the words "any such nation." The difference was vital, for all connotation of inviting formal agreements with other nations disappeared. Lord Lansdowne at once accepted this form of the amendment, which he wrote, "seemed to us equally efficacious for the purpose which we had in view, namely, to insure that Great Britain should not be placed in a less advantageous position than other Powers, while they stopped short of conferring upon other nations a contractual right to the use of the canal."

The minds of the two governments had now met. The amendments proposed on each side, with the modifications noted, were agreed upon. The treaty was reduced to final form, engrossed for signature, and on November 19, 1901, Lord Pauncefote had the honor to inform the Marquis of Lansdowne that on the preceding day he had visited the State Department and had "signed the new treaty for the construction of an interoceanic canal." The Senate ratified the treaty on December 16, following.

Venezuela had opened the way for Panama. The hand withdrawn from broad areas east of the Orinoco had relinquished its lawful rights under the canal partnership, and in both cases at our instance. In the one, Lord Salisbury's noble British contempt of our demands and our doctrine forced us into an unaccustomed attitude of firmness. In the other, the Marquis of Lansdowne's open-minded, amicable, and statesmanlike disposition favored our interest, and left us free to give to the communication what had been the dream of centuries. We had expressly set up the principle of the Monroe Doctrine as the warrant of our interference for the protection of Venezuela, and Great Britain gave heed by submitting to impartial examination titles she had insisted upon enforcing as though they were beyond dispute. Ill-judged concessions contrary to the spirit of the Monroe Doctrine, made in the Clayton-Bulwer Treaty, we recalled by a substitute agreement with Great Britain which left us with a free hand for the construction and control of the canal as an exclusively American work. The vitality, the continuing and constant applicability, of the Monroe Doctrine, at every stage in our National existence, as Mr. Cleveland put it, could hardly be more conclusively demonstrated than by the record of the American Government's part in bringing about the agreement to arbitrate the Venezuela boundary dispute, and in replacing the outworn Clayton-Bulwer convention by the Hay-Pauncefote Treaty.

WHY SOCIALISM IS IMPRACTICABLE

BY CHARLES R. MILLER

Century Magazine, April, 1910

The enduring charm of the literature of Socialism lies in its complete emancipation from the thraldom of reality and experience. No cringing deference to the teachings of human history chills the ardor or cramps the inventive fancy of a Socialist when he sits down to draw up a programme for the reconstruction of society. He sets his foot upon the neck of authority, and blithely repudiates established truths worked out through centuries of toil and strife in the organization of institutions. The immense and enviable advantage of this free position is self-evident. It exempts socialistic theory and utterance from conformity with a host of tiresome axioms; it dispenses with research, it shuts out the confusing past, and enables the Socialist to soar with light heart and unhindered wing toward his ideal. This sense of freedom and detachment colors all socialistic writing, and must, I imagine, bring to the expounder of that faith a joyful sense of the perfection of his work rarely vouchsafed to toilers in other fields of authorship and exposition.

I am not sure that the Socialists ever attempt to picture forth, even for themselves, the actual conditions under which the socialistic state would take up and carry on its work. I have nowhere found such a projection of the programme of the socialization of industry and production. A balance-sheet of Socialism, a Socialist budget is a thing unknown. No Socialist writer has told us how much his ideal government would cost, or has disclosed to us the sources of its revenue. I shall try to put before the readers of *The Century* some of these missing elements of the problem. For a thorough test of Socialism it would be necessary to construct a sort of working plan of a complete Socialist government, and put it in operation. No Socialist will do that; nobody else will have the hardihood to attempt it. I shall merely set forth some of the conditions that would confront a Socialist administration in the United States, in the hope that the showing may bring into view certain matters of which Socialism has taken small account.

There are no canonical books of the socialistic faith and practice, no body of doctrine anywhere proclaimed that is in all its parts everywhere accepted by Socialists as orthodox. Of current writers no two are in such agreement that it is possible to quote one as an authority on the "faith and morals" of Socialism, save at the risk of being reproached for misrepresentation by most of the others.

There is, however, a collective pronouncement of Socialism in this country which we may accept as authoritative, and which may safely be consulted by those who wish to know what Socialism is and what the Socialists really propose to do. Everybody should know that Socialism aims at the overthrow of the existing social and industrial system, the abolition of capitalism and the competitive wage-system. Jaurès says that the proletariate, the wage-earners, and the salaried classes, have now an ideal: "They desire not merely to cure the worst defects of society as it exists; they want to establish a social order founded on another principle. For individual and capitalistic property, which assures the domination of a part of mankind over the rest of mankind, they would substitute communism of production, a system of universal social cooperation which would make every man a partner by right."

This embodies in general terms the ideal of European and American Socialists. We find these principles concisely set forth in the platform of the National Convention of the Socialist Party, adopted at Chicago, May 17, 1908, the platform upon which Eugene V. Debs made his campaign for the Presidency. Two hundred and nineteen delegates, representing nearly all the States in the Union, had seats in that convention. The conflict of so many minds and four days of debate ought to have prepared the platform to resist triumphantly the impact of the exegesis of the faithful and the criticism of unbelievers. From this seasoned exposition of American Socialism I quote the general demands to which the convention and the candidates were pledged:

GENERAL DEMANDS

1. The immediate Government relief for the unemployed workers by building schools, by reforesting of cut-over and waste lands, by reclamation of arid tracts, and the building of canals, and by extending all other useful public works. All persons employed on such works shall be employed directly by the Government under an eight-hour work day and at prevailing union wages. The Government shall also loan money to States and to municipalities without interest for the purpose of carrying on public works. It shall contribute to the funds of labor organizations for the purpose of assisting their unemployed members, and shall take such other measures within its power as will lessen the wide-spread misery of the workers caused by the misrule of the capitalist class.

2. The collective ownership of railroads, telegraphs, telephones, steamship lines, and all other means of social transportation and communication, and all land.

3. The collective ownership of all industries which are organized on a National scale and in which competition has virtually ceased to exist.

4. The extension of the public domain to include mines, quarries, oil-wells, forests, and water-power.

5. The scientific reforestation of timber lands, and the reclamation of

swamp lands. The land so reforested or reclaimed to be permanently retained as a part of the public domain.

6. The absolute freedom of press, speech, and assemblage.

In this new world where everybody is to have everything, it seems to me that, to many weary souls, the most pleasing prospect must be that of rest—rest from the endless arguing and contention that have plagued our statesmen and our politicians for a generation. Are not all these problems solved in the twinkling of an eye by this inspired program of social reorganization?

The regulation of interstate commerce would be consigned to the limbo where the Wilmot Proviso and the Alien and Sedition acts have been forgotten. It is inconceivable that collective ownership would wink at unholy rebates, or in any other way stoop to the chicane of favoring one shipper over another. There would be no watered stock—nor any other. Monopolies in restraint of trade would be made forever impossible—an amazing paradox—by combining all the "combinations" under one ownership. Complete desuetude would be the fate of the Anti-Trust Act. All the land being collectively owned, no reformer could fasten upon his neighbor the guilt of unearned increment. Although banks and banking are not mentioned in these "demands," the control of the instruments of exchange has always been insisted on by Socialists. That would inevitably come, and early. The Monetary Commission could rest from its labors, and turn over to the Socialist Secretary of the Treasury its accumulation of texts and documents; for which, we may be quite sure, that functionary would have no use. The Socialist fiscal and currency system would be simple beyond belief.

There might still remain subjects for discussion by statesmen, by legislators, by orators, and by the press, but they would be new subjects. The matters we now take with such entire seriousness would interest only antiquarians.

These "general demands" call for the acquisition by the Government of a great deal of property now in private hands, owned by individuals and by corporations. About the terms of the bargain, the price to be paid to present owners, the platform is as silent as the grave. The test-writers differ on that point; some say that private property is to be paid for, not confiscated. The Fabians, the so-called "intellectual" Socialists of England, have proposed that the British railways shall be purchased at a price reached by capitalizing their earnings on a four per cent basis; that is, the purchase price would be twenty-five times the average dividends for three years. Let us assume that the Socialists of the United States intend to make payment for the property conveyed from private to collective ownership.

We are now in a position to apply the first test, to picture forth the effects of Socialism upon the commonwealth, and to bring clearly into view the conditions under which the Socialist government would take up its important work. All lands, all the instruments of communication and transportation, all except the minor industries, all the mines and the forests, all the water-power and oil-wells, are to be acquired by the Government. Banks, as I have said, are not included in the list, but Mr. John Spargo, who was Chairman of the Committee on Resolutions, says in his book, "Socialism," that "a monopoly of the monetary and credit functions, including coinage, banking, mortgaging, and the extension of credit to private enterprises," belongs to the irreducible minimum of Socialism's demands. Now let us count the cost, so far as the elements of computation are within our reach, of achieving collective ownership and of setting the new Government upon its feet.

According to the last report of the Interstate Commerce Commission, the entire outstanding capital of all the railroads in the country—stock, $7,373,-212,323, bonds, $9,294,332,504—amounted on June 30, 1908, to $16,667,544,-827. The securities, bonds and stocks representing the capital of the Western Union Telegraph Company amounted to $138,462,100. Of the Mackay companies, which control the Postal Telegraph and Commercial Cable companies, and many others, the outstanding capital is $91,380,400, and the Cable Company has outstanding bonds to the amount of $20,000,000. The American Telephone and Telegraph Company has, of bonds and stock, $369,587,300. The telegraph and telephone lines, therefore, foot up $619,-429,800 of capital.

The resources of all the banks, State, National, and private, and of the trust companies in the United States, amounted on April 28, 1909, to $21,095,054,420. If Socialism assumed the liabilities, it would feel at liberty to take the assets, I suppose, upon payment to the owners of the par value of their shares, and of the distributive value of the surplus and undivided profits. That item would be $3,637,972,240. In banks having a large volume of deposits other elements of value belonging to capital might very properly be included. But bankers must not expect too much from Socialism.

The value of the farm-lands of the country, with the improvements, was determined by the census of 1900 to be $16,614,647,491. The value of the buildings and improvements cannot be separately stated, but it would be only a small part of this sum, and the deduction on that score would be much more than made up by the increment in farm values in the last decade. The real property in the twenty-eight principal cities of the United States was assessed for taxation in 1909 at $12,838,399,024. Assessed valuation ranges from fifty per cent, or less, to one hundred per cent of actual market-value. The unvalued and unassessed margin, together with the billions of land-values in the smaller municipalities, would easily swell this total to twenty billions, even after the deduction of the value of buildings and improvements. The "Statistical Abstract," using the figures of the census of 1905, puts the capital employed in manufactures in the country, not including hand trades and minor concerns, at $12,686,265,673.

No trustworthy estimate of the property value of the steamships, oil-wells, mines, and water-power privileges in the United States is accessible.

APPENDIX

The merchant marine, including sailing-vessels, reached the total of 7,365,-445 gross tons in 1908. The energy yielded by the streams of the country, turning 52,877 wheels, is estimated at 5,356,680 horse-power. The oil-wells produced in 1908 crude petroleum to the value of $136,347,831. The Standard Oil Company, with a capital of $98,338,300, does not own the wells the crude petroleum of which it refines. In 1908, other mineral products reached a total of $1,469,982,914. These properties are worth many billions of dollars. They sustain their fortunate owners, some in comfort and others in luxury. But there is no basis for an estimate of their worth, and we need spend no time in vain regret over this blank in the statement of accounts. We have assembled so many more imposing masses of capital that these items may properly be omitted on the principle of de minimis. In this account, as I shall show, a matter of a few billions more or less is quite negligible.

We may now state the account in tabular form, and give ourselves up to the pleasure of contemplating the total initial liabilities of the Socialist government:

Railways	$16,667,544,827
Farm-lands	16,614,647,491
City lands	20,000,000,000
Manufacturing capital	12,686,265,673
Bank capital and surplus	3,637,972,240
Telegraphs and telephones	619,429,800
Total	$70,225,860,031

How would the Socialist government settle for these properties, bought at such colossal cost? Only by issuing its obligations. There would be no other possible way. Thus we should come to the unchallenged primacy among debtor nations, with a debt of seventy billions. The present public debt of all the nations of the world is only thirty-seven billions. The largest debt of all is that of France, amounting to $5,600,000,000; the United Kingdom owes $3,880,000,000. The annual interest charge on all the public debts of the world is $1,550,433,038. At three per cent, the interest charge on the Socialist government's debt would be over two billions, or more than twice our entire national debt, and more than three times our total annual treasury revenue. Much more than half the wealth of the nation would, by the Socialist programme, be transferred from private to "collective" ownership. We may grant that Socialism would cut down "capital's" account. It would make large deductions for inflation in stock and bond issues. But, even on the basis of a fair "physical valuation," the total would not be materially diminished.

The reader who is in any degree familiar with fiscal theory and practice will already have reached the conclusion that, to the present owners of the property to be acquired, it would not make the slightest difference whether the Socialist government proceeded by purchase or by confiscation. No government on earth could give value to bonds representing a seventy-billion debt, nor could it keep up the interest payment, meet other public expenditures, and maintain its credit. But Socialists point to the revenue features of their programme, "extension of inheritance taxes, graduated in proportion to the amount of the bequest and nearness of kin," and "a graduated income tax." It ought to be unnecessary to point out that, after the government had taken over all the land and the instruments of production, transportation, and exchange, a great deal more than half the whole wealth of the country, the people would find it hard enough to make a bare living on the remainder in their hands. There would be no incomes for the levy of the tax-gatherer, no estates to be bequeathed. There remains the possibility of profit in the operation of railroads, factories, telephones, and telegraphs by the government. Experience in municipal trading here and in England shows that to be a delusive hope. The highest skill and trained capacity of private railroad management secured in this country in 1907–08 a net return of 3.9 per cent. on railroad capital, and in England, in the period from 1901 to 1905, the net return to capital was 3.38 per cent. There is no source from which the Socialist government could get revenue enough to pay its bills. Its bonds would be worthless, and holders of them could never hope to receive any part of either principal or interest.

It would be just as well. What use could they make of their money? No field of possible investment would be open to them. There would be no shares to buy, no corporations to organize, no city-lots to be bought, no farm-lands, not an acre anywhere left to which they could acquire title. Only the smaller trades and occupations, and those mostly co-operative, would remain for the employment of private capital. To abolish capitalism is the fundamental intent of the Socialists. On that all else depends. To achieve that, their "demands" are made. Mr. Spargo says that when these enumerated activities are undertaken by the state, "private enterprise would by no means be eliminated, but limited to an extent making the exploitation of public interests and needs for private gain impossible." Again: "It may be freely admitted, however, that the ideal to be aimed at, ultimately, must be approximate equality of income, otherwise a class formation must take place, and the old problems incident to commercial inequality reappear." To check this deplorable tendency, Mr. Spargo would provide that the inheritance of acquired wealth should be denied, "society being the only possible inheritor of property."

Here reappears the bland, engaging aloofness from unconquerable fact and conclusion. Socialists plant themselves firmly on the postulate that present economic conditions, the unequal distribution of wealth, are responsible for the differing conditions of men. The redistribution of wealth would make all men equal, all men happy and contented. The Socialists overthrow, by paying no attention to it, the belief somewhat widely held that it is the inequality in the capacities and in the ambitions, temperaments, and dispositions of men that have made economic conditions unequal, that have brought the reward of accumulations to the industrious and the thrifty, and have visited the penalty of narrow circumstances upon the improvident and the prodigal.

Plainly, the Socialist ideal is a social dead-level, an organization of society in which no man would have either the incentive or the law's permission to surpass his neighbor in effort or in the fruits thereof. That dream of a state of social perfection can be attained by an act of their congress. The bees appear to be Socialists. They are industrious, they seem to be happy and contented. But they long ago enacted that the honey-cell should be constructed in a certain way; and that, it happens, is the perfect way in the mechanical as well as in the economic sense. Since then, very naturally and sensibly, the bees have given up the idea of progress. Somehow, since

"Man never is, but always to be blest,"

he cannot rid himself of the idea of progress. It is an ineradicable propensity, and he clings to that idea and yields to that propensity in proportion to his ambition and to his ability. Some men are happy in the static condition; others find content only in change, and change always with the idea of advancement.

The chief of all the many unconquerable conditions which the Socialists ignore is the nature of man. But they cannot change it, for it is about the most unchanging and unchangeable thing within our knowledge. Death alone—the death of all men, and the arrest of all organic forces—can bring about the ideal dead-level of Socialism. Mr. Herbert Spencer assures us that one of the laws of the vital universe is "the instability of the homogeneous," which may be transmuted into the homelier phrase, "the cream will rise upon the milk." Organic matter is never inert, and human society is only an organism. Socialism cannot annul the laws of its existence, paralyze its energies, or blast with sterility every atom and cell of its being, by decreeing that the government shall own the railroads, the farms, and the factories. Brains, industry, capacity, foresight, would assert themselves in a Socialist state as in any other, and laziness and improvidence would bring want and dependence, as they now bring and always have brought them. The Socialist state, even if it were possible to establish it, would tear itself asunder. Living men would dissociate themselves from the body of death.

Yet the doctrines of Socialism are taught to adults and to children in many schools established and maintained by Socialists in New York City, and in many other cities and States. Picture primers, reading-books, songs, little plays, serve to instil the abhorrence of capitalism and the present social order into infant minds, and into older ones as well. The doctrines are preached from pulpits and from the chairs of professors. In no Socialist writing that has ever come under my observation has any attempt been made to count the cost of collective ownership, or to show how the bill would be paid. Any candid inquiry into the problem leads to but one conclusion—that the bill would not and could not be paid at all. Collective confiscation must necessarily precede collective ownership.

We may therefore ask by what means the owners of half the national wealth are to be made to part with it for the common behoof. Evidently not by persuasion. Nothing in human experience, nothing in history, supports the theory of voluntary surrender. The Socialists say that the change is to come with the ballot. Socialist lawmakers, executives, and judges will accomplish the desired expropriation, paying no heed, of course, to the outcries of the despoiled. Armed revolution is no longer very much preached save by a fiery agitator here and there, and by those passionate declaimers, newly come to our shores, who bring with them the ardor of Continental Socialism. And they, it seems to me, are the only consistent Socialists, the only ones who really know what they want.

Socialists who have thought much about the adaptation of means to ends long ago came to understand that revolution by force was out of the question, because, as Karl Kautsky puts it, "of the colossal superiority of the weapons of the present standing armies, as compared with the weapons in the possession of civilians, which makes any resistance of the latter patently doomed to failure from the beginning." Is it not natural, therefore, that Kautsky should insist that "the abolition of the standing army and disarmament is indispensable, if the State is to carry out any important reforms"? Far above the great volume of Socialist utterance, that remark shines by the quality of consistency.

There is no antidote to Socialism. It was born in man when he first fought over the spoils of the chase and raged against his sturdier cavemate who seized the larger share. But there are checks and palliatives. A clear understanding of what Socialism means and what it seeks to do will tend to arrest the spread of its doctrines, now furtively making their way to a broader acceptance among dreamers and visionaries and children, and, above all, among those who are altogether uninformed as to what Socialism is. It is well, therefore, that there should be a clear understanding that the Socialist government would begin, must begin, by wholesale confiscation of property.

The palliatives are being administered all the time in every civilized land, by the action of public opinion upon the makers of the laws. A study of the legislation of the last century in this country and in England for bettering the hard conditions of toil, for the prevention of "man's inhumanity to man," for establishing the rights of wage-earners, and setting up safe-guards for them against oppression, extortion, injustice, and disease, for better housing, for schooling, for the relief of the needy, and importing heart and human feeling and conscience into a relation that, a hundred years ago, was based upon the relentless law of supply and demand which regulates the commodities market, would put into the heads of the theologians, the professors, the charity-workers, and the fashionable ladies who are dabbling in Socialism, a fund of knowledge which they now lack. They would learn that, under the existing social order, under our institutions as now established, through the working of public opinion, and by the orderly process of law, the evils of which Socialism justly complains are curable and being cured.

DEMAND AND SUPPLY IN LITERATURE

Address delivered before Goethe Society
February, 24, 1890

BY CHARLES R. MILLER

The terms Demand and Supply, I am aware, pertain rather to the operations of the corn market than to the relations of authors to publishers and to the public, and I confess that I have had some misgivings lest the theme of my discourse might offend the strict constructionists of this literary guild. If I were summoned before the Council of the Goethe Society to justify this intrusion of the sordid terminology of exchange into the purer realm of letters, I might find myself in some perplexity, and possibly I should emerge from the examination under merited censure for having attempted to degrade the rich fruit and golden grain of the imagination to the level of those coarser commodities which, in the phraseology of World's Fair bills, are comprehensively described as "products of the soil, the mine, and the sea." Shall we decree that the laws of trade are to have equal respect in the republic of letters? Shall we employ there the brisk demand for medium to light grades of novels, nominal quotations for prime poetry, and nothing doing in theology? Shall we ask the scholar to turn aside from the lofty meditations of his cloister and consult the literary price current before he decides to write a book? No, it is not quite that. We will not go so far toward a purely materialistic conception of the profession of authorship. I propose only to make a candid survey of the phenomena of exchange between author and reader, and to make it not as an offensive dogmatist, but in a spirit of an inquirer.

In truth, whoever takes the pains diligently to compare the calling of the author with the calling of the merchant will most likely become convinced that there are more points of difference than of likeness; that the complex machinery of trade has no analogue in the simple process by which the progeny of one brain becomes the property of another, and any attempt to formulate commercial laws for literary products must end in failure and confusion. We may frankly admit that some of the most familiar laws that govern the production and distribution of material commodities are inapplicable to the literary calling. Yet if any such laws are of force and effect in literature, it is worth the literary man's while to inquire what they are and how their operation may affect him and his work. That is as far as we need carry the inquiry.

About the first thing we discover is that demand is not the tyrant in literature that it is in trade. In the markets where natural and industrial products are dealt in there may at all times be what the political economists call an effective demand—that is, a demand that gets itself satisfied. At some price or other, higher or lower, the stores of supply are unlocked and the corn, or the iron, or the manufactured products begin to flow in. The products of the author's fancy are not of this obedient temper. Minds capable of creative work, of noble and lasting work, are subject to no outer command of enticement. The flame of inspiration that produced Milton's "Paradise Lost" was kindled by an inward spark and it burned steadily in his bosom for thirty years, through a time of tumult and revolution, when his countrymen were in no mood to concern themselves about epic poetry. It was an inward impulse even more potent and lasting that moved Goethe to express his philosophy of life in "Faust" begun at the age of twenty-five and completed at eighty. Poets of this eminence writing, as Channing puts it, with the conscious dignity of prophets, respond only to the stimulation of their own genius; exterior demand, in the commercial sense, they neither feel nor obey. For epic poetry, indeed for all great literary work, there is no conscious demand. The world does not call for it, asks no man to produce it. It cannot get epics written to order. In the humbler walks of literature, however, or, to employ Mr. Lowell's distinction, in respect to mere printed matter as distinguished from literature, there is such a thing as an effective demand. It is constant, voracious, insatiable. Yet so prodigious is the fertility of printed-matter minds that the supply ever outruns the demand and the equilibrium of exchange must at stated intervals be artificially restored by the deportation of unsold remainders from the booksellers' shelves to the vats of the paper maker.

And here, no doubt, we encounter the profoundest problem that my theme can suggest, a problem of pathetic interest to every inquiring mind, one which countless philosophers and men of letters have striven to solve, hopelessly striven, until, the quest abandoned, the philosophers have become cynics and the men of letters misanthropes. Why is it that the greater part of humanity is content with bad books when good books are just as cheap? That is a blunt, mercantile way of putting the question, but it is best put so. No man or woman, however poor or ignorant, will buy unwholesome provisions when wholesome provisions can be had for the same money. No man buys a deformed or vicious horse if he knows that a well-shaped and gentle animal may be bought at a price no greater. No farmer or gardener will buy for the cultivation of his soil an inferior and worthless instrument if in the same shop and at the same price he may buy an instrument perfect in design and construction. Then, why, in the purchase of books, does so discouragingly large a part of mankind display a blind, headlong, incorrigible liking for the unwholesome, the deformed and vicious, the inferior and worthless? Why is the privilege of discovering the mint-mark of genius reserved for the slender minority having sensibility and understanding, while a spurious coinage attains undetected the widest currency among the mass? If, upon each of our public news stands, where the throngs pass daily, there should be placed to-morrow fifty copies of a novel by some new and unheralded Thackeray, with such a sober title as Thackeray must choose for his novels, side by side and at an equal price per copy with fifty copies of a new work of fiction pumped out of the well-nigh inexhaustible springs of Mr. Rider Haggard's fancy, or bearing, we will say, a name altogether unknown, subjoined to a title suggestive of ill-regulated passion upon a page bearing a picture of a young woman insufficiently clad in an unadvisable attitude—if this free choice between the good and the bad in literature were offered, does any informed and candid person doubt or deny that the public with the utmost alacrity would seize upon the bad and eschew the good? The woman who goes with a shawl and basket to the butcher's or to the green grocer's for her day's supplies, inspects with an awakened and instructed judgment the wares displayed before her, wary of defects and exigent of good measure. The woman's daughter, freed at dusk from the bondage of the shop counter, approaches a curbstone literary emporium where our twin piles of books lie displayed, and without a moment's hesitation pounces upon Mr. Haggard and deigns not to honor even with a glance the undiminished stock of the new genius's work. Later on, to be sure, a month, a year, or ten years, or it may be when our man of genius, after an inexpensive and sparsely-attended funeral, had been laid to rest, the book of the sober title and glowing pages comes to its own, is read by everybody, gets unstinted praise, and perhaps like Don Quixote, becomes a book "to which the slightest allusion may be made without affectation, but not missed without discredit"; while Mr. Haggard and the young woman of passion have long since gone to swell the rubbish heap in wide Oblivion. Infallibly time brings this revenge to neglected genius—the mere printed stuff goes down to dusty death, while genius always and invariably gets itself recognized and comes sooner or later into its estate. There is sweetness and joy in this revenge if only genius can wait for it, if only it can keep the pot boiling meanwhile. But in the making of this late though unfailing distinction between printed matter and literature, the great mass only follow where the perspicacious few have led. Just as all the minor watchers of the skies find and admire the new planet, when the astronomer with the great telescope has announced its position, so the uncounted thousands of the reading public hasten to peruse and praise the book that has received the approving stamp of critical and authoritative opinion. Sometimes, as in the case of "Waverley" and the other tales that Scott put forth in that prodigious rush of composition, the great reading public presses hard upon and is almost abreast of the illuminati; more often, as with nearly everything that Milton wrote, it lags miles behind and accords only a late recognition.

The judicious find in this state of things a double grief—that good and worthy literary workmanship should find only tardy appreciation and a deferred reward, and that the mass of the reading public should voluntarily abase and harm itself with books that, when not positively vicious, have neither excellence in art nor truth to nature to commend them.

The clamorous demand for reading for immediate consumption is not less fierce in its assaults or harmful in its influence upon the periodical and newspaper press than in the field of literature proper. It is a disputed point between the austere censors and the defiant corrupters of the press whether the impulse which leads to the printing of scandals and sensational news originated with the public or with the press; whether reading man, being born in sin and desperately wicked, demanded this objectionable matter of his editors and publishers, and with a high hand and the allurement of gain compelled them to furnish it, or whether the crafty and covetous men of the press, foreseeing large circulations and resulting fortunes in the enterprise, have created this demand, beginning in a small way with inconspicuous trifles of unrighteousness and going on with calculated steps from paragraphs to pages until they have insidiously and with incredible patience and industry built up a wholly new department of human depravity. Personally I think the question not worth discussing, since the conductors of the press, like the readers of the press, are a part of fallen humanity. A person who habitually buys and reads a scandal-mongering newspaper would, if he should become an editor and publisher, make just that kind of newspaper himself. It must be remembered that a very considerable part of mankind is vulgar, tasteless, stupid, and unscrupulous. So long as this continues to be the case some men will write bad books and other men will read them; some men will preach dull sermons and other men will uncomplainingly listen to them; some men will make adulterated bread and other men will eat it, and some men will publish pernicious newspapers and thousands of other men will read them.

Nevertheless, no one will pretend that any newspapers have gone so far as some novelists and versemakers in disregarding the decencies and proprieties of life, or that they are chargeable with anything like the same degree of moral harm to the community. There may be editors shameless enough to seek to make vice attractive in their reports of its ravages, but they are commonly balked in their designs by the happy faculty their reporters have of adding to the frightful mien of the monster the new terrors of their own literary style. The journalists who engage in this class of work are usually not the most gifted beings or the most cultivated of their calling, while the novelists of the extreme naturalistic school have oftentimes unusual gifts of mind and a dangerously fascinating style. They permit themselves moreover, or society permits them, to make minute analytical studies of the subjects that the press, even as represented by its worst examples, can but vaguely touch upon. The worst vice of the sensational newspapers, I am convinced, is the utter emptiness and triviality of much of the matter that occupies their columns. It gives no information, it teaches no lesson, it is of no sort of consequence to any human being, and it is so entirely void of meaning and purpose that shallow minds grow only the more vacuous by feeding on it. There are so many shallow minds, however, that editors who will stoop to it drive a roaring trade in supplying their needs. But it is an unequal compact. The readers get nothing for their money, or nothing of equivalent value, and they are always finding this·out, so that whatever of prosperity may for a time attend a venture in sensational journalism it cannot be said that the business offers a return sufficiently assured to compensate a man to whom any honorable calling is open for all that he must abjure in entering upon it.

Since I may be reminded that, because in a briefer utterance before the Goethe Society some time since I asserted that newspapers were not literature, and gave my grounds for the assertion, I must now be held to have wandered from my subject, I ought to say that in the observations I have made and have yet to make about the periodical and newspaper press, I wish only to illustrate the operation of the laws of demand and supply that have wrought in literature the effects I have pointed out. Their rule extends wherever ink, types, and paper are brought together. In obedience to them reviews and magazines, both in this country and in England, have visibly changed within the memory of persons not yet grown to manhood. Their managers have taken rapid strides toward the popularization or, toward the vulgarization of their contents. The illustrated monthly magazines were never artistically so beautiful as now, and in respect to that quality they have made a notable advance; but if they are not practically devoid of literary value they have at least made no such progress in that department as in the art of illustration. Engravings that are the admiration of their readers, and until surpassed in the hot competition are the despair of their rivals, patches and catches of verse that may be read at a glance as the pages are turned, bright but sketchy articles upon subjects of transient and trivial interest, such as befit rather the quick gait of the daily newspaper than the deliberate pace of a monthly magazine, tales, and serial novels that with some welcome exceptions are of too slight a texture to bear with safety translation to the covers of a book—these make up the substance of the repast which the reader of the magazine finds set before him. Let me, one of a calling over whose shortcomings the editors of these monthly picture books have dropped tears fast as the Arabian trees their medicinal gum, lift up this wail at the intellectual and literary pauperism of the magazines.

How fast the process of popularizing a review may go on we know from repeated examples. Within my recollection there have existed in this country, and even in this commercial city, reviews whose contents might fairly claim to be literature—at least on this ground, if on no other, that they were indigestible and might defy the erosive tooth of time. I can recall one quarterly that discussed with unflagging spirits the meters of Pindar, and once or twice a year chased the ancient Aryans quite over the tops of the Himalayas to an original home which subsequent and more enlightened investigation has shown never could have been their home. I have no doubt that the review gave joy to some lone scholars here and there, and I have the impression that at one time it numbered among its corps of contributors men whose names stand upon the roll of literature. For reviews of that type, indeed for reviews or periodicals of whatever kind that are, in the main, made up of articles interesting to scholarly minds or having some claims to permanent literary value, there is but a narrow field in this country. The meters of Pindar, the homes and habits of the Aryans, and all that class of articles which our fathers called the "higher" and we call the "heavier" writing, have been banished from the pages of our reviews, repeated bankruptcies having proved, with the certainty and the remorselessness of a mathematical demonstration, that there was no demand for them. The reviews of today reek with actualites. Their editors seek out topics that are piping hot in popular interest, put them into the hands of men who are eminent, prominent, or notorious in some walk of life, little matter what one, and at the end of the month lay before their readers a publication that throbs with timeliness and pushes the sensational newspapers a hard race for the first place in the business of supplying diverting reading matter for idle moments. Reviews of this class, like almanacs, perish with the issue of the next number. The writing that fills them is in the main argumentative, the writers are politicians and partisans, professional contenders, the themes are the day's or the afternoon's burning questions. In the nature of things, the burning questions burn themselves out, the contenders seek some fresh dispute, the arguments are presently forgotten, and last month's review, wrapped in yesterday's newspaper, goes with other refuse of the immediate consumption habit at one cent a pound to the junkman.

Some few persons predisposed to gloom and retrospection now and then break out into lamentation over this tendency of the reviews toward assimilation in matter and method with the daily newspapers. But why should any review editor waste and impoverish himself in producing unsalable wares? Why should he continue impertinently to thrust before the public what the public does not want to buy and would not accept gratis? In England, as in this country, the reviews of that old-fashioned kind to which a livelier generation has given the title of "The Heavies" have been kept alive for years by a kind of artificial respiration, the editors paying the contributors nothing, or perhaps paying a few of them next to nothing, and the proprietor contentedly drawing his check for the monthly deficit, proud of the distinction of being a patron of the higher literature. That sort of thing is grossly irrational. From a business point of view it is less defensible than intelligently-directed burglary, and from any point of view, moral, social, or literary, it is futile. It is an insult to ask a professional man of letters to write without payment; it is larceny to ask a review editor to serve for a pittance and expectations; and the man who owns the company which continues to issue a review or any other publication that is hopelessly incapable of paying its way is a fool. A literary enterprise that cannot be established and maintained on a business basis does the cause of literature no service. It is worthless as a standard, misleading as an example, and deserves to die. We will grant, if you please, that this world would be more beautiful and agreeable if a great many more of its people were habitual readers of reviews of the highest order of merit. But that is another question. We are considering this world as it is. We cannot materially change it by spending our substance in the publication of reviews which it will not buy. The experiment has been tried and it has failed miserably. Moreover, it is well, I think, for men of letters to take a just account of their part in the world's work, and of the relation of that part to the whole. There should be no conceit or extravagance in estimating the place of literature. Mr. John Morley has aptly described taste as one of the most serious of the world's superficial interests. Literature is a serious interest, it is a beneficent and ennobling force, but it is not fundamental, it is not vital. In the relentlessly-logical order of nature the vulgar bread-and-butter arts take precedence over it. In times of peril to the individual or to the body politic the impulse that produces it is stilled, the taste that calls for and enjoys it is suspended. It may be that a temporarily declining or perverted appetite for literature is not compatible with material advancement that augments the sum of human happiness.

Above all, no author should despair of the world because it declines to read his books. Personal failure, however humiliating and painful, is not a broad enough basis for pessimism. Some comfort may come from speculation about the causes about the present debasement of popular taste, but this is to be undertaken rather as a pastime than in the hope of reaching sound conclusions. Burke, in his "Essay on the Sublime and Beautiful," attempted to construct a theory of taste and he satisfied himself, apparently, though the reasoning of his immature essay has not satisfied others, that there are grounded and certain principles of æsthetics, common to all, and that it is only from difference in knowledge that difference in taste arises. "The cause of a wrong taste," says Burke, "is a defect of judgment, and this may arise from a natural weakness of understanding, or, which is much more commonly the case, it may arise from want of proper and well-directed exercise, which alone can make it strong and steady. Besides that, ignorance, inattention, prejudice, rashness, levity, obstinacy, in short all those passions and all those vices which pervert the judgment in other matters, prejudice it no less in its more refined and elegant province. And, indeed, on the whole, one may observe that there is rather less difference upon matters of taste among mankind than upon most of those which depend upon the naked reason, and that men are far better agreed on the excellency of a description in Virgil than on the truth or falsehood of a theory in Aristotle." A study of the phenomena of taste in reading at the present day would probably lead one not afraid to face the truth and speak it to differ with Burke as to the extent to which the principles of correct taste are diffused, and utterly to dissent from his view that a defective judgment and false taste are more commonly due to a want of proper exercise of the understanding than to its incurable weakness. It has been held that there are only about ten thousand persons in this city who are capable of thinking; who are possessed, that is to say, of the cerebral mechanism necessary for the manufacture of original judgments. Of these, perhaps three or four thousand are too indolent to employ their faculties, so that if this estimate be true the audience in New York to which literary work of a profound, of a subtle, or of a loftily imaginative character can appeal is brought within discouragingly narrow limits. If any aspiring man of letters accepts this view, let him bear its consequences like a philosopher. It is vastly more important that some men should be hewers of wood and drawers of water than that all men should read good books.

When the facts, and so far as we can formulate them, the laws, of demand and supply, in literature have been studied and pondered, how is the actual or intending author to profit by it? If at all, precisely as the coffee merchant or the manufacturer of dress goods profits by his careful observation of the state of the market; save that the merchant and the manufacturer have a free choice, while the author's choice is sometimes impeded by considerations of conscience and pride in his art. If the public taste demands less Mocha and more Old Government Java, or tires of bright-hued raiment and asks for sombre shades, it may be gratified without reproach to the purveyor. But a man of letters who is conscious of great gifts may not put them to ignoble uses without a sacrifice of self-respect and some sinking in the esteem of others. Happily, the field of literature is a broad one and traversed by many paths. The literary form lends itself to many purposes not strictly literary, yet in themselves worthy of pursuit and yielding abundant reward. The book that made the name of Harriet Beecher Stowe known through the whole world is not literature. "Uncle Tom's Cabin" is at best a piece of pamphleteering, yet the cause it championed was of immense importance to humanity. It had an immeasurable influence, and its sale of more than half a million copies brought to its author a reward of fame and direct remuneration with which any literary man or woman might be content. The inculcation of religious truth or the recital of religious history in books professing to be novels or tales is one of the shortest and surest ways to popular favor. Two writers in our own country have freely employed the spiritual element in this way, and though in respect to form and style their books have only the slenderest claim to the attention of persons of taste, the success they have attained is astonishing. Two English books of the contrary tendency that have lately set all tongues wagging throughout the opposing camps of belief and rationalism may be instanced in further evidence of the sure reward that comes to any one who successfully appeals to the deep human interest in spiritual things. Yet a moving spiritual interest and conviction on the part of the writer as well as on that of the reader must be exacted undoubtedly as an indispensable condition. The truest and sincerest literary art put to the service of a simulated spirituality would inevitably betray itself in a thousand passages of hollow hypocrisy and sham fervor. We have, to be sure, the great example of Milton deliberately weighing the advantages of a historical theme for the English epic he was to write, deciding that "the events narrated must be of general national concernment," rejecting the Arthurian legend upon which his choice had first been fixed and finally choosing a Scriptural subject, the Fall and Redemption of man, because of its being "every man's property and concernment and having also the highest guarantee of truth." But Milton had a deeply religious mind.

While modern criticism affirms that art has no duty to teach morality and commonly suffers in the attempt, there are in this crowded and bustling world a multitude of social problems which literary art may legitimately seek to illuminate. But he who undertakes this work must be amply equipped for it, since all men and all women have their opinions in these matters and will not attend to a writer who has not the power either to present their own ideas in so suggestive and striking a form that they have, when read, all the charm of novelty, or else so to confute and overset their prepossessions that they are compelled to read the book through from sheer indignation. If the writer's art earns no reward or appreciation in imaginative work, or in spiritual teaching or in the service of his reasoning powers, let him survey the field anew and seek further for some demand which he may be able to supply. One of our most painstaking and brilliant writers on American history, at the outset of his literary career, devoted himself almost exclusively to evolution and kindred subjects. His essays were fascinating in style; few writers in that field surpassed him in breadth of view or approached him in clear, logical, convincing treatment of the subject in hand. Yet I fancy he found that path too narrow, the popular demand for instruction in evolution and sociology too limited for his ambition, and turning to another class of subjects of equal dignity and wider interest, he has won for himself a place among the soundest, the most fertile, and the most widely appreciated American historical writers of the present time. Or, if the imaginative writer, neglected and unsuccessful, shrinks from a test of his powers in the sober realm of fact, or in any other than his native realm, let him there attentively study the shifting currents of popular fancy, and set his sails to catch the favoring breeze. There is no use in trying to drive your craft, with its precious freight of your own hopes and the bread for your children's mouths, in the teeth of the wind. If the novel-reading public wearily yawns and exclaims,

> "Those damsels of Democracy's
> How long they stop at every stile;
> They smile and we are told I wis,
> Ten subtle reasons why they smile,"

then, in Heaven's name, send your damsels over the stile with a flying leap and a deep-chested laugh, paint their robust figures upon your canvas with broad strokes of the brush or palette knife, make them glowing, natural, delightful animals, and invite the public, jaded with analytical character painting of drawing room figures, to come and enjoy their gambols. If only the art be true, if the characters be not copies, and the drama they play in have a breathable atmosphere of reality and living interest the public will accept the invitation. But I believe truth, originality, and living interest are qualities the novel writer does not hit upon simply by being told to do so.

Whether or not the man of letters who is discontented with his present lot finds his chosen sphere and hoped-for reward in any of these suggested ventures, a study of demand and supply in the literary market will infallibly teach him the futility of seeking to better his condition by descending to the production of tasteless and formless trash to meet the demand for immediate consumption. That way lie ruin and suicide. The material failure is no less certain and disastrous than the intellectual degradation. Though the minds that use literature only as the diversion of idle moments be legion, their demand yields no reward of fame or fortune to the writers who pander to their craving. The output of the stuff they feed on is too vast in the aggregate, the number of persons fit for no higher task than that of augmenting it is too great to leave room in the competition for any man capable of better things. The gains of authorship, whether in money or in repute, are dependent upon the sale of a large number of copies of one book; the best that any author can do in this field is to sell a few copies of many books—a game that is not worth the candle. As I read the literary signs of the times they show a tendency away from this kind of writing rather than toward it, a tendency to leave the wants of idle and mindless readers to be supplied by persons who have neither the art nor the ambition for any higher work, and a disposition more and more evident among the young and studious men of the craft to appeal by finer art to finer taste, to satisfy at least their own consciences, and to give the public the best that is in them. The spirit of intellectual integrity visibly guides and animates a considerable group of American imaginative writers of the present day whose work is of constantly increasing value and who have long surpassed in achievement, as they still surpass in promise, nearly everything that we have, or are likely to get, from the present generation of English writers. The standards set up, faithfully observed, and continually advanced in American literature at the present time give witness in refutation of those despairing mortals who foresee nothing but the extinction of the literary taste and faculty because this is an age of materialism and newspapers. Materialism is by its nature the foe of all art, and the newspapers have no doubt much to reproach themselves with. But the most formidable enemies of literature are ignorance and the military spirit, and notwithstanding some recent discouraging showings of the results of common school education, this is an age of enlightenment, and it is not an age of war. It is an age in which no man who speaks with competence and authority is long unheeded, and one in which those who do so speak are not few.

HAS THE SENATE DEGENERATED?

BY C. R. MILLER

Forum, May, 1897

When George F. Hoar first took his seat in the United States Senate, bringing up from the House the fruits of eight years' experience as a Representative and that serious interest in the public business that for more than a quarter of a century has made him a conspicuous figure at Washington, he gazed about him upon a body of men of whom nearly one-half were already distinguished for their ability and influence, while several of them were destined to still higher honors and larger responsibilities in the service of the nation.

It was on March 5, 1877, at the first meeting of the Senate of the Forty-fifth Congress, called in extraordinary session by President Hayes for the confirmation of executive appointments. There sat Anthony, whom Rhode Island obeyed and the country respected, and Allison, then as now one of the most just-minded men of his party. Thomas F. Bayard was there, a man of gifts and true democracy, whom a Democrat President was to call to his aid as Secretary of State and, later on, to the first ambassadorship. The lamented Beck sat there for Kentucky, and Newton Booth, the finest mind ever placed at the service of the State of California in either House of Congress. Mr. Blaine, whom Mr. Hoar did not like, and Roscoe Conkling, who did not like Mr. Hoar, were the two most powerful partisan chieftains in the Chamber. David Davis, a very able man, was equally noted for his independence of party. Edmunds and Thurman, good friends in private, fair foes in politics, expounded the Constitution with a breadth and soundness of learning unknown to the Senate since they retired leaving no successors. Windom, Lamar, Howe, and Kirkwood were later on to be called to Cabinet places, and Stanley Matthews to the bench of the Supreme Court. Other men of real strength were Oliver P. Morton, the eloquent Benjamin H. Hill, of Georgia, Justin S. Morrill, Angus Cameron, Hannibal Hamlin, Francis Kernan, and Plumb, of Kansas.

Here were twenty-two men every one of whom was a moving force in the work of the Senate. Every one made his influence felt in committee or in debate, and imposed himself upon the public attention as a distinct and energetic personality.

As the eye of Mr. Hoar roams about the Chamber in quest of the notables who take part in the proceedings of the more numerous Senate of to-day, it rests upon no figure so great and striking as the greatest of these, nor marks out more than a score who are in any way distinguishable from the mute herd whose senatorial activities are limited to the hunting of patronage and the care of private pension bills. As I study the list, I see no names but these that, under the most liberal interpretation of the term, could be

APPENDIX

called distinguished: Morgan, Allison, Hale, Frye, Gorman, Hawley, Lodge, Hoar, C. K. Davis, Chandler, Platt, Hanna, Foraker, Quay, Aldrich, Elkins, Tillman, Mills, Gray, and Stewart—twenty in all.

There are no great names here. What Senator among them can pretend to a tithe of Blaine's power to stir the hearts of the people? How unpersuasive in leadership would the ablest of them be if he should set his heart on the Presidency and sally forth among the masses to build up a following. They would be impotent, ineffective, absurd. What constitutional lawyer is there here to match Edmunds or Thurman? Platt may be the equal of Conkling in political leadership, and Quay may offset Oliver P. Morton as the boss of a State: but the moral weight of Bayard, Beck, Booth, David Davis, Windom, and Lamar, or of Edmunds and Thurman already mentioned, has no counterpoise; and the Senate of to-day must kick the beam.

Let us broaden the comparison. If, as Mr. Hoar so strenuously contends in *The Forum* for April, the Senate has not degenerated, it must now be of such high distinction that we may, without fear, set it over against the Senate of a time, now remote, when the roll bore names so illustrious that our children know what they stand for in the nation's history. I trust Senator Hoar will not accuse me of taking an unfair advantage if I go back half a century to a decade when the slavery question roused the patriotism and kindled the passions of the country, and centred its attention upon the giants contending in the Senate Chamber for the settlement of sectional differences that only later and sterner disputants could adjust. I will select the most conspicuous names that stood on the rolls of the Senate during the ten years from 1843 to 1853, the Twenty-eighth to the Thirty-second Congress, inclusive, and, for comparison and contrast, the most shining names among those elected to the Senate from 1889 to the term ending with 1899 —the ten years including the Fifty-first Congress and the Fifty-fifth.

From 1843 to 1853: Senators Thomas H. Benton, James Buchanan, Rufus Choate, Daniel S. Dickinson, John A. Dix, Levi Woodbury, Silas Wright, John C. Calhoun, Lewis Cass, Simon Cameron, Sam Houston, Reverdy Johnson, Daniel Webster, Thomas Corwin, Jefferson Davis, Stephen A. Douglas, R. M. T. Hunter, Salmon P. Chase, Henry Clay, Thomas Ewing, John C. Frémont, John P. Hale, Robert C. Winthrop, William H. Seward, James A. Bayard, Solomon Foot, Henry S. Foote, Hamilton Fish, Hannibal Hamlin, Charles Sumner, and Benjamin F. Wade.

From 1889 to 1899: Senators Morgan, Allison, Hale, Frye, Gorman, Lodge, Hoar, Sherman, Foraker, Hanna, Aldrich, Justin S. Morrill, Pugh, Teller, Palmer, Voorhees, Vest, W. E. Chandler, David B. Hill, Brice, Quay, Don Cameron, Mills, Elkins, Hawley, Cullom, Peffer, Vilas, Evarts, Stewart, Vance, and John P. Jones.

I do not expect Senator Hoar to throw up his brief after an inspection of these lists. No doubt he does intellectual homage to Webster and Clay and Calhoun and the men who were grouped about them in the 'forties. He reveres them as he reveres the second aorist, something majestic and pervading, but shadowy and far off; while the Senators with whom he now every day sits or strives look big to him and dwarf the figures farther down the gallery. Besides, I am afraid the Massachusetts Senator is not imbued with the scientific spirit. To a candid world, the comparison I have made will be convincing, I think. In the laboratory of social and political science, these exhibits will suffice for a demonstration that the Senate *has* degenerated. To employ the lingo of the neoscientific charlatanry, the stigmata of degeneration are visible upon the body and in the behavior of the Senate. I prefer the reasoning and the terminology of the older and sounder men of science, the Darwins and Spencers and Tyndalls who have traced for us the laws of change in the organic world. Accordingly, I should say with them that the Senate has undergone a variation from the type. The upper House of Congress is an organic structure: it is one of the organs of the Republic. Its present form and functions are the result of evolution, up or down, from the original type. If we would measure the possible changes it has undergone, we must examine the early structure in comparison with the structure of to-day, and note the divergences.

The Senator admits that "the Senate must be justified by the behavior of the men who compose it now, and not by the behavior of the men who composed it in the time of our fathers"; and he finds it "interesting to examine anew the original constitution of the Senate, and to see how far it has met the expectations of the Fathers."

We know what were "the expectations of the Fathers." In the Federal Convention of 1787, Edmund Randolph, of Virginia, in giving his views as to the constitution of the "second branch" of the Congress, declared that "it ought to be made much smaller than the first, so small as to be exempt from the passionate proceedings to which numerous assemblies are liable"; since, in tracing to their origin the evils under which the Federation labored, "every man found it to be in the turbulence and follies of democracy," and a good Senate seemed most likely to answer the purpose of a check against "this tendency of our governments." No part of the creative work of the Convention was the subject of more anxious consideration, or was more carefully matured. In order to insure a measure of experience and soberness of judgment, no person was to be elected Senator until he had attained the age of thirty years. As the Senate was, with the President, to exercise control over foreign relations, it was prescribed that Senators must have been for nine years citizens of the United States; while a citizenship of five years, with a minimum age limit of twenty-five, sufficed to qualify for election to the House. In those days the possession of wealth brought no reproach upon any man; and General Pinckney seriously proposed, and Dr. Franklin seconded the motion, that Senators should have no salary, since that body ought to be composed of men of wealth and position. The authors of the *Federalist* essays, writing in support of the Constitution and with the purpose of procuring its adoption by the States, dwelt with expository fulness and visible pride upon the constitution of the Senate. Historic precedents of Greece and Rome and all nations that had set up a second house of legislature were marshalled to show that the Convention had profited by the wisdom of the ancients, and had improved upon it. Hamilton wrote:—

"Through the medium of the State Legislatures—which are select bodies of men, and which are to appoint the members of the national Senate—there is reason to expect that this branch will generally be composed with peculiar care and judgment; that these circumstances promise greater knowledge and more extensive information in the national councils, and that they will be less apt to be tainted by the spirit of faction and more out of reach of those occasional ill humors or temporary prejudices and propensities which, in smaller societies, frequently contaminate the public councils."

What a picture of the Senate as it appeared in February last when Senator Cameron was pressing a resolution that would have brought on a war with Spain, and Senator Morgan was stamping on the Arbitration Treaty to relieve a spirit overburdened with hatred of Grover Cleveland and Richard Olney! Was Jay any nearer the mark when he prophesied that in the choice of Senators the votes of the State Legislatures "will be directed to those men only who have become the most distinguished by their virtue and in whom the people have perceived just grounds for confidence"?

Was it in this spirit that the New York Legislature chose Edward Murphy, Jr.? Was it after a prayerful search for men of virtue and ability among the available male population of the State that the choice of the Albany Solons fell on Mr. Platt? And did the Pennsylvania legislators send Quay to the Senate because they discovered in him "just grounds for confidence"?

Here is the original type of the Senate as clearly present in the minds and pictured forth in the language of the framers of the Constitution; and along with that delineation I have presented some individual deviations that show how it has failed to meet "the expectations of the Fathers." It is not in individual variations, however, that we can best trace degenerative changes, but by a study from time to time of the behavior of the entire body when engaged in the performance of its functions.

The Senate is now fighting for its place, and angrily protesting that it ought to have the respect and confidence of the country.

In the old days, Presidents were fain to consult at every step the wise, experienced, and eminent men of the upper branch. The people reverenced them and, by their greatness, proudly affirmed the greatness of America.

In comparison with the heroic age when Webster and Calhoun and Clay and Douglas and the fiery tribunes of the "peculiar institution" compelled the attention of every intelligent man and woman in the country and quite overshadowed the Executive by their comminating contentions, the Senate nowadays is a parvenu family, struggling for social place and recognition, sure neither of its clothes nor its manners, ignored by the great, rebuffed at every door, and ridiculed by the whole community. You can find fairly intelligent men who would be unable to name more than two or three Senators of the United States. It could not have been so in Webster's time.

"We are selfish men.
Oh! raise us up, return to us again;
And give us manners, virtue, freedom, power."

Not long ago Senator Hoar personally listened to most conclusive evidence of the degeneracy of the Senate. During the discussion of the resolutions providing for the recognition of the sovereignty of the "Republic of Cuba," when Senators were mad with jingo frenzy and sober-minded people were apprehensive, Secretary Olney contemptuously remarked that the recognition of sovereignty was none of the Senate's business. It was exclusively a Presidential prerogative; and he very plainly intimated that the President would pay no attention to any resolutions relative to Cuban recognition which the Senate might be pleased to pass. Immediately there was a great ruffling of feathers among the Senators. The declaration of the Secretary of State was denounced as an affront, an outrage upon the Senate's dignity, and an attempt to abridge its constitutional powers. I do not know why Secretary Olney chose the unusual medium of a newspaper interview for this important utterance; but it is probable that there was at the moment no official channel through which he could communicate to the jingo Senators the salutary and needed information. The form and manner, no less than the matter, of the communication roused his and the President's enemies in the Senate to a pitch of rage, in which they freely exhibited themselves in full possession of the passions and the factious spirit from which the Fathers fondly imagined they would be free.

This very question of the respective powers of the legislative and the executive departments in the recognition of the sovereignty of newly created governments comes up in the first Administration of Monroe, and again, in 1836, in the Administration of Jackson. Clay, while still a member of the House, in 1817, began to urge a prompt recognition of the revolted colonies of Spain in South America; and nearly twenty years later it fell to him, as chairman of the Senate Committee on Foreign Relations, to press for a speedy greeting to the Republic of Texas as a nation. In each case the Executive took its time: but in the courteous exchange of views each branch behaved with the dignity of conscious power; and in the case of the Spanish Republics it was not the Senate at all, but the House, that attempted to force the President's hand. President Tyler's plans for the annexation of Texas were checked by the Senate, which defeated his treaty. He could not control so strong a body: he could do nothing without it. He canvassed the strength of the opposition at every step, and sought to win over its members. Finally he was obliged to abandon the treaty, which required a two-thirds vote, and to ask that Texas be admitted by a joint resolution, for which a majority was sufficient. The weakness of Tyler, and the power of the Senators, both those who were for and those who were against annexation, were apparent throughout the contest. Polk could despatch General Taylor to the Rio Grande, with instructions that meant war; but the moment Mexico prepared to accept the challenge he hastened to put the responsibility on Congress. To be sure, the Constitution required him to invoke the help of Congress if war was to be declared; but the support of Congress was necessary to make his war policy acceptable to the people. "Polk's war," they called it; but he was fortified behind the Senate's vote of 40 to 2 for money and troops. Both these Presidents intrigued and manœuvred to win the cooperation of a body that was strong enough to have destroyed them, had they been rash enough to defy it. They were wise; and they consulted the Senate, as the Executive will always do when the Senate is also wise.

When Seward, annoyed by House resolutions declaring that the United States could not longer tolerate the presence of the French troops of Napoleon III in Mexico, wrote to Minister Dayton in Paris that "the question of recognition of foreign revolutionary or reactionary governments is one exclusively for the Executive and cannot be determined internationally by congressional action," the Senate did not shriek out that President Lincoln was a usurper and Seward his willing tool. On the contrary, Charles Sumner, as chairman of the Committee on Foreign Relations, rendered valuable assistance in carrying out the policy of the Secretary of State by discreetly pocketing every resolution about Mexico that was referred to his committee. Both the President and the Senate being inspired by the highest patriotic purposes, relations of confidence and cooperation naturally existed between them, by which the national welfare was promoted.

It has thus far been shown that the Senate has now no party leaders or constitutional expounders of such power as those whom Senator Hoar found in that Chamber when he entered it twenty years ago; that while some of the greatest names that have adorned the pages of American history were upon the roll of the Senate half a century ago, there is now no Senator, and in the last decade there has been none, who has impressed the world by his abilities or made the age illustrious by his achievements; that the Executive, instead of seeking the aid and counsel of the Senate, as was the earlier custom, is obliged to rebuke it for its officious and offensive meddling, and must resort to extraordinary means to thwart its mischievous intentions; that, in place of spontaneous tributes to its greatness, it constantly receives popular testimonials of want of confidence and respect, which provoke its members to undignified exhibitions of resentment; and that, by its obstructive and fractious behavior, the Senate has become a body totally unlike the type planned and created by the Fathers. These changes constitute degeneracy. The organism has undergone a marked modification of form and function.

But it is not alone by obstinate ill-doing that the Senate has forfeited the public respect. In what it refuses to do, or does grudgingly under the lash of compulsion, it is unbearably exasperating. The mulish stubbornness with which it has resisted the will of the people in respect to the Treaty of Arbitration is a flagrant example of degenerate practices. That treaty was conceived in the spirit of higher civilization, of advancing humanity. It was of that indisputable expediency that is an inherent quality of truth and honesty and justice. No right-minded man sufficiently advanced to have laid aside skins, and discarded the stone hatchet and the club, could have refrained from acclaiming the principle of arbitration as a happy means of escaping the barbarism of war. The instrument had been perfected by the diligent labors of men incomparably abler and broader than any that now sit in the Senate. It was such a pact as an enlightened branch of the treaty-making power would have ratified after a delay sufficient only to allow its chief statesmen to express worthily their pleasure at joining in a work of such beneficence.

Yet, from the moment it received the Treaty from the hands of the President, the United States Senate has railed at it and rent it savagely, as though it were a league with death. Senators of twenty years' service have shown themselves not ashamed to plead the general issue against it; openly avowing a hostility to arbitration and to England, which it was their judgment the country also ought to feel. Others have opposed ratification as a means of revenge upon Mr. Cleveland and Mr. Olney, and have been unable to conceal their detestable motive. Still others, and I grieve to say that Senator Hoar is one of these, have put upon the Treaty unsightly and perverting patches of amendment that well-nigh extinguish its usefulness, and endanger its acceptance by England.

These are the characteristic procedures of a degenerate Legislature. It is impossible that in any Senate where sat a Webster or a Sumner the meaner and uncivilized half would, in so grave a business, achieve an almost unresisted triumph. The savages would slink away before the majesty of their countenances, or be persuaded by the eloquence of their lips.

I suppose that when Senator Hoar invented the new social stratum which he describes as the American "populace"—a rank neologism as he employs the term—he had in mind the thousand or more bishops, clergymen, college presidents and professors, philanthropists, authors, jurists, and prominent men of affairs, who recently sent to the Senate their fervent prayer that the Arbitration Treaty might soon be ratified. This "cultivated and lettered populace" of ours is described with circumstance in Senator Hoar's *Forum* article:—

"Our populace does not come from the poor or ignorant classes. It is made of very different material. It has white and clean hands. It parts its hair in the middle. . . . It prates and chatters a good deal about the sentiment of honor and political purity; but it is never found doing any strenuous work on the honest side when these things are in peril. . . . It contributes to public discussions nothing but sneers, or expressions of contempt or pessimistic despair. It is found quite as commonly on the wicked side as on the honest side."

APPENDIX

On the heads of these learned blatherskites the Senator pours out his wrath with sacerdotal austerity as though he were the high-priest pronouncing upon the people the penalties of their impious conduct. Is not the Senate, by constitutional designation and the mode of its election, set far above the people to protect them from their own gusts of passion? May it be importuned by petition like a dirty little board of aldermen? Must it listen to lectures as to its duty from the turbulent milksops of the colleges and pulpits? Shall its precious freedom of debate be abridged or its sage deliberations be hurried by the irresponsible clamor of bishops and judges? Every feeling heart will sympathize with the evident sense of injury under which the Massachusetts Senator declaims his arraignment of the white-handed and lettered mob. His position is deplorable, his task difficult. Nothing is so injurious to a man's dignity as to have it questioned. And when the dignity with which the Senators solemnly invest themselves is stripped off with irreverence and jeers they must be pardoned if they show some irritation.

Upon two other occasions within the last four years the Senate has stood out in stiff-necked opposition to the sentiment of the country. If its attitude toward the Arbitration Treaty was barbarous, its prolonged haggling over the repeal of the Sherman Silver-Purchase Act in 1893 was wicked. The nation was in the throes of a financial convulsion. Upon the urgent recommendation of the President, the House of Representatives passed a repeal bill promptly. The Senate held it under pointless and inane debate for two months, while confidence fled the country and business went to rack and ruin. Even when this immeasurable harm had been done, it was only in obedience to extraordinary outside pressure and by a narrow majority that the Senate finally assented to the repeal. In its treatment of the Wilson Tariff Bill of 1894 it showed the same unreasoning disregard of the public wish and interest. Considerations of low tariff and high tariff do not enter at all into my condemnation of its behavior. The Bill was held in the Senate not for amendment along the lines of either policy, but for individual and disconnected assaults upon its schedules of such strange persistency that men grew suspicious, and at length became convinced that no honorable motive could actuate certain of the Senators in their highwayman-like attitude toward it.

If a comparative study of the personnel and efficiency of the Senate at different periods and the record of its malfeasance and non-feasance afford insufficient proof of its degeneracy, some light may be thrown upon the problem by observation of its manners. Here Senator Hoar feels himself upon solid ground. "Talk about the degeneracy of the Senate!" he exclaims, to a man who is writing at the very desk beside which Charles Sumner was struck down by the ruffian's bludgeon, who remembers that Foote—the same Foote who drew a pistol upon the indispensable Benton—in debate warned Hale that he would be hanged upon the tallest tree in the forest, if he should visit Mississippi, and who recalls the days when honorable but convivial Senators came into the Chamber "with whiskey-soaked brains."

Alas! men had their failings even in the heroic age. It is true that the passions of the Southern Senators were sometimes violent and ungovernable. It is true that Brooks was a coward and a ruffian; and it is true that at various periods in the history of this nation United States Senators have been too much given to the indefensible practice of alcoholic stimulation. We hope Senator Hoar is right in his assumption that no Senator now ever drinks more than is good for him. But, deplorable as were the exhibitions to which he refers, they were perfectly compatible with the concentration in the Senate Chamber of more brains and force and greatness and general efficiency than can be assembled there from forty-five States in the days of decorum and degeneracy. The politest little man in the world may be a less interesting example of a nation's virility than the swaggering fellow who can "clean out" a caucus. Tom Jones was a sad dog and got into no end of scrapes; but we can put up with his frank irregularities better than with the meaner vices of the sanctimonious Blifil.

Daniel Webster, in that seventh of March speech in which he made the "grand renunciation" of his former views against the extension of slavery, gave more convincing proof of the greatness of the Senate than a dozen statesmen of the present senatorial calibre could do by years of perfectly consistent and irreproachable public conduct. The prostrate trunk of some centennial oak speaks more eloquently of the majesty of the forest than the scrubby exuberance of the living underbrush. Webster's fall awakened echoes that have not yet died away from our historical discussions. Of the present Senate, the perversities of one day are forgotten the next.

> "All else is gone; from those great eyes
> The soul has fled;
> When faith is lost, when honor dies,
> The man is dead."

No muse is stirred to such a glow of indignation by our modern Ichabods. We impale them with a paragraph, and let them squirm while we turn to weightier things.

To sum it up,—the Senate lacks moral authority and holds no leadership of opinion. Once it had both.

Senator Hoar, admitting some of the defects in the body he so skilfully defends, casts about rather helplessly and hopelessly for a remedy. It is not to be found in a change of the rules or in the manner of electing Senators. The evil lies deeper,—in the social conditions and tendencies of the time. The Senate was once the goal of every bright young man's aspirations. It no longer attracts them; and public life in all its stations has lost much of its old allurement. For one thing, the great questions that stirred the popular heart and roused those emotional fervors so dear and so necessary to the platform orator have mostly been settled by the growth of the country. During the slavery agitation strong men entered public life as devout young men entered the ministry,—in obedience to an inward call. But, with our tremendous industrial development, invocations more numerous and compelling come from other directions. To the young man casting about for the choice of a calling in life, the rewards which brains and ability can command in business or the professions seem far more generous and substantial than any degree of public fame to be won in discussing the sordid questions of tariff and free coinage. Great lawyers no longer go to the Senate. They cannot afford to give up corporation practice.

If Webster were alive to-day he would be neither in the Senate nor in debt.

FOR THE GERMAN PEOPLE, PEACE WITH FREEDOM

New York Times, December 15, 1914

Germany is doomed to sure defeat. Bankrupt in statesmanship, overmatched in arms, under the moral condemnation of the civilized world, befriended only by the Austrian and the Turk, two backward looking and dying nations, desperately battling against the hosts of three great Powers to which help and reinforcements from States now neutral will certainly come should the decision be long deferred, she pours out the blood of her heroic subjects and wastes her diminishing substance in a hopeless struggle that postpones but cannot alter the fatal decree. Yet the doom of the German Empire may become the deliverance of the German people if they will betimes but seize their own. Leipsic began and Waterloo achieved the emancipation of the French people from the bloody, selfish and sterile domination of the Corsican Ogre. St. Helena made it secure. Sedan sent the little Napoleon sprawling and the statesmen of France instantly established and proclaimed the Republic. Will the Germans blindly insist upon having their Waterloo, their Sedan—their St. Helena, too? A million Germans have been sacrificed, a million German homes are desolate. Must other millions die and yet other millions more before the people of Germany take in the court of reason and human liberty their appeal from the imperial and military caste that rushes them to their ruin?

They have their full justification in the incompetence and failure of their rulers. German diplomacy and German militarism have broken down. The blundering incapacities of the Kaiser's counselors and servants in statecraft at Berlin and in foreign capitals committed Germany to a war against the joined might of England, France and Russia. Bismarck would never have had it so. Before he let the armies take the field, before he gave Austria the "free hand," he would have had England and Russia by the ears, he would have isolated France, as he did in 1870. The old Emperor, a man not above the common in capacity, surpassed the wisdom of his grandson in this, that he knew better than to trust his own judgment and he was sagacious to call great men to his aid. Wilhelm II. was wretchedly served at Vienna by an Ambassador blinded by Russophobia, at St. Petersburg by another who advised his home Government that Russia would not go to war, and at London by the muddling Lichnowsky, whose first guesses were commonly wrong and his second too late to be serviceable. Germany literally forced an alliance for this war between England and Russia, two Powers often antagonistic in the past and having now no common interest save the curbing of Germany. The terrible misjudgment of the General Staff hurled Germany headlong into the pit that incompetent diplomacy had prepared. The Empire went to war with three great nations able to meet her with forces more than double her own.

Then the worth of that iron military discipline and of the forty years of ceaseless preparation to which Germany had sacrificed so much of the productive power of her people was put to the test. Again the colossal imperial machine broke down. It was not through incompetence. The German Army was magnificent in its strength, in equipment, and in valor. It was overmatched, it had attempted the impossible. That was the fatal blunder. The first rush upon Paris was intended to be irresistible; that was the plan of the General Staff; France crushed, Russia could be sent about her business. It was not irresistible, it was checked, it was repulsed. When the invaders were driven back from the Marne to the Aisne and the Belgian frontier Germany's ultimate defeat was registered in the book of fate and heralded to the watching world. Germany's battle line had been forced back to where it stood when it first encountered the French. Calais is freed from her menace, Tannenberg was but an incident to the swarming hordes of Russia. What boots it if she enters Lodz, if she seize Warsaw, what even if by some unlooked for turn of fortune she again approach the walls of Paris? Kitchener's new million of trained men will be in France before the snows have melted in the Vosges, and Russia is inexhaustible.

There is within the German view an even more sinister portent. The world cannot, will not, let Germany win in this war. With her dominating all Europe peace and security would vanish from the earth. A few months ago the world only dimly comprehended Germany, now it knows her thoroughly. So if England, France and Russia cannot prevail against her, Italy, with her two millions, the sturdy Hollanders, the Swiss, hard men in a fight, the Danes, the Greeks and the men of the Balkans, will come to their aid and make sure that the work is finished, once for all. For their own peace and safety the nations must demolish that towering structure of militarism in the centre of Europe that has become the world's danger-spot, its greatest menace.

The only possible ending of the war is through the defeat of Germany. Driven back to her Rhine stronghold, she will offer a stubborn resistance. Even with the Russians near or actually in Berlin she would fight on. But for what? Why? Because the German people, the very people are resolved to get themselves all killed before the inevitable day of the enemy's triumph? Not at all. The weary men in the trenches and the distressed people merely obey the orders given by imperial and military authority. For the men in those high quarters defeat would be the end of all. Desperation, with some possible admixture of blind confidence, will continue the war. But why should the German people make further sacrifice of blood to save the pride and the shoulder straps of German officialdom? It means a million more battle field graves. It means frightful additions to the bill of cost and to the harshness of the terms. Since the more dreadful ending is in plain view why not force the better ending now?

But this is revolution. That may be so; call it so. Definitions are useful, they are not deterrent. Is there in all history any record of a whole people rising against their rulers in the midst of a great war? Let the historians answer the question. Is it conceivable that the loyal German people, made one by the love of the Fatherland and devoted to the accomplishment of the imperial ideals, could be stirred to revolt while still unconquered? That concerns the prophets. We are concerned neither with precedents nor with prophecies. We have aimed here to make clear the certainty of Germany's defeat and to show that if she chooses to fight to the bitter end her ultimate and sure overthrow will leave her bled to exhaustion, drained of her resources, and under sentence to penalties of which the stubbornness of her futile resistance will measure the severity. We could wish that the German people, seeing the light, might take timely measures to avert the calamities that await them.

It may well be doubted that they will see the light. But have not the men of German blood in this country a duty to perform to their beleaguered brethren in the old home? Americans of German birth or of German descent should see and feel the truth about the present position of Germany, the probability for the near, the certainty for the remoter, future. At home the Germans cannot know the whole truth; it is not permitted them to know. It will be unfraternal and most cruel for German-Americans further to keep the truth from them, or to fail in their plain duty to make known to them how low the imperial and militaristic ideal has fallen in the world's esteem, and to bring them to understand that the enemies they now confront are but the first line of civilization's defenses against the menace of the sword that forever rattles in its scabbard. The sword must go, the scabbard, too, and the shining armor. If the Germans here have at all the ear of the Germans there, can they not tell them so? They have come here to escape the everlasting din of war's trappings; they have come to find peace and quiet in a land of liberty and law, where government rests on the consent of the governed, where the people by their chosen representatives, when there is a question of going into the trenches to be slain, have something to say about it. Have they ever tried to get into the heads of their friends in the Fatherland some idea of the comfort and advantages of being governed in that way? Instead of vainly trying to change the well-matured convictions of the Americans, why not labor for the conversion of their brother Germans?

The State is Power, said Treitschke. He would have written Tennyson's line, "The individual withers, the State is more and more." In the German teaching the State is everything, to the State the individual must sacrifice everything. With us the State is the social organization by which men assure to themselves the free play of individual genius, each man's right in peace and security to work out his individual purposes. If the German-Americans prize the privileges they have enjoyed under our theory of the State, ought they not to tell the Germans at home what it means for the individual to be free from quasi-vassalage? There is no people on earth more worthy to enjoy the blessings of freedom than the Germans. Germany has taken her place in the very front of civilization; freed from the double incubus of imperialism and militarism, the German genius would have a marvelous development. It is not in the thought of Germany's foes to crush the German people, the world would not let them be crushed. It has for them the highest esteem, it will acclaim the day when it can resume friendly and uninterrupted relations with them. But the headstrong, misguided, and dangerous rulers of Germany are going to be called to stern account, and the reckoning will be paid by the German people in just the proportion that they make common cause with the blindly arrogant ruling class. When representative Americans and men of peace like Dr. Eliot and Andrew Carnegie insist that there can be no permanent peace until an end has been made of German militarism, soberminded Germans, here as well as in Germany, ought not to turn a deaf ear to such voices, for they speak the opinion of the world. The bill of costs mounts frightfully with every month's prolongation of the war and the toll of human lives is every day ruthlessly taken. It may be a counsel of unattainable perfection to say that the German people ought now to end the war. But for their own happiness, for their own homes, for their interests and their duty it is true. The truth of the counsel is unconquerable.

WOODROW WILSON

The New York *Times*, February 27, 1921

It made a world of difference whether throughout the war and at the end of the war we had in the White House a common man, or a man above the common. A President content to patch up the shattered world and set it spinning again in the old grooves would have been overlooked altogether. He never would have helped the nation to find its soul, he would not have found his own. He would have had no part in the work of reconstruction; Europe was full of complacent men of no force or initiative, no imagination, no new ideas—why summon another from overseas? But in this American nation gifted men come to the fore whenever some great public business calls them. They came forth, each at his appointed time, for the achievement of our independence, for the making, interpreting and expounding of our Constitution, for saving the Union and doing away with slavery, even for revoking the edict of banishment decreed against a great party, and for chastising "culpable wealth." As if by predestination, when the war came, one was at the post of duty and of trial who, by his gifts and abilities, seemed to be designated above all others for a service such as no American had ever before been summoned to undertake.

Through the carnage and welter in Europe, above the ruined fields and blackened temples, Woodrow Wilson had sight of a different world, where, as he was to phrase it later, this agony would "not be gone through with again." He was resolved that it should be different, better, and to the work of making it better he devoted all the powers of his mind. Mr. Wilson was prepared for what he undertook by beliefs and convictions matured through a lifetime of labor, study and thought. It was the foundation article of his creed that "the greatest forces in the world and the only permanent forces are the moral forces." He had full faith in constitutional government, no faith in any other; government by military authority he abhorred. He believed in democracy, the rule of the people, but always under constitutional forms and restraints. "Liberty is a privilege of maturity, of self-control," he wrote nearly a score of years ago, "some peoples may have it, others may not." And again in his Columbia University lectures: "Self-government . . . follows upon the long discipline which gives a people self-possession, self-mastery, the habit of order and peace, and common counsel which will not fail them when they themselves become makers of law."

Here we see the reason why at Paris he held that "self-determination was not for all peoples, only for those fit for it." From his studies in history, from the faith that had ripened in his mind, from his firm belief in liberty as a natural right, his love of constitutional government, and his distrust of all government not responsible to the people and administered in their interest, was born that aspiration to serve mankind by striving to give it a safer and saner world to live in which burned in his bosom throughout the war and through the peace negotiations which followed it. In these things we find the sources of his policies and of his acts.

In what manner he was to serve the world and his fellow-men could not be clearly revealed to him until we had joined in the fight against Germany. He had to guard our neutrality. The notes of inquiry and protest respecting our rights as a neutral Power, which our Government dispatched during the first two years of the war, were read with little patience in the London and Paris Foreign Offices; in that time of anxiety and of danger, how could anybody be expected to bother with such matters as illegal searches and seizures? At home there was a like impatience because of the notes, but only among the thoughtless. Belligerents will respect no right of neutrals unless respect is compelled. At his peril the neutral overlooks encroachments, for precedents are created that may prove awkward in some future time of war; and sympathy with the offender's cause cannot justify neglect to call him to account. Nevertheless, amid the flood of current business during the first two years of the war—notes of warning to Germany concerning the crimes of submarines, correspondence with the Allies about the rights of our ships upon the seas, and the reorganization of our military and naval forces—Mr. Wilson was taking thought for the future, of that time when the nations should "be governed by the same high code of honor that we demand of individuals." How far they were from that standard of conduct in 1914! His mind was occupied with a project, already long under discussion here and abroad, of an international agreement to banish war. The ethical basis and outline plan of the League of Nations were set forth in his address at the first annual meeting of the League to Enforce Peace, in Washington on May 27, 1916: (1) the right of every people to choose the sovereignty under which they shall live; (2) the right of smaller States to enjoy that respect for their sovereignty and territorial integrity which the powerful nations insist upon; (3) the right of the world "to be free from every disturbance that has its origin in aggression and disregard of the rights of peoples and nations." Further, he was sure the people of the United States would be willing to become partners in any feasible association of nations formed in order to realize these objects and make them secure against violation. These are the foundation concepts of the League of Nations—the rest is but means for their effectuation.

Faithful to this "unceasing purpose," Mr. Wilson, even in asking of Congress on April 2, 1917, a declaration that the state of war existed between Germany and the United States, renewed the expression of his hope for "a steadfast concert of peace," but he clearly saw that "no autocratic government could be trusted to keep faith within it, or to observe its covenants." That thought took concrete form just before the armistice in his proclamation to all the world of the principle that no peace could be made with the Hohenzollerns.

We had been less than a year engaged in war and victory was not yet within view when Mr. Wilson was able to formulate with wonderful foresight and precision the basic principles of the peace. We speak advisedly, for his Fourteen Points, embodied in the address to the two houses of Congress on Jan. 8, 1918, accepted by the Allies with two minor reservations and assented to by Germany in the negotiations for an armistice, actually became the basis and framework of the Treaty of Versailles and the Covenant of the League of Nations. Mr. Lloyd George, three days earlier, had stated the war aims of Great Britain, but the scope of his pronouncement was limited, far less comprehensive, and there was no such clear definition of intent as in Mr. Wilson's Fourteen Points.

Those who find their chief joy and occupation in decrying Mr. Wilson have insisted both that the Fourteen Points were rejected altogether at Paris and that the Treaty was totally vitiated and made odious because they were taken into it bodily. A Treaty that put an end to the bloodiest of wars and has become the public law of the greater part of the world through its ratification by some half a hundred nations now needs no defenders. It is true, incontestably true, that the body of political principles formed in the mind of Woodrow Wilson in the years when he was a student, teacher and writer of history, and at the last a chief figure in the greatest events of all history, became the soul of the Treaty. Sir Ernest Satow says of Mr. Temperley's "History of the Peace Conference at Paris" that "it shows clearly that with the exception of the reservation of the European allies with respect to No. 2 of the famous Fourteen Points, namely, the so-called 'freedom of the seas,' the President had been allowed to formulate the terms upon which peace should be concluded." Germany, on Oct. 19, three weeks before the armistice, declared that she "accepted the terms laid down by President Wilson in his address of Jan. 8, and subsequent addresses, as the foundation for a permanent peace of justice." The allied Governments, after a careful consideration of the correspondence with Germany, declared their willingness to make peace with the German Government on the terms of peace laid down in the President's address to Congress of January, 1918, and the principles of peace enunciated in his subsequent address. The dominance of Mr. Wilson's ideas and principles at Paris was made evident in the sharp conflict over reparations. The European Premiers stood out for assessing upon Germany the whole cost of the war and all direct and indirect damage resulting therefrom, for which in signing the Treaty she had acknowledged full responsibility. The American contention was that the pre-armistice agreement limited the demand to reparation for damage to civilian populations and property. Lloyd George came to Paris fresh from an electoral campaign in which the platform demanded "shilling for shilling and ton for ton." France, Italy and Serbia supported him. The Americans not only pointed to the agreed basis of the armistice, but insisted that, if anything was to be collected from Germany, the reparation total must be fixed at a sum she could reasonably hope to pay. Lloyd George, Clemenceau and Orlando were at last won over to the American position. While the plea of the Americans that the sum to be demanded should be definitely fixed was denied, it is interesting to note that their estimate of approximately $15,000,000,000 approaches the capital sum agreed upon by the Supreme Council at Paris last month.

All this is history. It would have been a different history had Mr. Wilson not been engaged in its making. He met at Paris the statesmen of the Old World, bred in its traditions. They were prepared to make a treaty much in the old way; each member of the Conference looked out chiefly for the interests of his own country, all with an eye to immediate advantage— Fiume, Shantung, Yap, Mesopotamia, the Rhine provinces—giving little heed to remote and perhaps dangerously disturbing consequences of transferring territory without regard to the wishes of its owners and inhabitants. Mr. Wilson was thinking more of the future, of the permanence of the peace. His great aim was to make a treaty that would breed no new wars. He put practical ends above the fierce joy of vengeance; it was better to ask $15,000,000,000 of Germany and get it than to demand $120,000,000,000 and get nothing. The Treaty in its details is not all he would have had it, but in its structural provisions it embodies his principles, it was largely influenced and definitely shaped by his labors. The League of Nations Covenant was the fruit of a righteous propaganda of peace originating long before the war and engaged in by enlightened men of many nations. Mr. Wilson strove with others at the Conference for its inclusion in the Treaty; it was his foremost aspiration, its adoption was the crown and triumph of the cause of which he had made himself the champion. At the Paris Conference, says Sir Ernest Satow, having in mind the great figure of Alexander I. at the Vienna Congress, President Wilson was "perhaps a more powerful personage than even a Russian Emperor." He was powerful not only as the representative of this nation, but because of the moral force of his ideas.

Surely there was good reason for a feeling of pride in every American bosom when the head of this Republic, a Government of the people, and he a man chosen by the people, became during the war, by common consent, the chief spokesman of the Allied and Associated Powers in presenting their demands and their aims to the enemy. It was an occasion for even greater pride that in the most momentous international business in the world's history he should have held so high a place, should have exercised an influence surpassed by none in molding the Treaty of Peace, should have impressed deeply upon the great pact the stamp of American genius and American respect for law and right.

II

Almost universally Mr. Wilson is discussed and judged in terms of the war. The events and consequences of the great struggle so far transcended the business of our own household that the public seldom calls to mind acts and policies that would have lent distinction to any peace-time Administration. Chief among them all is the establishment of the Federal Reserve System, urged upon Congress and the country in his first inaugural address. For decades the defects of the banking and currency system established during the Civil War had been known and pointed out; the Republicans had talked much of reforming it; in the Monetary Commission Report of Senator Aldrich they had drawn up a plan embodying the chief features of the Federal Reserve System, but, to the great disappointment of the author of that report, who was really the father of the Federal Reserve plan, they had done nothing further. It fell to the party which had three times named as its candidate for the Presidency the apostle of all that is unsound and unsafe in finance to formulate and enact the measure that met triumphantly the test of the war's enormous demands, and that within the last critical year has proved its strength and soundness and value.

Mr. Wilson eagerly embraced the opportunity that awaited him to substitute a reasonable tariff law for that protectionist Republican device for the enrichment of a favored few at the expense of the many—the Payne-Aldrich act; and he must smile grimly as he now contemplates the preparations of that party again to expose itself to odium and overthrow by the enactment of a new tariff measure dictated by the old spirit of private greed. The Panama tolls repeal, which enabled us without a blush or any prick of conscience to denounce the German "scrap of paper" theory of treaties, was another of Mr. Wilson's triumphs which Republicans, if their chosen leader keeps to his announced purpose, will expunge—a propitiatory move which must be expected to inspire other nations with a sudden enthusiasm for "an Association of Nations."

In these matters, as in others of major concern during his two terms, Mr. Wilson, with an openness and directness beyond the wont of Presidents, used his influence to obtain the compliance of Congress. It was a theory he long had held that the President of the United States is also virtually Prime Minister, charged with the duty and responsibility of carrying his measures and policies to fruition by direct appeal and pressure. It is a practice for emergencies, not for all occasions. It may be approved by the people when a President spurs a laggard and perverse Congress to action as in the case of the repeal of the Silver Purchase act, compelled by Mr. Cleveland. It may be disapproved as it sometimes was, though not always, when Mr. Roosevelt constrained Congress to give effect to what he called "my policies." It involves the risk of sharp reminders to the Executive that the three departments of the Government are not only co-ordinate but independent. Inasmuch as this theory necessarily implies a Congressional majority always favorable to the Executive, and since it connives immediate ministerial responsibility to Congress and to the country, it is manifestly alien to our constitutional system.

III

Intending to present here not a panegyric, not a review confined to great achievements, but a just estimate of Mr. Wilson's services to the world and to his country, it is of obligation that we take account of his defects as well as of his qualities; that we give place in the record to his errors of judgment and procedure; in particular, that some attempt be made to find a reason for the attitude toward him, transitory we are convinced, of a great part of the public; for the loss of popular favor that was overemphasized during the last two years of his second Administration—in short, for that "hatred of Wilson" openly displayed in season and out of season by so many of his opponents. The prime source of this bitterness, of this dislike of Mr. Wilson, is to be sought in that most ancient and enduring of all the forces that move men in politics—party passion. Ever since the Civil War, Republicans of the older type have looked upon the election of a Democrat to office as a monstrous solecism, a terrible slip in the orderly processes of nature. Mr. Wilson's first term could be forgiven, for it was due to a Republican quarrel; his second election was a summons to all Republicans to take measures, desperate if need be, to restore power to that party in whose keeping it should always repose. The partisan spirit spares none, not even the highest. Washington was first in war, first in peace, first in the hearts of his countrymen, but many of his countrymen assailed him with a foulness and indecency of vituperation that far surpassed the ingenuity or the daring of Mr. Wilson's foes. Jefferson wrote the Declaration of Independence, but the Federalists abused him as though he were the meanest malefactor. Lincoln, savior of the Union, was slandered not only by the men of the opposite party, but by the abolitionists, and he himself was at one time doubtful of his re-election. Grover Cleveland, a great President, a man who stood "foursquare to all the winds that blew," who delivered the country from the perils of that silver delusion that had seized upon both parties, was malignantly traduced; ministers of religion who prayed for him were threatened with dismissal from their pulpits. The severe censure visited upon Mr. Roosevelt, most severe from members of his own party, has not been forgotten. It needed but the touch of Time's finger to redress the balance of public judgment upon all these men. They stand secure in their high places.

Not wholly to the heat and license of partisan spirit, but in no small measure to ill-judged and too well remembered utterances made before our declaration of a state of war, must be attributed the earlier manifestations of disfavor. The first of these were words spoken at a meeting of newly naturalized citizens in Philadelphia in June 1915: "There is such a thing as a man being too proud to fight." In a time of public tranquillity they would have passed unnoticed. Spoken three days after the sinking of the *Lusitania,* they shocked the country. Less than a year later he said, "With the causes and objects of the great war we are not concerned"; and again that the objects which both parties to the conflict had in mind, "as stated in general terms to their own people and to the world," were "virtually the same," which was true in a sense too strictly literal for general understanding. He wrote, too, that "a peace worth guaranteeing and preserving" must be "a peace without victory," which was the worst of all.

These things ought never to have been said, and could have been said only by a President so far preoccupied with the processes of his own mind as to be inattentive to the currents of public thought. They may not be excused, they can be explained. Mr. Wilson, it is plain, confidently believed that it was our destiny not to fight in the war, but to end the war by our good offices in mediation. It was a mistaken belief, shared doubtless by millions of Americans; not, however, by those who from the beginning better understood the German purpose and the German spirit as well as the German power, and felt deep in their hearts the promptings of a sacred duty to use our might in common with the other defenders of liberty against the assaults of an odious despotism. It was this belief that prompted Mr. Wilson in his proclamation of neutrality to say, "We must be impartial in thought as well as in action," lest we disqualify ourselves for the "proper performance of our duty as the one great nation at peace, the one people ready to play the part of impartial mediator." This is the key to his thought and the explanation of the phrases for which he was so severely censured. It may be said that he atoned for them by other memorable words in a more welcome sense after we entered the war. It is not forgotten that the world was to be made "safe for democracy," and that to the Hohenzollerns there was but one answer, "force to the utmost, force without stint or limit."

Mr. Wilson should have profited by the story of the lawyer who when admonished from the bench that he was showing contempt for the court replied that he was doing his best to conceal it. For those "pigmy minds" in the Senate he too plainly showed the disdain he felt. His was a mind of another order. He moved in another world to which they were strangers. The Senators who fought him upon the issue of the Treaty and the Covenant were little concerned with the peace and safety of the world, with international good faith and morals. There was a devil's dance of all the carnalities; there was, month after month, an infernal rigadoon where hypocrisy footed it with impudent false pretense, calumny with malice and the whole brood of hates with all the evil sisters of uncharitableness, until the Treaty was torn to tatters beneath their feet. The heart of the world might burst its auricles and its ventricles, but Woodrow Wilson must be put down. They might have beaten his party without beating the Treaty, as they well knew, but it was personal vengeance they sought.

All this Mr. Wilson might have spared himself had he bridged the chasm between him and them by the forms of politeness, by some manifestation of interest as to what ideas had found lodgment in the chambers of their minds. They raged at him because they knew he disdained them. It is impossible for anybody to show to a United States Senator the full measure of respect which the customary manner of some of them seems to exact, but it is unwise and inexpedient for a President ever to let a Senator know just what he thinks of him.

Although the wisdom of Mr. Wilson's decision to take part personally in the peace negotiation was at first much questioned, it soon became evident that his presence at Paris was essential to the making of a sound treaty. But it was probably the worst of his mistakes to go there alone. Everybody saw and said long ago that he should have invited one or two eminent Republicans to share with him the labors of treaty making. Beyond all question, Mr. Root should have been associated with him in the work at Paris. Samuel J. Tilden, a politician more deeply skilled than any that ever sat in the White House, would have chosen that wiser course. He would have made it his own treaty, as Mr. Wilson did, but he would have encouraged his Republican associates to believe that it was their treaty. Thus the Treaty would have been ratified, even though word for word and line for line it had been the instrument that Mr. Wilson brought back from Paris. The disappointment he had just encountered in the Congressional elections should have warned him of the gathering storm. It was a danger signal to which he should have given instant heed by a calculated effort to allay opposition to the Treaty in the Senate.

IV

The right of appeal to posterity may be invoked by every statesman misjudged by his contemporaries. Already the public judgment has vindicated Mr. Wilson in respect to one decision which has often been brought up against him for censure. Great numbers of Americans felt that we should have declared war against Germany after the sinking of the *Lusitania*. Throughout the East public feeling ran high, there was a passionate demand for hostile action, and justification was not wanting. "Mr. Wilson was right," said Mr. Choate a few days before his death, "the rest of us were wrong." It is exceedingly doubtful whether the President could have carried the country with him had he then demanded a declaration of war. Congress would have been divided, it might have refused, which would have been an almost irreparable disaster. While the East was hot, the West and South at that moment were more than cool. A year later the Republican National Convention was not warlike, the Democratic Convention at St. Louis went wild over Martin H. Glynn's keynote speech upon the text, "He kept us out of war." The great Mississippi Valley was not for war. Mr. Wilson correctly judged the temper of the country.

And so, as the years roll by and the last traces of party feeling and personal prejudice disappear, and men forget the small things and have memory only of the great ones that really matter, the country will correctly judge Mr. Wilson. A great and high place is reserved for him. There can be no doubt of it. When Truth sits at her elbow History bears false witness against no man, and the true record of Mr. Wilson's service to the world will be an open book. The future inquirer will not be at a loss to discover the sources and appraise the merit of the accusations hurled against him; he will judge them, dismiss them. When a score of years have passed, will any man call his own sanity in question by insisting that Woodrow Wilson sought to override the Constitution, destroy our sovereignty, and embroil us in all the wars in Europe? For one thing it can never be charged against him that he was false to his ideals, that he ever betrayed his principles and his followers. To falter at the supreme moment, to desert a cause through timidity or for selfish advantage—that is a blunder that has blighted many a high career. Mr. Wilson was lion-hearted in defending and forwarding his great purposes. He found new courage as foes multiplied, fresh reserves of strength as their assaults grew fiercer, until at last he fell, grievously stricken, upon the very field of battle, giving the last hours of his manhood's full strength and vitality to the American people in his effort to make them understand what his noble aspirations meant for them. It was a dark hour for the world's millions when he faltered and fell. He might not have been able to accomplish all that he desired, yet we cannot but feel that, had he been spared to continue the struggle, his powers of appeal and his resources of leadership would have compelled a different result.

But Mr. Wilson's ideas survive, the Covenant lives, the cause for which he strove is deathless. The Old World reels and is shaken by alarms because misguided men defeated his plan to unite all the peoples of the world in the compact of peace. The nations again beseech us to give them the help he promised, to hold aloof no longer, but join them in determining the grave questions that remain unsolved. Join them we shall and must; it cannot be otherwise, unless men have gone altogether mad. And when the noble work for which he toiled with unflagging zeal and devotion is achieved, even though men who come after him may give it their name, it will stand through all time as the memorial of its chief builder, a great American President.

INDEX

INDEX

Adams, C. H., 53
Adler, Julius Ochs, on editorial council of *The Times*, 81; 185
Agar, John G., Mr. Miller's honorary pallbearer, 185
Alloway, Harry, of *The Times's* Wall Street staff, 65
American, The Baltimore, comment on *The Times's* Senate investigation, 135
American, The New York, handling of Ship Purchase bill, 132
American-Hellenic Society, Mr. Miller serves on executive council of, 101
Armaments Limitation Conference, sponsored by Harding, 120
Armstrong, H. E., on editorial council of *The Times*, 185

Barker, Augustine V., judge: scapegrace at Dartmouth, 18; persuades Mr. Miller to return to college, 26; solicitous of Mr. Miller's future, 28
Barlow, Francis B., 107
Bartlett, Edwin J., classmate of Mr. Miller's at Dartmouth, 12
Beecher, Henry Ward, sued by Theodore Tilton, 45
Bennett, James Gordon, blazes trail of sensationalism, 58; Mr. Miller confers with, 94
Birchall, Frederick T., assistant managing editor of *The Times*, 81; 185
"Black Crook, The," 33
Blooming Grove Fishing Club, Mr. Miller a member of, 92
Bonner's New York Weekly, 25
Bowles, Samuel, the elder, 31
Bowles, Samuel, 2d, "the great Sam Bowles," 30–41
Bowles, Samuel, 3d, letter of congratulations to Mr. Miller, 51; death, 101
Bradford, E. A., on editorial council of *The Times*, 185
Brevoort Hotel, 139
Brougham, H. B., Mr. Miller's secretary during the war: confidential interview with President Wilson, 141
Bryan, William Jennings, Democratic convention of 1904, 87

Bryce, Lord, urges William Howard Taft to speak in England, 144
Butler, Nicholas Murray, appoints Mr. Miller to advisory board of Columbia School of Journalism, 100; confers degree of Doctor of Letters on Mr. Miller, 102

Cary, Edward, political editorial writer on *The Times*, 49; partner in New York Times Publishing Company, 61; prevents creation of Times-Recorder Company, 67; friendship with Grover Cleveland, 106
Century Club, Solomon Bulkley Griffin and Mr. Miller at, 41; George Haven Putnam proposes Mr. Miller for membership, 55; Mr. Miller's love of club life, 55; Alexander Dana Noyes writes of Mr. Miller's outrageous handwriting, 77; Mr. Miller's mornings at, 80
Century Magazine, Mr. Miller contributes article on Monroe Doctrine, 201; Mr. Miller's article, "Why Socialism Is Impracticable," 217
Clark, Champ, possible nominee for President, 115
Clement, Charles H., 28
Cleveland, Grover, Mr. Miller fights for, 60; his friends help *The Times*, 61; *The Times* supports him, 63; basis of intimate friendship with Mr. Miller, 104; Mr. Miller's editorial analysis of Cleveland as president, 189
Cleveland, Mrs., admired by Mr. Miller, 105; activity in behalf of international copyright, 106
Cobb, Frank, his *World* editorials read carefully by Woodrow Wilson, 119
Co-education in the Sixties, 4–9
Coffin, Haskell, portrait painter: paints Mr. Miller, 180
Coleman, Warren, consulting physician in Mr. Miller's last illness, 182
Columbia University School of Journalism, Mr. Miller's relationship with, 100; Mr. Miller tells students what makes an editorial writer, 166

INDEX

Corbin, John, on editorial council of *The Times*, 185
Courant, The Hartford, 52
Courier-Journal, The Louisville, 77
Crane, Charles R., 185
Crowder, Rev. Dr. Frank Warfield, reads Mr. Miller's funeral services, 185
Cunliffe, John W., excerpt from his book, "Writing of Today," 125
Curie, Marie, Mr. Miller's comment on her visit to the United States, 182
Curtis, George William, New York civil service reform, 107

Daily Herald, The Grand Rapids, 18
Dana, Charles Loomis, elected assistant librarian of Social Friends library, Dartmouth, 16; letter of praise to Mr. Miller, 53; toastmaster at Mr. Miller's birthday dinner, 181; 185
Daniels, Frances, meets Mr. Miller at Kimball Union Academy, 5; at Dartmouth commencement, 29; love affair with Mr. Miller, 34; marriage, 48. *And see Miller, Frances (Daniels)*
Daniels, William Henry, father of Mrs. Miller, 48
Daniels, Mrs., mother of Mrs. Miller, discourages daughter's love affair, 34, 48; helps in *The Times's* purchase, 63
Dartmouth College, description, 10; Mr. Miller an undergraduate, 10–29; library system, 15; *The Dartmouth* revived, 15; social life in the Sixties, 17–18; confers Doctor of Laws degree on Mr. Miller, 102
Davis, Elmer, on editorial council of *The Times*, 185
Davis, John W., 185
Davis, T. Wallis, consulting physician in Mr. Miller's last illness, 182
Drummond, I. Wyman, 185

Edison, Thomas A., Mr. Miller teases his questionnaire idea, 178
Editor and Publisher, The, Mr. Miller interviewed by, 174
Eliot, Charles W., president of Harvard, war letters in *The Times,* 139; reassures Mr. Miller on "Austrian Peace Overture" editorial, 149
Ely, Alfred, attorney, receiver of *The Times,* 67
Evening Post, The New York, attacks *The Times* and retracts, 61; Godkin's alliance with the Villards, 72; Rollo Ogden leaves to join *The Times* editorial staff, 177

Figaro, The, 141
Finley, John H., associate editor of *The Times:* quatrain on H. H. Kohlsaat, 122; joins *The Times* editorial staff, 177; quatrain on Mr. Miller, 184
Fisherman's Advocate, The, of Newfoundland, 177
Flint, Charles R., helps New York Times Publishing Company, 61; sues New York *Evening Post,* 61; opinion of Mr. Miller as internationalist, 91
Foord, John, appointed to fill vacancy on *The Times,* 46; editor-in-chief, 49; leaves *The Times* for Brooklyn *Union-Argus,* 50
Forum, The, Mr. Miller contributes "A Word to the Critics of Newspapers," 161; Mr. Miller's article, "Has the Senate Degenerated?" 235
Fowler, Robert Ludlow, writes for *The Times* during the war, 139
Frederick, Harold, *The Times's* representative in London: Mr. Miller preserves letters, 79; full life, 91

Globe, The Boston, 37
Godkin, Lawrence, 61
Goethe Society of New York, Mr. Miller addresses, 155; the address in full, 225
Grant-Greeley campaign: Springfield *Republican* supports Greeley, 31; Grant's executive incompetence, 40; a plot to get control of *The Times,* 46
Grant, MacCallum, Lieut.-Governor of Nova Scotia, entertains Mr. Miller, 176
Graves, Ralph, on editorial council of *The Times,* 185
Greeley, Horace, atrocious handwriting, 78
Green Mountain Institute, 6–9
Gridiron Club, Mr. Miller attends famous 1906 dinner, 112
Griffin, Solomon Bulkley, on staff of Springfield *Republican,* 32; enthusiastic French student, 36; managing editor of Springfield *Republican,* 41; inspects New York with Mr. Miller, 42; sends congratulations to his first journalistic friend, 52; joins Columbia School of Journalism advisory board, 101
Gunnison, Almon, 6
Gunnison, Herbert F., 6

Harding, Warren G., election, 120
Harper's Weekly, 43
Harris, Sir William Alexander, governor of Newfoundland, entertains Mr. Miller, 176
Hay, John, respect for *The Times,* 109

INDEX

Hearst, William Randolph, coming of yellow journalism, 59
Herald, The New York, first sensational newspaper, 58; Mr. Greeley's handwriting, 78
Hill, David B., governor of New York, *The Times's* attitude toward, 76; Mr. Miller telegraphs, 87
"History of the New York Times," excerpt from, 68
Hooker, Richard, 39
Hoover, Herbert, H. H. Kohlsaat dies at the home of, 122
House, Edward M., Colonel, informs Woodrow Wilson of the attitude of *The Times,* 119

Jennings, Louis J., 45
Jones, George, partner of *The Times's* great editor Raymond, 42; makes Mr. Miller assistant telegraph editor on *The Times,* 43; becomes majority share holder, 46; decides *The Times's* presidential stand in 1884, 54; his business methods, 60; death, 60
Journal, The Albany, edited by Harold Frederick, 91

Kimball Union Academy, 4-6
Kingsbury, E. M., on editorial council of *The Times,* 185
Kohlsaat, Herman H., Chicago friend of Mr. Ochs, 66; sends *Times* editorials to Colonel House, 119; intimacy with President Harding, 120; informal "ambassadorship" between *Times* and White House, 120; visits Mr. Miller in last illness, 182; death, 122

Lafayette Hotel, 139
League of Nations: early indications of Woodrow Wilson's idea, 142
Lloyd George, David, rebuked by Woodrow Wilson, 153
Lord, Chester, Mr. Miller's opponent in poker, 47; letter to Mr. Miller, 53

MacGeorge, Betty, friend of Madge Miller, travels with the Millers in Europe, 96; holiday with the Millers, 176
Macpherson, Cluny, Colonel, C. M. G., Mr. Miller's guide in St. John's, Newfoundland, 176
McKinley, William, friendliness toward *The Times,* 106
Mercury, The New York, 65

Metropolitan Club, Mr. Miller a member, 80; Mr. Miller holds club in regard, 97; Mr. Miller's birthday party, 181
MILLER, CHARLES RANSOM, editor-in-chief of the New York *Times:* birth, 1; early education, 3; Kimball Union Academy, 4-6; Green Mountain Institute, 6-9; delights of feminine society, 7-8; love for Frances Daniels, 5, 29, 34, 35; Dartmouth College, 10-29; writer of poetry, 15, 20; power of concentration, 24; first visit to New York, 25; recreations—fishing, 2, 6, 8, 47, 92, 176, tennis, 47, 98, golf, 47, 80, baseball, 47, poker, 47, 180, woodcarving, 50, billiards, 56, novels, 92; personal finances, 27, 61, 72, 179; on the staff of the Springfield *Republican,* 30-41; on the telegraph desk of *The Times,* 42-47; in charge of the weekly edition, 47; writes editorials, 47; marriage, 48; appointed regular editorial writer, 49; made editor-in-chief when thirty-four years old, 51; club life, 55, 80, 97; president of New York Times Publishing Company, 61; the fires of defeat, 64; meets Mr. Ochs, 64; retained as editor-in-chief under Ochs ownership, 68; friendship with Mr. Ochs, 71; new office, 75; habits of work, 84; treatment of editorial visitors, 85; relationship with staff, 86; love of languages, 89, 101; first trip to Europe, 94; second trip to Europe, 96; dislike of crowds, 97; country home at Great Neck, Long Island, 98; advisor, Columbia School of Journalism, 100; honorary degrees from Dartmouth and Columbia, 102; friendship with Grover Cleveland, 104; contacts with other presidents, 104-122; defender of *The Times* against the United States Senate, 123-136; brilliant editorial interpretation of World War, 137-152; honored by France, Belgium, Greece, 152; works for League of Nations, 154; holiday in Nova Scotia and Newfoundland, 176; illness, 181; death, 183
Miller, Chastine Hoyt, mother of Mr. Miller, 1
Miller, Edward, Mr. Miller's half-brother, 3
Miller, Elijah T., father of Mr. Miller: New England farmer, 1; believed in education, 26
Miller, Fanny, Mr. Miller's half-sister, 3
Miller, Fayette, Mr. Miller's elder brother, 3

INDEX

Miller, Frances (Daniels), wife of Mr. Miller: companionship, 48, 62, 92, 98; puts all her money into *The Times*, 61; entire management of home and children, 61; takes lodgers, 61. *And see* Daniels, Frances

Miller, Hoyt, son of Mr. Miller, born in Brooklyn, 62; recalls father's scorn for dictionaries, 91; travels with father in Europe, 96; holiday in Nova Scotia and Newfoundland, 176

Miller, John, Mr. Miller's uncle, 2

Miller, Madge, daughter of Mr. Miller, born in Brooklyn, 62; travels with father in Europe, 96; holiday with her father in Nova Scotia and Newfoundland, 176; with her father during his last illness, 182

Miller, Captain Thomas of Bishops Stortford, Mr. Miller's earliest American ancestor, 1

Mills, John Bailey, 18

Mitchell, E. P., serves Columbia School of Journalism advisory board, 101; goes to Princeton with Mr. Miller, 170

Monroe Doctrine, Mr. Miller's views on its relation to Venezuela dispute, 201

Morgan, Pierpont, at Gridiron Club dinner, 112

Morris, "Bob," Springfield's clerk of court, 40

Mortimer, F. C., on editorial council of *The Times*, 185

New York Times Company, created by Mr. Ochs in 1896, 68

New York Times Publishing Company, purchases *The Times* in 1893, 60

Niles, Walter L., consulting physician in Mr. Miller's last illness, 182

Northcliffe, Lord, rumored as *The Times's* backer, 124

Noyes, Alexander Dana, 77

OCHS, ADOLPH S., meets Mr. Miller, 64; becomes owner and publisher of *The Times*, 68; friendship with Mr. Miller, 71; hospitality, 80; negotiates to purchase New York *Telegram* and *Herald*, 95; friendship with President McKinley, 106; friendship with President Taft, 113; lunches with President Wilson, 117; 62 per cent of *Times* capital stock, 124; mourns Mr. Miller's death, 184

Ogden, Rollo, editor-in-chief of *The Times* after Mr. Miller's death: editorial on H. H. Kohlsaat, 122; joins *Times* editorial staff, 177

Oxley, F. H., Colonel: Mr. Miller's guide in Halifax, 176

Paige, Mrs., aunt of Frances Daniels, invites niece to Dartmouth commencement, 29; encourages love affair, 34

Paladium, The New Haven, 37

Park Avenue Methodist Church, Mr. Miller discusses history of journalism from pulpit, 168

Peace Conference at Paris, 119

Perkins, Edward N., 185

Phillips, O., on editorial council of *The Times*, 185

Piping Rock Club, Mr. Miller a member, 98

Powers, Samuel L., Congressman, his description of President Smith of Dartmouth, 11

Princeton Graduate School, Mr. Miller defends the classical faith at, 170

Pulitzer, Joseph, *World* strong in sensationalism and editorials, 58; founder, Columbia School of Journalism, 100; sits for Rodin in sulky silence, 180

Putnam, George Haven, proposes Mr. Miller for Century Club, 55; opinion of Mr. Miller's handwriting, 78; tells of Mr. Miller's dislike of society, 97; New York civil service reform, 107

Putnam's, G. P., publishers, ask Mr. Miller to write history of Greece, 89

Recorder, The New York, 67

Reid, John C., a great news editor, 45; *Times* managing editor, 50; an ardent Republican, 54

Republican, The Springfield, Mr. Miller works for, 30–41; applauds *The Times's* attack on Tweed ring, 43; a "paper that had found its soul," 47; word portrait of Mr. Miller, 51; read by Woodrow Wilson, 119

Richards, John H., Mr. Miller's physician, 182

Rogers, H. H., at Gridiron Club dinner, 112

Roosevelt, Theodore, Mr. Miller preserves his hurried notes, 79; New York civil service reform, 107; pays Mr. Miller great compliment, 108; quarrels with *The Times*, 109; writes for *The Times* on "What America Should Learn from the War," 139

Root, Elihu, friendship with Mr. Miller,

INDEX

114; opposed by New York *World*, 114; needed at Peace Conference, 153
Root, Frank, 37
Rosen, Baron, killed by taxicab accident, 102
Russell, Charlie, member of Congress for Connecticut, 37

Savage Club, of London, Harold Frederick member of, 91
Schiff, Jacob H., congratulates Mr. Miller on honorary degree from Columbia, 103; war letters in *The Times*, 139
Schurz, Carl, advises Theodore Roosevelt, 108
Seitz, Don, writes "Life of Joseph Pulitzer," 59
Senate, The United States, committee investigates *The Times*, 123–136; Mr. Miller's article in *The Forum*, "Has the Senate Degenerated," 235
Shepard, George, 49
Ship Purchase Bill, opposed by *The Times*, 123; comment by Woodrow Wilson, 143
Smith, Asa Bodge, president of Dartmouth College, 1863–77, 10
Smith, Charles Emery, 67
Smith, Sallie, 27
Socialism, Mr. Miller's opinions on, 217
Spinney, George F., 61
Spring-Rice, Sir Cecil, British ambassador to the United States: writes on "official deathbed" to Mr. Miller, 152
Steele, Sandford H., 47
Stokes, Anson Phelps, New York civil service reform, 107
Stone, Melville E., 185
Sultzberger, Arthur Hays, on editorial council of *The Times*, 81; 185
Sun, The New York, Chester Lord on staff, 47; first paper to humanize the news, 57; editorial—"Larry a Confessed Liar," 61

Taft, Henry W., 185
Taft, William Howard, friendship with Mr. Ochs, 113; congratulates *The Times* on Sixtieth anniversary, 113; invited by Lord Bryce to make war talks in England, 144; needed at Peace Conference, 153
Telegram, The New York, Bennett threatens to kill, 94
Theta Delta Chi Fraternity, 25
Tilton, Theodore, sues Henry Ward Beecher for alienation of wife's affections, 45

Times, The Chattanooga, 65
Times, The London, editorials present the news, 59; cordial relations between Delane and the Walters family, 72; praises Mr. Miller's editorial on Germany's sure defeat, 141
TIMES, THE NEW YORK, defeats Tweed ring, 42; prosperity in late Seventies, 44; decline, 60; Mr. Miller as president and editor, 61; purchased by Adolph S. Ochs, 68; new buildings, 74; the editorial conference, 81; supports Woodrow Wilson, 83; relations with White House, 104–122; a national newspaper, 106; investigated by United States Senate, 123–136; during the World War, 137–152; supports League of Nations, 152–154; tribute to Mr. Miller, 183
Tribune, The New York, 77
Tweed ring, 42

Union, The Springfield, 31
Union-Argus, The Brooklyn, 50

Van Anda, Carr V., applauds Mrs. Miller, 50; on *Times* editorial council, 81; appears at Senate investigation of *The Times*, 123

Walsh, T. J., Senator, chairman of *The Times* investigation committee, 123
Wanamaker, John, 107
War, the World, *The Times* cable tolls, 44; *The Times's* service during, 137–154; Mr. Miller's editorial, "For the German People, Peace with Freedom," 244
Wark, Rev. A. N., 25
Watterson, Henry, 77
White, Horace, New York civil service reform, 107
Whitman, Walt, visits Dartmouth College, 16
Wickersham, George W., seeks explanation of Roosevelt bombshell, 112; Attorney-General in Taft cabinet, 112; comments on Mr. Miller's treatment of Senate, 136
Wiley, Louis, business manager of *The Times*, 81; visits Democratic convention in 1904, 87
Williams, George Fred: Mr. Miller's freshman roommate at Dartmouth, 11; Mr. Miller's letters to, 34, 93, 99, 103, 115, 136, 173; in journalistic lunch club, 37; Mr. Miller's unique correspondent, 99; Mr. Miller's executor, 179

INDEX

Wilson, Woodrow, *The Times* stands behind his administration, 83; supported by *The Times* for nomination, 115; luncheon with Mr. Ochs and Mr. Miller, 117; indifference to press, 118; succinctness of exposition, 141; at Peace Conference, 153; mysterious estrangement from *The Times*, 153; Mr. Miller's estimate of, 247

Winter, Edward W., 185

World, The New York, founded by Joseph Pulitzer, 58; opposes Elihu Root, 114; editorials read by Woodrow Wilson, 119; Ship Purchase bill, 132; comment on *The Times* investigation by Senate, 135

Youth's Companion, The, article on "Training for Journalism" by Mr. Miller, 156

4871.M49 B6 1931